Without Walls or Barriers

Without Walls or Barriers

The Speeches of Premier David Peterson

Edited by
Arthur Milnes and Ryan Zade

Library of Political Leadership Series
School of Policy Studies, Queen's University
McGill-Queen's University Press
Montréal & Kingston–London–Ithaca

School of Policy Studies
Robert Sutherland Hall
138 Union Street
Kingston, ON K7L 3N6
www.queensu.ca/sps/

The preferred reference for this book is
Milnes, Arthur, and Ryan Zade, eds. 2017. *Without Walls or Barriers: The Speeches of Premier David Peterson,* Montreal and Kingston: Library of Political Leadership Series, McGill-Queen's University Press.

Library and Archives Canada Cataloguing in Publication

Peterson, David, 1943-
[Speeches. Selections]
    Without walls or barriers : the speeches of David
Peterson / edited by Arthur Milnes and Ryan Zade.

(Library of political leadership series)
Includes bibliographical references.
Issued in print and electronic formats.
Text chiefly in English; some French text appears as part of
some speeches.Without walls or barriers.
ISBN 978-1-55339-525-6 (softcover).--ISBN 978-1-55339-526-3
(EPUB).--ISBN 978-1-55339-527-0 (PDF)

    1. Peterson, David, 1943-. 2. Ontario--Politics and
government--1985-1990. 3. Speeches. I. Milnes, Arthur, 1966-,
editor II. Zade, Ryan, 1985-, editor III. Title. IV. Series: Library
of political leadership series

FC3076.1.P48W58 2017   971.3'04   C2017-903128-7
                                                C2017-903129-5

TABLE OF CONTENTS

PREFACE

Dr. Thomas S. Axworthy and Arthur Milnes first conceived the Library of Political Leadership occasional book series in 2008. At the time, Dr. Axworthy headed the Centre for the Study of Democracy (CSD) of the School of Policy Studies at Queen's University. Milnes had joined Axworthy's CSD that year as fellow, shortly after completing his work as research assistant to the Right Honourable Brian Mulroney on the latter's 2007 *Memoirs*.

Both Axworthy and Milnes believed strongly that present and future students of Canadian public policy would benefit if the words of political figures were made available. Milnes, for example, as a young man had been inspired by historic political speeches after discovering volumes of the published addresses of leaders such as Arthur Meighen, Sir Wilfrid Laurier, and John Diefenbaker in his high school library in Scarborough.

Part of the series' vision has been to allow past historical figures to "speak" directly to future students through the speeches they delivered on platforms throughout Canada's rich political history. As a result, the volumes feature a minimum of footnoting and present-day commentary.

A veteran speechwriter, who had worked closely with Pierre Elliott Trudeau, Axworthy best outlined the aims and goals of the Library of Political Leadership Series with the following passage in *Politics of Purpose: 40th Anniversary Edition*, a collection of the speeches by Canada's 17th prime minister, the Right Honourable John Napier Turner:

"One of the first questions to ask about any leader is what are his or her priorities and do they run with or against the grain of history? An essential way of determining this is to research the public record and then compare dreams versus accomplishments. It is the public record of measured words that remains the most reliable barometer of either consistency or change in one's purpose. As Lord Acton wrote to the contributors to the Cambridge Modern History Project, 'archives are meant to be explored.' And because the written word is the key to describing ruling currents and interpreting sovereign forces, 'we must provide a copious, accurate, and well-digested catalogue of authorities.' To understand a public figure like John Napier Turner [or in this case, David Peterson] it is necessary to start with what he said and what he wrote."

As this volume started to become a reality, Milnes turned to Ryan Zade, the former lead research assistant on the Paul Martin Oral History Project, which formed the basis of Mr. Martin's 2008 memoirs. Zade too had been inspired by political figures early in his life, reading the speeches of Trudeau, Clark; and Mulroney to supplement his grandfather's political teachings. For this project, Zade spent weeks in the Ontario Archives gathering Premier Peterson's addresses. Together, the editors endeavoured to provide a comprehensive primary source of both depth and breadth that speaks to the issues faced by the Peterson government.

For this volume in the series, the editors turned to journalist, author, and authority on Ontario politics, Steve Paikin of TVOntario. He has provided an in-depth introductory essay explaining the life and political times of Premier Peterson and his government between 1985 and 1990. Readers will agree that Paikin has done so in a way that demonstrates his impressive knowledge and analytical ability that has made him the most respected journalist covering Ontario politics today. We salute him for his contribution to this book and his ongoing dedication to educating Ontarians about their province.

Steve was on the lawn of the legislature on June 26, 1985 as a reporter when David Peterson was sworn in as premier. As Steve describes, it truly was a new day for Ontario. After forty-two years of rule by Ontario's Progressive Conservatives—a reign that produced six premiers from George Alexander "Colonel" Drew to Frank Miller—Peterson became the first Liberal to occupy the corner office at Queen's Park since the middle of the Second World War. "David Peterson the Politician"—one of five sections in this book—provides a narrative through Peterson's voice of the remarkable political change in Ontario that started in 1985.

In "Breaking Down Walls and Barriers: David Peterson as Policy Maker," readers will explore the activist agenda the London, Ontario lawyer led through his premiership. We have provided speeches on education, health care, the environment, the public service, and conflict of interest. His agenda sought to ensure all Ontarians were able to participate fully in provincial society. When we asked Peterson what he viewed as his most important accomplishment, he thought for a brief moment and then whispered with obvious emotion: "breaking down walls and barriers."

In "Peterson the Federalist," we see the premier on the wider Canadian stage addressing the economic challenges faced by the federation, most notably free trade. Peterson distinguished himself and Ontario through the alliances and friendships he built with premiers across Canada. These premiers came from all political parties; Alberta's Don Getty, New Brunswick's Frank McKenna, and Quebec's Robert Bourassa were particularly close friends and colleagues. Through his efforts, he continued in the proud tradition of past Ontario premiers such as John Robarts and William Davis: He put Canada first.

The debate that consumed Canadians during those years is featured in "David Peterson and the Meech Lake Accord." Despite the fractures within his own caucus caused by Meech Lake, Peterson never wavered in his support of the agreement that was designed to bring Quebec into the constitutional family. Politically, it would have been much easier for him if he had done just that. In a prophetic moment, minutes before Premier Peterson was to offer his fellow premiers six Senate seats, he phoned his wife, Shelley, and said "I could lose my job because of this decision I'm going to make."[1] His efforts to save the Accord, featured prominently in the section, would be in vain. Even today, he continues to say he regrets Meech's demise even more than losing the Ontario election later that year.

Peterson's views on Meech would be foretelling; the failure of Meech Lake—followed by the 1992 rejection of the Charlottetown Accord—created, as the premier put it, a "house divided against ourselves."

The speeches we have included in the section on international affairs attest to the pace of geopolitical change that Peterson and his ministers faced. In 1985, the federal government of Brian Mulroney was less than a year into its mandate, a relatively unknown Mikhail Gorbachev had just emerged as general secretary of the Soviet Union, and the Macdonald Commission had yet to release its report recommending free trade with the United States, which called on Canadians to take a "leap of faith." By 1990, the Berlin Wall had fallen, Europe was speaking integration, a fragmented Soviet Union was beginning to collapse, the Canada-United States Free Trade Agreement was in full force and effect, and the age of globalization had begun.

Finally, in the "Paying Tribute" section, we provide a selection of addresses where Premier Peterson spoke about the leading figures of Ontario, Canada, and the world. We have provided an interesting cross section of personalities from former premiers, to his political contemporaries, to the British royal family. Particularly powerful tributes include Nelson Mandela's first visit to Canada and Peterson's eulogy for MPP Dalton McGuinty, Sr., the father of Ontario's 24th premier.

---

[1]Gagnon, Georgette and Dan Rath. 1991. *Not Without Cause: David Peterson's Fall from Grace*, p. 174. Toronto: HarperCollins.

Certainly Peterson's government had its ups and downs; its successes and its disappointments. Nevertheless, it is fair to say that in breaking down walls and barriers, the 20th premier led and shaped Canada's largest province during a crucial period, leaving all Ontarians well positioned for the challenges of the coming decades.

There can be no higher tribute to his public service than that.

ACKNOWLEDGEMENTS

This volume grew out of discussions between the Honourable Brad Duguid and his long-time friend from Scarborough, Arthur Milnes. Duguid and Milnes felt it would be appropriate and fitting to honour this significant leader's role in Ontario political history with a collection of the 20th premier's addresses. Minister Duguid assembled a first-rate group of like-minded individuals who met for breakfast on June 3, 2010 to plan the necessary fundraising efforts to secure the funds to enable Queen's University to undertake this project. They included Tom Allison, Brent Duguid, and Paul Pellegrini. As noted in this book, a group of generous donors quickly provided funds so the project could begin.

Our first acknowledgement, therefore, is to Minister Duguid, his colleagues, and our donors. Without them, this volume would not have been possible. In addition, Gordon McCauley, Premier Peterson's popular and hard-working executive assistant while at Queen's Park, and the Honourable Elinor Caplan, took time out from busy schedules to write essays for Milnes which provided excellent background to assist and guide Milnes in his research. Jim MacLean assisted in this process as well. Joel Heard also provided advice and support. Queen's Park political staff Hratch Aynedjian, Andrew Block, and Chris Yaccato also provided timely and valuable assistance.

After discussions with Mr. Peterson, a wide variety of associates of the former premier, as well as leading academics and journalists, took valuable time to provide advice and their memories of the Peterson years. These discussions were extremely beneficial. Participants included Vince Borg, Sean Conway, Professor Kathy Brock, George Hutchison, Robert Prichard, and Professor Jonathan Rose.

Queen's Principal Daniel Woolf, himself a leading historian, joined by his executive director Sheilagh Dunn, took a great interest in this project and we are very much in their debt. The editors would also like to salute the dedicated staff of the Ontario Archives and the Legislative Library at Queen's Park, copy editor Anne Holley-Hime of Kingston and Mark Howes, publishing coordinator, at the School of Policy Studies at Queen's University. Mark, in fact, deserves special recognition and thanks from Milnes. Many thanks to Dr. Kim Nossal for his keen editing eye and thoghtful recommendations as this volume neared completion. We are also indebted to Queen's University Archivist Paul Banfield and Susan Office, also at the Queen's University Archives. Dr. David Walker and Lynn Freeman of the Queen's School of Policy Studies also deserve the high praise and thanks for their roles in bringing this book to fruition.

Thanks to Jay Collins and Hillary Ryde-Collins for their editing assistance *en français*. Marta Bedard's publishing and formatting advice was just a fraction of the good counsel she provided throughout this process. And this being Ryan's first foray into the published world, he begs your indulgence as he thanks his family—Sherry, Penny, Jeffrey, and Holly—for their unwavering and unconditional support.

Finally, both editors would also like to pay tribute to all MPPs, of all parties, who served Ontario between 1985 and 1990. Public service is a higher calling and our society is richer for all those who put their names forward and engage in the political process.

Arthur Milnes
Kingston and Scarborough

Ryan Case Zade
Toronto and Aurora

FINANCIAL CONTRIBUTORS

This volume would not have been published without the generous financial support of the following:

Jeff Smith and Ellis Don (lead corporate sponsor)

Julie Burch and John Phelan

George Cooke and the Dominion Insurance Company

Gordon and Cathy McCauley

The Honourable Frank McKenna and TD Financial Group

Lawrence Tannenbaum

Scarborough Centre Provincial Liberal Association

INTRODUCTION: THE DAVID PETERSON YEARS

INTRODUCTION: THE DAVID PETERSON YEARS
by Steve Paikin

In Ontario's 145-year history, there has never been a day like June 26, 1985.

For it was on that day that one of the most successful political dynasties anywhere in the world came to an end.

The joke in political circles was that there were two remarkably successful political machines around the globe. The first belonged to Enver Hoxha, who ruled Albania's Communist Party with an iron fist from 1941 until his death in 1985.

The second was the Progressive Conservative Party of Ontario, which had managed to find the magic formula for staying in power from 1943 to 1985—a whopping 42 consecutive years.

But on a beautiful, sunny, summer day on the south lawn of Queen's Park, something took place that most Ontarians had never seen before: the swearing-in of a *Liberal* as premier of Canada's most populous province.

David Robert Peterson was born five months after the beginning of the Tory dynasty, on December 28, 1943. In other words, there wasn't one moment in Peterson's life—from his birth in London, Ontario, to his graduating from the University of Western Ontario and then the University of Toronto Law School, to his running the family electronics business, to his election as the MPP for London Centre in 1975, to that first moment with his hand on the Bible being sworn in as Ontario's 20th premier—that David Peterson lived under anything other than Tory governments at Queen's Park.

Peterson's rise and subsequent fall has all the elements of one of the country's most dramatic political stories. When he took over the lead-

Without Walls or Barriers: The Speeches of Premier David Peterson, Library of Political Leadership Series, by Arthur Milnes and Ryan Zade, Editors. Montreal and Kingston: McGill-Queen's University Press,

ership of the Liberal Party of Ontario in February 1982, he was an un-
gainly, awkward-looking fellow, just 38 years old, whom nobody would
have given a chance in hell of finishing off one of the country's great
political institutions.

Three years later, he was premier.

Two years after that, he was arguably the most popular politician in
the country.

Three years after that, he was out of politics altogether.

Now *that's* a dramatic story.

• • •

The Liberal Party that David Peterson inherited in 1982 was hardly a
threat to take over the government. Despite efforts by outgoing leader
Stuart Smith to make the party more relevant and popular in urban Ontario, it still had a distinctly rural membership and caucus.

In fact, some elements of the party were downright backwards. Peterson and Hamilton East MPP Sheila Copps were on the final ballot at the
1982 leadership contest. When one delegate was asked whom he'd be
supporting on that ballot, the Toronto Star's Jim Coyle remembers that
delegate responding: "It ain't the broad."

On many issues, it felt as if the Liberals were more like conservatives
than the Conservatives. Perhaps that's because the Tories were so skil-
fully led by the province's 18th premier, William Davis, whose instincts
for tacking left or right on issues was unparalleled. His debut as PC
leader was a great success, winning a larger majority government in
1971 than the one he inherited from his predecessor, John P. Robarts.
Eventually, Davis would go on to become the longest-serving premier
of Ontario in the 20th century.

But in 1975, in his second campaign as leader, Davis faltered and was
fortunate to hang on to a minority government. Nineteen seventy-five
was also the year David Peterson was elected for the first time, in the
riding of London Centre. An ill-advised attempt by Davis to recapture
his majority in 1977 fell short, and resulted in another hung parliament.

But by the 1980s, Davis had figured it out. After ten years in power,
he enjoyed his most satisfying triumph, returning the Tories to majority
status in the 1981 election with the same 44.5 percent of the total votes
cast as he achieved in 1971.

It was a new decade and Davis was at the top of his game. Politically, he was more popular than ever, almost untouchable. On policy, he
was one of the single-most important architects behind the repatriation
of the Canadian Constitution, with a Charter of Rights and Freedoms,
one of the country's most historic achievements. And he had the benefit
of knowing that the next time he went to the polls, he'd be facing two
untested, first-time opposition leaders: David Peterson, and Bob Rae of

the New Democratic Party, who won his leadership contest exactly two weeks before Peterson became Liberal leader, in February 1982.

But then, Davis made a decision that would set in motion a chain of events, which would forever alter Ontario politics. On Thanksgiving weekend in 1984, with party members, Cabinet ministers, and some close advisers begging him to go back to the polls and win another certain majority government, the man from Main Street in Brampton decided, instead, that he'd had enough. He had been in public life for 25 years, and premier for 14 of them. He was 55 years old. It was simply time to do something else.

Bob Rae has often joked that had Davis decided to fight another election, "He'd have wiped the floor with both Peterson and me."

There's plenty of evidence to suggest Rae is right. While Davis was at the height of his political prowess, his two opponents in the legislature had significant problems of their own.

Go back to the summer of 1984. Peterson's actress wife Shelley was performing in a play. The couple had an agreement. She would do one play a year and he'd hold the fort while she did. So she left her husband and three kids (two of them in diapers) at a cottage the family rented in Grand Bend on Lake Huron.

One day, with a pot of chicken stew on the stove and one child with a very full diaper, the phone rang at the cottage and the news wasn't good. Four of Peterson's key MPPs—Sheila Copps, Don Boudria, Albert Roy, and Eric Cunningham—were all quitting his Liberal caucus. John Turner had just taken over the leadership of the federal Liberal party. Turner's polling numbers were sky-high. All four MPPs concluded that their best chances of sitting on the government benches were in Ottawa. Poor David Peterson looked like he was going nowhere. And so they bolted for what seemed like a much better opportunity.

Ian Scott, a Toronto lawyer and perhaps the most brilliant intellect ever to sit in the Ontario legislature, was also having doubts. Having already run unsuccessfully in 1981, he wasn't keen on doing the same thing for a second consecutive election. So he got in his car and began to drive to Grand Bend to tell Peterson in person that the Liberal leader couldn't count on him running again either.

But half way there, Scott turned the car around. "After those other four had quit, and he was taking care of all those kids, I just didn't have the heart to do it to him," Scott told me years later.

Nevertheless, "This was *the* low point of my entire life," Peterson laughed as he told me about the goings-on of 1984, during an interview on TVO's *The Agenda with Steve Paikin*.

Things weren't much better for the leader of the NDP. Bob Rae had come to Queen's Park as both a saviour and a boy wonder. In 1981, former leader Michael Cassidy had led the party to a very disappointing finish, losing 12 seats and capturing just 21 percent of the total votes cast.

Enter Bob Rae, the 33-year-old brainy finance critic from the federal NDP, who had captured national attention both for his skill in the House of Commons, and for moving the motion in 1979 that pulled the plug on Joe Clark's nascent minority government.

Expectations were high that Rae would be able to breathe new life into Ontario's New Democrats. Instead, he came off like a whiny kid when juxtaposed to the poise and skill of Premier Davis. Suddenly, the media were writing stories about why Rae was either ineffective at the provincial level, or just non-existent.

But William Davis's surprise retirement announcement created a new dynamic. In the past, Progressive Conservative Party members, in the main, chose well when replacing their leaders. George Drew gave way to Leslie Frost. Frost retired in favour of John Robarts. And Robarts passed the torch to Bill Davis. In each case, a younger man, not too far from Ontario's ideological centre, replaced an older man. And generational change ensured that the dynasty continued.

However, the majority of delegates to the January 1985 leadership convention in Toronto may have felt that their party was so strong and their opponents so weak that they could ignore history and indulge themselves. And so, they chose Cabinet Minister Frank Miller from Muskoka. Miller was a delightful guy, who despite being highly educated, bilingual, and from Toronto, preferred to wear loud, plaid jackets, play up his Scottish roots in an increasingly multicultural province, and portray himself as the champion of rural Ontario.

He was also two years *older* than Davis, and openly expressed admiration for US President Ronald Reagan, a very un-Ontario thing to do. It was a pretty significant hint that Miller intended to take the Ontario PC Party away from its traditional "tack left-tack right, centrist philosophy," into something much more small "c" conservative.

Even so, the notion that the Conservatives were somehow vulnerable was still a stretch. They entered the 1985 election campaign with a 25-point lead on the second place Liberals. Forty-two straight years of Tory government meant the roots of Ontario Progressive Conservatism ran deep. So no one, least of all David Peterson, had any reason to suspect a different outcome.

And yet, there was something about Frank Miller. He was affable, fun, and humorous. But he was also a common sense revolutionary ten years before Mike Harris made that a winning platform. The knock that he was just too right wing would not go away. And Miller wasn't doing anything to dissuade people from believing it. He was proud of it.

Ernie Eves, who had been nicknamed "Landslide Ernie" because of his six-vote margin of victory in 1981, was nervous. His Parry Sound riding was right next door to Miller's Muskoka riding. And too many of Eves's constituents were complaining that they didn't know Miller well enough to go to the wall for him. If his neighbours in central Ontario didn't know Miller, despite his having been treasurer, minister of industry, and minister of health, how well could the rest of the province have known him?

It was the first of many signs that all may not have been well in blue paradise. Other things started happening that suggested the PCs weren't as invulnerable as everyone thought.

For example, on June 12, 1984, Premier Davis rose in the legislature to inform Ontarians that he was changing his mind on a policy that had the potential to stick a dagger right into the heart of the Tory core.

For more than a century, Ontarians had walked an uncomfortable tightrope on the issue of funding religious schools. The original Confederation deal required Ontario to provide public funding to Roman Catholic "common schools" (essentially, to the end of Grade 8), while the Quebec government had to do the same for Protestant (read: English) schools.

Over the years, public funding for a couple of extra grades was added. But the Conservatives successfully withstood a full court lobbying press from the Catholic Church and refused to extend full public funding to the separate school system to the end of Grade 13. In fact, Bill Davis won his first election in 1971, some think, by expressly refusing to extend full funding to the Catholic system.

But in June 1984, just a few months before he would announce his retirement, Davis shocked everyone by announcing he was changing his mind, and that his government *would* fully fund the Catholic system.

The opposition parties were pleased. They'd been on record as supporting full funding for decades. Rumour abounded that the Tory caucus wasn't particularly pleased. But when it came time to vote on the issue, every single Conservative MPP (except Carleton-Grenville's Norm Sterling) voted in favour.

But a near unanimous vote in the Ontario legislature couldn't obscure the fact that many Ontarians, particularly long-time Tory supporters, couldn't stand the decision. So, just under the surface, the occasionally toxic mix of education policy and religion in Ontario was doing a slow boil.

That slow boil turned into a certifiable explosion during the 1985 election campaign. At a news conference, Anglican Archbishop Lewis Garnsworthy responded to a question from yours truly by launching into a full blown attack on the Tories and their full funding policy.

"This is how Hitler changed education in Germany, by exactly the same process, by decree," Garnsworthy said to an astonished assemblage of media. "And I won't take that back."

It was left to a seething Frank Miller to describe Garnsworthy's comments as "odious" and "totally unfounded." However distasteful the comments were, they signaled a kind of "open season" on Miller's Conservative government.

Suddenly, the Conservatives looked mortal. The previously accessible Miller, who always enjoyed fun banter and repartée with reporters, now complained to those same wags that his handlers wouldn't let him schmooze with them anymore. The back room boys wanted a safe, peek-a-boo campaign, keeping Miller away from reporters, lest his penchant for saying colourful things get him in trouble. That strategy even went so far as to have Miller decline to participate in a leaders' debate, something that may have been a frill at one time, but which voters now expected to happen as a matter of course.

The effects of all of the above were immediate. Tory polling numbers began to sink. Media reports were getting more and more negative. Conservative campaign events were held in half-empty rooms, and even then, without much enthusiasm.

Into this volatile mix stepped David Peterson. But not the old David Peterson. Not the guy with the goofy glasses and jackets with the patches on the elbows. No, the new Peterson dressed smartly. He ditched the glasses for contact lenses. And borrowing a sartorial tip from former Liberal Premier Mitchell Hepburn (1934–42), Peterson's media guru, Gabor Apor, told him to wear red ties because they looked modern and snappy. Those red ties would soon become almost as iconic with Peterson as those red roses were for Pierre Elliott Trudeau.

Now, the Tory party with its deep roots in the Ontario political firmament seemed mortal. Frank Miller was looking every bit of his nearly 58 years of age. Meanwhile, if you watched television, you frequently saw pictures of the 41-year-old David Peterson and his beautiful, much younger blond wife Shelley, out jogging, playing with their young children, and feeling a wind at their backs that Liberals hadn't felt in more than four decades.

If one Liberal campaign policy captured the public's imagination more than any other, and summed up how the party had tossed off its rural rump roots in favour of a new, modern urbanity, it was a promise Peterson unveiled one day at a corner store belonging to Martin Baranek on Keele Street in North York.

Peterson harkened back to the days when anyone wanting to buy a bottle of wine or spirits would go to a Liquor Control Board of Ontario outlet and fill out a form to make the purchase. The spirit of temperance still ran deep in Ontario. Many still clung to the notion that Ontarians couldn't quite be trusted to handle alcohol responsibly, and so LCBO outlets were prohibited from actually having any alcohol on display. It was all secreted away in the back rooms, lest even its availability to be seen by the public might somehow start a drunken revolution.

Peterson suggested Ontario had come of age. He floated the crazy notion that halfway through the 1980s, Ontarians might actually want more convenience in the way they purchased their beer and wine. He talked about busting up the monopolies of the LCBO and the Brewers

Retail, and suggested Ontarians were ready for the convenience of purchasing their alcohol in the corner store, as Quebecers and Americans did.

Naturally, there was opposition, and the idea had a lot of practical problems with it. But perhaps more than any other Liberal policy floated during that 1985 campaign, beer and wine in the corner stores captured a huge chunk of the public's imagination. And it was perfectly consistent with what the Peterson Liberals were about: modern, urbane, demonstrating trust in the electorate, and changing the old (read: Tory) ways in which Ontario had always done things.

"I knew things were changing," Peterson told me on TVO, 25 years after that campaign.

The election "presented us with an opportunity to present a fresh face. It was my first campaign so you've got nothing to protect, so you let it all out there. And it kind of worked. It kind of came together."

There may have been one other thing working in Peterson's favour. In 1985, there wasn't a single Liberal government anywhere in Canada. Not a one. In every provincial capital, Liberals were in opposition. And nationally, just eight months before the Ontario election, Brian Mulroney had led his Conservatives to the biggest majority government in Canadian history with 211 seats.

Conventional wisdom has held that Ontarians like to hedge their bets. When they vote in Liberals in Ottawa, they like to balance that by electing Conservatives in Toronto. Would the theory hold again? Now that the Tories were in charge in Ottawa, did that create an opening for Ontarians to consider a different party at Queen's Park?

Apparently so.

• • •

The results of the May 2, 1985 general election were fascinating. Despite the Ontario Tories running one of their worst campaigns ever, they actually won the largest number of seats. But they didn't get the largest number of votes. David Peterson's Liberals outpolled Frank Miller's PCs by one percentage point: 38 to 37 percent. But because of the way the votes split, the Liberals actually won four fewer seats: 48, to the Tories' 52.

In essence, the election was a tie.

Parliamentary convention was such that the Conservatives deserved the right to try to continue governing, since they won the most seats, albeit a minority of seats. But there was nothing conventional about these results and almost instantly, the back room boys and girls knew these numbers were different. In fact, they provided for an extraordinary new scenario.

What it meant was, Bob Rae's twenty-five New Democrats were in the driver's seat. Since the voters didn't make it abundantly clear who they wanted as their next premier, the NDP would decide for them.

Rae decided, in essence, to create a bargaining committee of key New Democrat MPPs. That group's job was to meet with representatives of both the PCs and Liberals, and then advise the NDP caucus whom they should support.

The politics were deliciously unprecedented and complicated. Ironically, many New Democrats and Conservatives have always felt they had more in common with each other than with the Liberals, despite the fact that ideologically, both of those parties were closer to the Grits than each other.

But New Democrats and Conservatives think they actually stand for something on the political spectrum, and so they tend to respect each other more than they do Liberals, whom they see as spineless, overly-pragmatic, bend-with-the-wind politicians with no particular principles. So there was a body of opinion within the NDP caucus that maintained: we must support the PCs. They won the most seats. They know how to do government. We can achieve some victories as we did in the mid-1970s, when constant pressure from the opposition parties on the minority Bill Davis government resulted in new policies such as rent controls on apartment buildings.

Besides, many New Democrats felt, the Liberals are completely untrustworthy. They'll take and get credit from the electorate for every policy victory we help them achieve. And the second their poll numbers go up, they'll pull the plug on the legislature, go back to the people for another election, and probably win a majority government.

But Bob Rae had another idea. He had always rued the fact that both federally in Ottawa and provincially in Toronto, New Democrats had never even had a sniff of power. Yes, they could be the conscience of the legislature. They could raise hell to try to move the policy yardsticks forward. But, frankly, they never had to be responsible for anything. Rae thought the discipline of actually having to have a hand in shaping government policy and seeing it through would be good for the party and the province.

And when the Liberal and NDP bargaining committees sat down to talk, they discovered they actually agreed on a lot. The notion of social democrats propping up not Leslie Frost's or John Robarts's or Bill Davis's moderate Tories, but Frank Miller's unabashedly right wing Republican wannabes, was a bridge too far for most New Democrats to cross. Given a chance to end the 42-year-old PC dynasty and experiment with something truly different, the NDP simply had to cross their fingers and cast their lot with the Grits.

And so, the Liberals and New Democrats agreed on something that became known as the Accord—a long list of policy initiatives the Liberals promised to introduce, and for which the NDP would support passage through the legislature. In addition, the Liberals promised to govern for at least two years without calling an election.

No one had ever tried this before. This wasn't some vague Speech from the Throne that the governing party could fudge on. The promises were quite specific. The Liberals, with NDP support, would fully fund the Roman Catholic school system to the end of Grade 13, completing Bill Davis's commitment. They would ban doctors from "extra billing," the practice some doctors employed of directly charging their patients above and beyond what the province's health insurance fee schedule paid them. They would bring in pay equity, offering women equal pay for work of equal value. They would bring in a freedom of information law, so the public could have greater access to what transpired behind the scenes. They would create a Spills Bill, requiring companies to be responsible for cleaning up (and paying for the cleanup) of their own chemical messes.

And so, when the Progressive Conservative government was defeated on the floor of the legislature, Frank Miller visited the lieutenant governor and no doubt, with considerable regret, told John Black Aird to give David Peterson a chance to command the confidence of The House. With the Accord in hand, Peterson had the proof that he could.

It's probably worth mentioning two other events that took place behind the scenes, which added to the intrigue of this time. At one point in the negotiations, Bob Rae floated the idea of forming a full-fledged coalition government with the Liberals, in which some NDP members would sit in the Cabinet.

But the idea never took off. Many New Democrats couldn't abide the idea of being governing partners with a "capitalist party." And Peterson, himself, refused to consider the idea even for a second.

"At some point it sort of bubbled up," Peterson recalled. "And someone suggested we should have a coalition. But I said 'Absolutely not.' I was not prepared to share the executive power, because I thought it would go nowhere."

Here, Peterson's experience in the legislature mattered. In his first election in 1975, Ontarians chose a minority Davis government. They did the same thing in 1977.

"I had seen minority government work," Peterson says. "So I wasn't fearful of that and didn't think we had to do anything dramatic in terms of a coalition."

The other backstage drama dealt with how the Accord should be signed. Rae may have considered the Accord proof that the Liberals and New Democrats were partners, of a sort, which is why Rae wanted a joint announcement of the two leaders signing the agreement together.

Again, Peterson was having none of it. He didn't want to leave the impression that this was a coalition government. It was a *Liberal* government with one man at the helm as its premier. There would be no signing ceremony with the two leaders.

In case anyone wasn't absolutely 100 percent certain, David Peterson and David Peterson alone was about to become Ontario's 20th premier.

• • •

What David Peterson didn't know on June 26, 1985 was that in his efforts to show how much more transparent and open his government would be than its predecessors, he was almost responsible for a near disaster at the Ontario legislature.

Channelling the spirit of the moment, Peterson was sworn in as premier, and then invited the thousands of people on the south lawn at Queen's Park on hand for the ceremony to come inside to see their beautiful, historic, seat of government. After all, he said, the Liberals would offer Ontarians a government "without walls or barriers."

Little did he know damned near everyone there would take him up on his offer. In they came, thousands of Ontarians, to see the inside of a building that probably many had never seen before. And that was the problem. Queen's Park is and was a very old building, which had no doubt seen hundreds of visitors at any one time, but never *thousands*. As the throngs gathered inside, nervous Liberals crossed their fingers and prayed that the second floor wouldn't collapse under the weight of all those visitors. Fortunately, nothing untoward happened.

June 26 was a memorable day for so many reasons. Yes, the swearing in of the first Liberal government in 42 years was historic. So was the size of the crowd. Governments in the past were sworn in with much less fanfare, inside the legislature. But a stage had been set up in anticipation of Canada Day celebrations, which would happen five days later. And Peterson, whose nose was running most of the day thanks to allergies, invited the thousands of civil servants who worked in the neighbourhood, to stroll by on their lunch hour to see their new government sworn in. The weather was perfect, which added to the crowd size, and the majesty of the day.

"There was just a sense of the dust being blown out of the place," Peterson said. "There was a whole new sense of energy and optimism. It really was a glorious day."

There were so many delightful stories in that first Cabinet swearing-in ceremony. Robert Nixon took the oath of office to become treasurer and minister of economics (today's minister of finance). Nixon was a living link to the last Liberal government back in 1943. His father, Harry Nixon, was the last Liberal premier before Peterson, and the longest-serving member of the legislature of all time (MPP for Brant from 1919-61). Even Bob Nixon himself had been an MPP for twenty-three years at that point, of course, all of it on the opposition benches.

Ontarians also saw the first black man ever take the Cabinet oath of office. Alvin Curling, born in Jamaica, now from the riding of Scarborough North, became minister of housing. Elinor Caplan became the first Jewish woman ever to become a cabinet minister as chair of the Management Board of Cabinet. Sean Conway, who was still a month away from turning 34 years old, would be tasked with implementing the promise William Davis made, to provide full public funding for Catholic schools. (Conway would go on to serve for almost three decades at Queen's Park, having got himself elected ten years earlier at age 24).

David Peterson talked a lot about the Conservative government being made up of a bunch of old, white guys, smoking fat cigars down at the Albany Club, Toronto's tony Conservative hang-out since the days of Sir John A. Macdonald. But years later, he would also acknowledge that those Tory governments were also made up of some pretty decent, moderate folks, who weren't ideologically driven. Having said that, more than four decades of governing had made the Tories, from time to time, a rather snoozy bunch. They certainly hadn't embraced two emerging phenomena—multiculturalism and feminism—with the enthusiasm that Ontario's Liberals had.

Peterson and his small team of rookies were determined to drive Ontario into the future. They promised the most activist government in the province's history, and they set out to deliver on that promise with a vengeance.

The Liberals entered the 1985 election campaign not expecting to win. Nevertheless, fifty-five days later, they were the government. That might have been a daunting challenge, given that none of the Liberals' forty-eight MPPs had any governing experience at the provincial or federal level (a few, such as Elinor Caplan, had some municipal experience). But thanks to having signed the Accord with the NDP, the Grits had a well-defined road map indicating exactly where they would go and how they would get there.

One of the first things the Liberals did was drain the press gallery. Conservatives, who had always been wary of the media and its overly fawning coverage of Peterson's campaign, had all of their worst suspicions confirmed when half the gallery quit to staff the "communications director" jobs for many new Cabinet ministers.

Ethics would also be important to this new government. Peterson insisted that his Cabinet ministers adhere to the highest standards. He boasted that his ministers wouldn't be tripped up by some of the lax ethical standards of which he believed the Tories were guilty.

Peterson would run an aggressive, activist, youthful, modern, progressive government in the normally politically sleepy Ontario. It was an irresistible story line. And for the first couple of years, it seemed as if the Liberals could do no wrong.

Even when scandals hit, they caused barely a ripple in Peterson's popularity. One year into his term, the premier learned that his minister of northern affairs and mines, René Fontaine, failed to disclose that he owned 17,000 shares of a mining company. It was a blatant screw up, and an obvious conflict of interest. But Fontaine admitted his mistake, resigned his seat, and ran again in the ensuing by-election. The New Democrats and Tories refused to field candidates, saying they wouldn't play along with what they considered a Liberal stunt. Fontaine won re-election and eventually got his old job back. Simply stated, public expectations were appropriately low for this group with no experience.

The Tories, meanwhile, were in the midst of an internecine battle, still not knowing what had hit them. Many were furious at Frank Miller for running a terrible campaign, failing to secure the NDP's support, and letting the dynasty die.

No doubt, many also believed this "illegitimate" partnership between the Liberals and New Democrats wouldn't last, the opportunistic Peterson would jump at the first chance to jettison the Accord and call an early election, or the government would fall due to its own incompetence, and the electorate would beg the Conservatives to return to the place to which they were so richly entitled.

Just one problem. None of that happened.

Peterson, with Rae's support, followed the Accord every step of the way, implementing item after item, as promised. Full funding for Catholic schools: done. Banning doctors from extra-billing: done. Pay equity: done. A *Freedom of Information Act*: done. Banning housing discrimination based on sexual orientation: done. And for the first time ever, the public could watch the debates in the legislature, live and in living colour, on television.

It truly was a new day in Ontario.

• • •

Almost two years into Ontario's first Liberal government in more than four decades, the verdict seemed to be in. David Peterson was, perhaps, the most popular politician in the entire country. He led a government that was activist and proud of it. Spending was way up, but the Liberals raised taxes to pay for their new programs. The NDP alternately played the role of tough-talking opposition party and legislative partner, ensuring Peterson had the votes to implement the Accord, and keep the disheartened and disorganized Progressive Conservatives on their heels.

That was not the script the PCs anticipated. As expected, the Tories dumped Frank Miller, and had a second leadership convention in 1985, but it was a very different affair. Unlike the last time, the prize wasn't the premiership, but rather the job of opposition leader.

Having said that, the contest was thrilling, with two senior Cabinet ministers from Toronto—Larry Grossman and Dennis Timbrell—duking it out on the last ballot. Grossman prevailed by just 19 votes out of nearly 1,700 cast.

The prevailing view among Conservatives was, now that the Miller mistake was behind them, a sharp cookie like Grossman would expose the Liberal-NDP alliance for the illegitimate bargain-with-the-devil it truly was, and the electorate would put the PCs back into power at their first opportunity.

But it was a measure of how out of touch the Tories really were that none of the things they had forecast would come to pass. Peterson had not opportunistically called an early election to disrupt the NDP. By sticking to the tenets of the Accord, his rookies, while not perfect, provided a government that garnered solid public support. The public was not begging the Tories to rescue them from an incompetent Liberal regime. And the Ontario Parliament buildings did not crumble to the ground without the Tories in power. Larry Grossman may have been a better leader than Frank Miller. But his timing was lousy. The electorate learned they could live without the Tories in charge. The party's support was in free fall.

It was the summer of 1987, and a perfect time for Peterson to go to the people. He wanted the public to render its judgment on the previous two years. And, frankly, the polls suggested he could win a majority government outright, and not have to depend on the NDP for his legislative survival.

So Peterson called an election for September 10, 1987. It meant most of the campaign would take place during the summer, when the premier could roll up his sleeves, attend barbeques, and bask in the glow of some very high public opinion surveys. It also meant that it would be harder for the opposition parties to chip away at Peterson's popularity, since much of the electorate simply turns off politics during July and August. By the time they started paying attention again after Labour Day, the campaign would essentially be over.

It's hard to imagine things could have gone better for David Peterson and his troops. Ontarians, in general, were happy. The economy was chugging along nicely and would improve. Both Grossman and Rae tried hard to chip away at the Liberal leader, but none of their attempts hit home. Peterson, who was a boxer during his days at the University of Toronto, was never in danger of hitting the canvas. In fact, when the Tories sent trouble-makers to Peterson's campaign events to start arguments with the Liberal leader by criticizing his record, he skillfully disarmed the confrontation by simply saying, "You're obviously unhappy with my record, so you should vote Conservative." It is a confident leader who ends a debate by saying vote for my opponent. But not many did.

The results of the 34th general election were, plain and simply, incredible. Peterson's Liberals took an astonishing ninety-five out of 130 seats, capturing more than 47 percent of the total votes cast. For the NDP, the news was mixed. On the one hand, the party moved past the Tories into second place and became the official opposition, a role it had played only twice before in its history (once as the CCF back in 1943, the other time against Bill Davis in 1975). But in coming second, the NDP also lost six seats, confirming the fears of those who worried that the party would help make the government better, but get none of the credit.

The undisputed losers were the Conservatives. They lost 36 seats including Grossman's own, which had been in the Grossman family since 1967 (Larry's father, Alan, had held the seat for eight years before his son took it over in 1975). The Tories also lost more than 12 percent of their votes, and were relegated to third place in the legislature for the first time since the United Farmers of Ontario formed the government. That was in 1919.

You would think that winning one of the largest majority governments in Ontario history would have made David Peterson the happiest man in Canada. While there was no question election night was an occasion for celebrating, Peterson was smart enough to know that winning too many seats is as much of a problem as winning too few. Expectations for his first government were extremely low, so meeting or surpassing those expectations was doable. Such is not the case when you control nearly three-quarters of the seats in the legislature as Peterson did after the 1987 election. In the first Peterson government, half the MPPs were in Cabinet. This time, only a quarter of the members would make it on to the executive council, meaning there would be more underutilized MPPs stewing on the backbenches, feeling underappreciated by the premier and his inner circle.

Peterson understood all this, which may be why he made what must have seemed, at the time, like an unusual first speech to his new, huge caucus.

"I got most of you elected this time," he told them. "But next time, I'm going to need you to get me elected."

Was it false modesty? Maybe. But it was also remarkably prescient.

•••

David Peterson's second term was nothing like the first one. For starters, it just couldn't have been as much fun. The Liberals were no longer the plucky underdogs, astonished at their good fortune to be occupying the government benches to the right of The Speaker of the legislature. With almost three times as many seats as the two opposition parties combined, they were firmly in charge of every lever of power at Queen's Park. They no longer needed their Accord partners, the New Democrats, for their political survival.

Liberals saw that as a good thing. Perhaps they shouldn't have. Removed from the discipline and strictures of their partnership with the NDP, the Liberals got into trouble. Part of their problems stemmed from the fact that Peterson had raised the ethical bar for his ministers so high, that many of them failed to meet the new, tougher code of conduct. And unlike in the first term, when ministerial resignations seemed to be taken in stride, they suddenly became a big deal after 1987. The Liberals were no longer the new kids on the block.

There was also a sense among the media covering Queen's Park that the opposition was so decimated after the 1987 election, that they had to get over their "bromance" with Peterson and start covering his government much more critically. Unfortunately, for the Liberals, they handed the media that gift on a silver platter, when some political contributions masterminded by a woman named Patricia Starr came to light.

"Patti" Starr, as everyone called her, was desperate to be a player. She ran the Toronto chapter of a relatively anonymous charity called the National Council of Jewish Women, which had been around for almost a century, and provided social services in the Jewish community. But Starr had greater ambitions for her charity and herself. So she started befriending Liberal government members and eventually got herself appointed chairman of the board of Ontario Place, the province's summer fun spot on Toronto's lakeshore right beside the Canadian National Exhibition. Along the way, she organized a bunch of fundraisers, cut a few corners, and funnelled money to some of her favourite politicians. Problem was, charities aren't supposed to give money to politicians, let alone a free refrigerator and a home paint job to the Liberals' campaign director. Yes, that happened too.

Before you knew it, Starr had been charged with breach of trust and violations of the *Elections Expenses Act*. And David Peterson was calling an emergency late night news conference, saying the revelations felt like a kick in the gut. He was ordering a judicial inquiry into the whole illegal campaign contribution mess.

In the grand scheme of things, it was a relatively minor scandal. But the media, anxious to overcompensate for its past overly-obsequious coverage of Peterson, went to town on the scandal. They would play it for all it was worth.

Eventually, Starr would go to jail for six months, write a bestselling book, and become *persona non grata* in Liberal circles, despite raising quite a bit of money for Cabinet ministers and members.

But it didn't end there. Even when the government thought it was on solid ground with progressive, new policies, it got hammered. An example of that would be when Peterson announced that hundreds of good-paying, permanent jobs at the Ontario Lottery Corporation would be moved from the corner of Yonge and Bloor Streets in downtown Toronto to Sault Ste. Marie. The thinking was, not every government job had to be in Toronto, where rents were sky high and unemployment was low. If the jobs really didn't need to be in Toronto, then why not export them to somewhat more vulnerable cities, where their impact could be enormous?

It was an unambiguously good news story in The Soo when it was announced in July 1986. But by late 1989 and early 1990, when the economy started to deteriorate, suddenly the media became interested in the hundreds of jobs Toronto was losing. It no longer seemed like such a good news story.

(For the record, the Ontario Lottery and Gaming Corporation opened its new headquarters in Sault Ste. Marie in 1992. There are 900 permanent jobs there making OLG the city's fourth largest employer. And while most Torontonians didn't make the move north with the company, the wisdom of the decision, and the huge impact those good-paying, permanent jobs have on The Soo's economy almost 20 years later seems obvious).

Decentralizing government made a lot of sense in communities outside Toronto. But there was one occasion when the effort truly did blow up in the government's face. Consistent with his "government without walls or barriers" philosophy, Peterson wanted to demonstrate that he was still "out there," not secluded in his office at Queen's Park. And so for the first time in years, the Liberals would hold caucus meetings or Cabinet retreats *outside* the legislature, in communities around Ontario. The move served a double purpose: first, getting away from the overly critical eyes of the Queen's Park press gallery in Toronto; and second, getting ministers and MPPs into Ontario's heartland, conveying the impression that the Liberal government was still very much connected to the people who gave it such a huge mandate.

No doubt, that was all in David Peterson's mind when he put his caucus on a train and had them roll a few hours east to Brockville. What was waiting for him and his fellow Liberals were six members of an anti-bilingualism group called APEC: the Association for the Preservation of English in Canada. They used the occasion to protest their opposition to Quebec's language laws, and Peterson's efforts to extend French language services to more Franco-Ontarians. In doing so, however, the protesters went one step too far. A few of them took a Quebec flag, tossed it to the ground, and trampled on it. Undaunted, Peterson gave a speech in Brockville—entirely in French.

Ironically, the incident received not much coverage immediately. But several months later, when Canadian first ministers were hip deep in negotiations with Quebec on the Meech Lake Constitutional Accord, that footage somehow miraculously appeared over and over and over again on Quebec television stations. And yes, it certainly had an impact then.

Former British Prime Minister Harold Macmillan was once asked what the greatest challenge facing leaders was. "Events, dear boy. Events."

Such was the case for David Peterson's government as well. His first term was dominated by Ontario issues, many of which were covered in the the Accord with the NDP. But his second term became dominated by national events, many of which were beyond the premier's control.

The clearest example of that was the national debate over free trade. When Prime Minister Brian Mulroney looked south, he saw an increasingly protectionist neighbour in the United States. Given that Canada did 85 percent of its trade with the US, securing access to the American market for Canadian goods and services became job one for Mulroney.

Politically, it was a bold gambit for two reasons. Mulroney had won the leadership of the national Progressive Conservative party in 1983, in part, because he so staunchly opposed free trade. In addition, as a student of history, Mulroney also knew that in 1911, Liberal Prime Minister Wilfrid Laurier lost his government after fifteen years by trying to pass a "reciprocity treaty" with the US—in effect, the free trade agreement of its day. For more than seven decades, no Canadian government would touch the free trade issue over fears of suffering the same fate as Laurier.

But America's increasing protectionism changed Mulroney's mind, and in the process, hurled David Peterson into the middle of a national debate, over which the 1988 Canadian election would be decided.

International agreements are clearly within the purview of the federal government to negotiate in Canada. But Peterson, deeply concerned about what a new free trade agreement might do to Ontario's manufacturing heartland, weighed in even though he had no seat at the table. He and his officials considered Mulroney's trade deal not to be in Ontario's best interests, and so the premier, backed with a majority government mandate comprising 73 percent of the members of the Ontario legislature, campaigned against free trade.

But Mulroney had an even bigger mandate of his own, comprising 75 percent of the seats in the House of Commons. And when the prime minister called an election after bringing free trade negotiations to a successful conclusion, he essentially left it up to the people of Canada to decide whether free trade would sink or swim.

Seventy-seven years after Laurier's Reciprocity Treaty went down to defeat in the 1911 election, Canadians finally opted for free trade. On November 21, 1988, Mulroney became the first Conservative prime minister since Sir John A. Macdonald to win back-to-back majority governments. Free trade was now a fact of Canadian life. Peterson may have opposed it. But the reality was, there wasn't a thing he could now do to stop it and he knew it.

• • •

There was another debate over national issues that Peterson could and did play a huge role in: the effort by Canada's eleven first ministers to get Quebec's signature on the Constitution, completing the task initiated by Prime Minister Pierre Trudeau earlier in the decade when he repatriated the Constitution with an accompanying Charter of Rights and Freedoms. This new effort was called the Meech Lake Constitutional Accord.

"Meech" would come to overshadow everything during Peterson's second term. In June 1987, Canada's eleven first ministers agreed on a series of constitutional reforms. During the previous round of talks under Trudeau in 1981, Quebec, which was led by a separatist government under Premier René Lévesque, refused to sign the Constitution. Quebec was legally bound by the agreement, but it stuck in Brian Mulroney's craw that his home province felt left out of the Canadian constitutional family. He wanted Quebec in, "with honour and enthusiasm." (Besting Trudeau wouldn't have been a bad thing for Mulroney's legacy either).

When the first ministers signed the agreement at the Langevin Block in Ottawa in 1987, it started a three-year clock, within which all eleven legislatures in Canada (ten provincial, one federal) had to ratify the agreement, or it would expire.

Without going into chapter and verse here, it became clear as time was running out that "Meech" was going to fail. Over the three-year ratification period, some governments changed and were less keen, even hostile to the Accord. The eleven first ministers gathered in June 1990 at the Government Conference Centre in Ottawa in hopes of making a last ditch attempt to salvage the agreement. When it looked as if all hope was lost, Peterson in effect rode in on a white horse and offered a compromise that appeared to save the day.

The problem was the composition of the Senate. Quebec's share of the population was declining, and yet it enjoyed a disproportionately high number of seats in the upper chamber. Quebec insisted on its historic 25 percent share of the Senate's representation. Peterson's eleventh hour play was to have Ontario offer to give up six of its Senate seats. Quebec would be satisfied, and so would the rest of the country. Ontario would look generous, making the supreme sacrifice for the good of national unity.

When Peterson was asked what the ramifications of giving up Senate representation would be, he said (probably echoing most Ontarians' sentiments), "Nothing at all." Frankly, who could quarrel with him? Did Ontarians ever care about the Senate? Would they miss the six seats? Would they feel underrepresented in Ottawa? Hardly. So Peterson gave something away that no one would miss and in the process, basked in the limelight of playing a historic role in the negotiations.

While the people of Ontario have traditionally expected their premiers to play a role on the national stage, they also expect them to stick to their knitting. Crudely put, it means if you want to fly off and play Captain Canada, you'd better make sure things are okay on the home front.

Problem was, they weren't. By 1990, when Peterson was neck-deep in constitutional negotiations, economic storm clouds were already gathering. Economists everywhere were forecasting a tough recession on the horizon. When one of his ministers tried to meet with him to talk about a growing crisis with skyrocketing auto insurance premiums, Peterson shot back, "I didn't get elected to deal with auto insurance."

In fact, he did. But understandably, with an unprecedented opportunity to resolve a constitutional quagmire, which had bedeviled first ministers for decades, Peterson's focus was on national unity.

Ironically, despite all his efforts, despite his sacrifice of Senate seats, despite all the political capital he spent to get Meech Lake passed, the agreement ultimately failed when the Newfoundland and Manitoba legislatures declined to ratify it.

In the midst of that political storm, David Peterson decided to call an election, two years before he had to.

• • •

Dalton Camp, the former president of the national PC Party and Toronto Star columnist, said at the time: "The first politician that picks his head up after Meech's failure will live to regret it."

What he meant was, the electorate was getting increasingly cranky. Most of the political energy in the country seemed to be focused on a constitutional agreement the public didn't care about, and not on the recession that was just around the corner, a recession that would kill tens of thousands of jobs in the process.

That first politician to "pick his head up"—in other words, call an election—was David Peterson.

"I was very worried after the death of Meech Lake that we were heading into a very difficult period," Peterson recalled. "I needed a strong hand to deal with Ontario's problems. And the separatist sentiment in Quebec was running as high as 75 percent. It was a very volatile time and I needed a strong hand to deal with that."

So, less than three years into his mandate, at the end of July, Peterson called an election for September 6, 1990. He was still light years ahead of the NDP and Conservatives in public opinion surveys. And the last summertime campaign had been very good to him. But something was different this time 'round.

In hindsight, it seems obvious that the premier shouldn't have called that 1990 election two years early. But all that wisdom wasn't so clear at the time. In fact, the conventional wisdom of the day was, *of course* Peterson should call an early election. The political reasons for doing so were simply too compelling.

First, the recession was coming. Any smart politician knows if you can avoid having an election in the middle of bad economic times, you should do so. If Peterson had called the election at the traditional four-year mark, it would have taken place smack in the middle of the worst recession since the Great Depression. That was considered too risky.

Second, the traditional challengers to the Liberals, the Progressive Conservatives, had just chosen a new leader in April 1990. He was Michael Dean Harris from North Bay. Harris was preaching what seemed like a platform more akin to the US Republican Party. Deep tax cuts. Spending cuts. Firing civil servants. More personal freedom. It was a very un-Ontario platform. An early election call would catch the third place Tories off guard with an unknown leader and no money in the bank.

Third, there were the New Democrats. The NDP would never be the government in Ontario. They were simply too far outside the mainstream. Ontarians had never voted for an NDP government, nor would they, the Liberals thought.

Money in the bank. A huge lead in the polls. A weakened opposition. Add it all up, and it seemed like a strategic slam-dunk to go to the polls early.

•••

When David Peterson raised the issue of the advisability of an early election call at one of his weekly Cabinet meetings in 1990, he wasn't bowled over with an enthusiastic response. His ministers did appreciate the strategic value of going early. But they worried that it would look opportunistic and that many good MPPs would lose their jobs in the process. Mind you, the Liberals could afford to lose a whopping thirty seats and *still* have a majority government. And frankly, it would be easier to run the government with fewer members.

So the Cabinet, with some reluctance, endorsed the premier's idea for an early election call. As health minister Elinor Caplan later described it, "We thought, let's just get it over with."

It didn't take long for the Liberals to realize that the early election call wasn't such a good idea. Just seconds after Premier Peterson launched into his campaign kickoff address in the Queen's Park media studio, a protester from Greenpeace, with an audio playback machine chained to his wrist, hijacked the news conference. He plunked the tape machine onto Peterson's desk, refused to budge, and played the previously recorded message, which offered a stinging indictment of the government's environmental record.

It was a strange issue to attack the Liberals on, since their environmental record was perhaps the most exemplary of any government in Ontario history. But it was a sign that this election would be anything but conventional.

Peterson froze. His safety wasn't in jeopardy. But he clearly wasn't in control of the situation. (The protester, Gord Perks, would go on to become a two-term Toronto city councillor). Inexplicably, the president of the press gallery, Gene Allen of the Globe and Mail, allowed Perks to finish his disruption without calling in security and having the protester removed. At one point, Peterson looked sheepishly at Allen and said, "Is this really how you want to run this thing?"

Allen timidly asked Perks to finish up, which he did. Peterson then looked into the assemblage of reporters, saw the dean of the press gallery, CITY-TV reporter Colin Vaughan (whose son Adam is now a Toronto city councillor as well), smiled, and said, "I told you it was going to be an interesting campaign."

That would turn out to be a massive understatement.

An objective look at the five years David Peterson's Liberals were in power would show that Ontario took some significant steps forward on several major files. The items in the Accord had been achieved in the first two years. On the environmental front, St. Catharines MPP Jim Bradley was being hailed as the best environment minister the province had ever seen. His ministry developed the blue box recycling program, the first of its kind anywhere in the world.

In addition, Bradley ordered the worst polluters in Ontario to clean up their emissions or risk being shut down. Such threats in the past were routinely ignored. But Peterson's government wasn't bluffing. And so, Inco, Ontario Hydro, Falconbridge, and Algoma Steel spent millions of dollars on pollution scrubbers, taking tons of noxious emissions out of the air. And yet, environmental groups blasted Peterson, saying it wasn't enough.

The Liberals, under education ministers such as Sean Conway and Chris Ward, ramped up public spending significantly, both for the Catholic school system, and to hire more teachers. And yet, the teachers' unions were omnipresent on the hustings, saying none of it was enough.

The Liberals extended French language services where numbers warranted, and yet, the blowback was intense. In January 1990, Sault Ste. Marie, which was such a beneficiary of economic development with the OLG move, passed a resolution confirming English was the sole working language of the municipality. It was the largest Ontario city to do so, and even though it claimed to be retaliating for a similar move in Quebec, it was hardly helpful to Peterson's efforts during the Meech Lake negotiations.

The court system was overhauled as never before by the brilliant attorney-general, Ian Scott. Welfare rates were significantly raised in response to cries from social service organizations that the poor needed additional assistance. Sunday shopping restrictions were eased, which only prompted the NDP to warn that social cohesion was at risk because too many family members would be forced to work Sundays (even though the bill stipulated no one would be forced to). Child care spaces were increased. Social housing units were built in unprecedented numbers.

The Liberals were the most activist government in more than half a century, but in every case, and on every file, their activism only served to prompt their critics to demand more and more.

The fact was, all these special interest groups were so positive the Liberals would be re-elected, they relentlessly and mercilessly attacked Peterson on the campaign trail at every turn. *Everyone* thought the Liberals were coming back to power, so this was simply a good opportunity to keep the heat on and keep their issue on the premier's front burner.

However, rather than keeping the Liberals modest, the protests served to portray a government constantly in the crosshairs. Night after night, the local news would broadcast images of Peterson getting hammered by one group or another. The Liberal campaign team hoped the image conveyed was one of an accessible leader, not hiding in a bubble, but rather unafraid to engage with Ontarians.

But that wasn't what the voters saw. What they saw was a premier under constant assault. Many concluded: maybe this guy's no good after all.

And then the mother of all missteps took place. Yes, the Liberals ramped up spending significantly compared to the Davis years. But they also created new taxes and raised existing ones to pay for their plans. The result was the first balanced budgets Ontario had seen in nearly two decades. But many thought the Liberals spent like drunken sailors and weren't fiscally prudent enough. The economy was firing on all cylinders, revenues were buoyant, and rather than just balancing the budget, critics thought the Grits ought to be running big surpluses and paying down more debt (which at the time was a modest $30 billion. Today, it's cruising towards $300 billion).

So, midway through the 1990 election campaign, Treasurer Robert Nixon announced if the Liberals were re-elected, he would cut the retail sales tax by one point, saving taxpayers hundreds of millions of dollars.

Years later, Nixon would confess the tax cut wasn't his idea. He would insist that it was forced upon him. He hated the idea because without that sales tax revenue, his next budget would be nearly impossible to balance.

In previous elections, offering a tax cut might be seen as the government bribing the electorate with its own money. But many electorates were happy to have that happen. Not this time. The outcry, first from the opposition parties, and then from others, confirmed something had changed. The public saw the move as too craven, and too desperate, by a party whose polling numbers had already started falling at alarming rates.

After the tax cut promise was announced, the Grits' popularity was in free fall. Still, this was Ontario. No one was prepared to forecast anything other than a much-reduced Liberal government.

At least, almost no one.

A few days before September 6th, Elly Alboim, the man responsible for producing CBC-TV's election night coverage, asked his anchor to leave his desk and huddle with him privately in one of the network's dark, small edit suites. The anchorman did so.

"I'm going to tell you something and I want you to keep this private," Alboim told the broadcaster. "Because when this happens on election night, I can't have you jumping up in your seat going, 'Holy shit, look at that,' as my anchor in Alberta recently did."

"Trust me, you have my attention," the host replied.

"OK, start to process the following information," Alboim continued. "The NDP is going to win a majority government, and David Peterson is going to lose his seat."

He said it calmly, and matter-of-factly, his face betraying no emotion as to whether he thought this was a good thing or not. He said it with the same level of drama as he might have told me to go get him a coffee.

"No way," I responded. "Not a chance." I had lived in Ontario for almost my entire life. And I knew this much was true: the NDP would never form a government. Not only that, only two sitting premiers had ever lost their seats, and in both cases, it was a fluke. William Hearst lost the election and his seat in 1919, after the United Farms of Ontario won an upset election that year. And George Drew lost his own seat in 1948, despite winning a majority government, because he upset the temperance crusaders in Toronto's High Park neighborhood by softening the province's liquor laws.

But both of those things were part of Ontario's long ago past. I was convinced history would not repeat.

"How do you know?" I asked him.

"I just know and you'll have to trust me on this," Alboim said.

I had to acknowledge that Elly knew a thing or two about politics, since he'd produced about two dozen federal and provincial election night broadcasts from his perch as chief of the CBC's parliamentary bureau. So I filed the prediction away just in case.

• • •

Election night, September 6, 1990, was one of the most shocking in Canadian political history. So many utterly unexpected things happened. The Liberals knew they were going to get a good spanking by the electorate. But they also figured, at the end of the night, they'd still be in charge. They expected to win, albeit with a reduced number of MPPs.

But election night wasn't a spanking. It was a smack-down worthy of the octagon.

As the returns started coming in, it soon became apparent that Ontarians didn't merely want to chasten the Liberals. They wanted to crush them. And, unlike in every previous provincial election, it wouldn't be the Conservatives who would benefit from the Liberals' poor showing. The electorate was about to do something unprecedented.

All across Ontario, current and former Cabinet ministers were going down to defeat. In Toronto, Scarborough's Ed Fulton, East York's Christine Hart, downtown's Bob Wong, and midtown's Chaviva Hosek went down to defeat. Ken Keyes lost in Kingston. Mavis Wilson and Ken Black were knocked out of their rural seats. In the Hamilton-Niagara region, Chris Ward, Lily Oddie Munro, and Harry Pelissero were ousted. In southwestern Ontario, William Wrye and Joan Smith were dumped.

Some who were members of the Liberal firmament were barely hanging on. St. Catharines' Jim Bradley, first elected in 1977 and now the dean of the Ontario legislature, squeaked back in by fewer than 1,000 votes. And Robert Nixon, whose roots in Brant riding went back to the year 1919, only managed to defeat Chris Stanek (a university student) by 1,500 votes.

Within an hour and a half of the polls closing, the broadcasters confirmed we were witnessing one of the most remarkable nights in history. The Liberals would lose fifty-nine seats and almost 15 percent of the vote, compared to their stellar performance of three years earlier. And most shockingly, one of those lost seats was indeed London Centre, where Premier Peterson went down to personal defeat. He was shellacked by New Democrat Marion Boyd, who bested the Liberal leader with more than 51 percent of the votes cast in that riding, compared with just 28 percent support for Peterson.

The debacle was complete.

Our first-past-the-post parliamentary system tends to exacerbate relatively small changes in popular opinion, and the 1990 election demonstrated that in spades. Bob Rae's New Democrats managed to win a solid majority government by capturing just 37.6 percent of the total votes cast. Conventional wisdom has always held that winning a majority in Ontario was impossible with less than 40 percent of the vote.

But on September 6th, conventional wisdom was on vacation.

(By way of comparison, Dalton McGuinty's Liberals won the exact same 37.6 percent of the vote in the 2011 Ontario election, and won just 53 seats and a minority government. Was Bob Rae incredibly lucky in the way the votes split? He sure was.)

In 1990, with just 5 percent more votes than the Liberals got, the NDP captured a total of seventy-four seats, an increase of a whopping fifty-five seats from 1987. They managed to take about 1.5 million votes compared to the Liberals' 1.3 million. But because of the efficiency of their vote—in effect, how those votes were distributed across Ontario—the NDP captured seats they'd never even dreamed of winning before.

Victoria-Haliburton, which had been represented by former Conservative premier Leslie Frost for more than a quarter of a century, went NDP. Halton North, where New Democrats routinely lost their deposit, ended up in the win column for the orange team. The agricultural riding of Lincoln, which had ping-ponged back and forth between Liberals and Conservatives in every election (except one) since Confederation, voted NDP. The same story repeated in riding after riding, across the province.

Almost lost in the evening's drama was the story line on the new PC Party leader. Mike Harris also had a rough night, losing just over 1 percent of the Tory vote compared to 1987, which was one of the party's worst showings ever. However, thanks to the way the votes split, Harris actually won four more seats and so his leadership was deemed safe.

When David Peterson finally appeared to give his concession speech, the former university boxer looked as if he'd barely been able to pick himself up off the canvas to deliver his remarks. Forcing a smile, he looked emotionally devastated as he no doubt wondered how it all ended so quickly.

And yet, on that night, Peterson gave an extremely classy speech. He took complete responsibility for the results, and yet made no apologies for getting knocked down (again, the boxing analogy). He suggested the only shame was in refusing to get back up again. Peterson insisted both he personally, and his party in general would do so.

Both statements proved prophetic, for in the carnage that was the 1990 election for the Liberal Party of Ontario, amidst all of the candidates going down to defeat, there was a single new Liberal MPP elected that night.

His name was Dalton James Patrick McGuinty, Jr. And the record will show that all he would go on to do is win three consecutive elections in 2003, 2007, and 2011—the first Liberal leader in 128 years to accomplish that.

• • •

Twenty-five years after the unforgettable 1985 election, David Peterson appeared on TVO's *The Agenda with Steve Paikin* to consider what had transpired.

"I don't beat myself up with recrimination about this," Peterson said. "Just as I didn't feel smug about winning, I didn't feel depressed about losing. The only bigger surprise to losing in 1990 was winning in 1985. That's the nature of the business."

As he looked back at his time in government, Peterson still can't say for certain what in particular caused his defeat. But, no doubt, a combination of the premature election call, a looming recession, and unhappiness over the Meech Lake negotiations played a part. While Ontarians have traditionally wanted their premiers to stand tall on the national stage, "Perhaps I didn't get that balance quite right," Peterson acknowledged. "Perhaps I spent too much of my own personal political capital on that (national unity) debate.

"It may also have been bad campaigning, and arrogance on my part. I didn't campaign with the same edge," he admitted.

One of the great debates emerging from the 1990 Ontario election has been, did the electorate really get the result it wanted? Did the people really mean to give the New Democrats a majority government? Did they really want to throw the Liberals out so dramatically, or just knock 'em down a peg?

"I really do believe—and maybe this is naiveté on my part—that people didn't want to kick us out," Peterson maintains a quarter century later.

"They wanted to chasten us. They wanted to slap our wrists. But if we could have done that election again the next day, they would have said, 'Holy smokes, do we really want to go there?' The government itself was actually fairly popular.

"I think I wasn't."

DAVID PETERSON
THE FEDERALIST

Premiers' Conference

St. John's, Newfoundland, August 21, 1985

Fellow premiers, I'm honoured to be at my first Premiers' Conference, at the same table with men I've read about and admired. Premier Peckford, before I say anything else I'd like to tell you how much I appreciate your hospitality, and how much Shelley and I have enjoyed your capital city in the short time we've been here.

I'm particularly glad to have the opportunity to attend this conference, because I am proud to have the chance to participate in at least one meeting with the current premiers of Alberta and Quebec. Although Ontario governments have differed from time to time with these leaders, in Ontario there is no disagreement over one point: two titans are departing the Canadian political scene.

Premier Lévesque, we appreciate that in waging a determined battle for your beliefs you have forced the entire country to recognize the strong and legitimate desire of francophones to maintain and enhance their linguistic traditions and culture.

Premier Lougheed, we appreciate that in standing up firmly for your province's interests you have forced us all to better define our economic objectives and strategies.

The people of Quebec and Alberta are no doubt experiencing the same feeling Ontario experienced when Bill Davis stepped down: the feeling an important era is coming to an end—leaving significant achievements that will provide ongoing legacies to these leaders.

There is no doubt in my mind about the most important legacy that has been left to my government, the Ontario leaders whom I've known and admired all had one thing in common: a philosophy that bridged a strong commitment to Ontario with a strong commitment to Canada.

Without Walls or Barriers: The Speeches of Premier David Peterson, Library of Political Leadership Series, by Arthur Milnes and Ryan Zade, Editors. Montreal and Kingston: McGill-Queen's University Press,
© 2017 The School of Policy Studies, Queen's University at Kingston. All rights reserved.

It has never been my practice to allow differences over this issue or that issue to diminish my respect for those who have done so much to fight for interests of importance to their province or raise questions of importance to the country. I do not believe in allowing policy differences to become personal differences, or confusing disagreements over process with disagreements over substance.

This is my first time at this table, and it is one at which I expect to learn much, but I realize that all of us here view many of the issues from different perspectives. That's only natural given that we view them from different points on the map. I will never criticize any premier for standing up for his province: like all premiers, I want the best for my province; like all premiers I want that to be consistent with what is best for all provinces.

We recognize the importance of common approaches to common problems; that is why we are here. We recognize that in the sea of federal-provincial relations, we are all in the same boat.

Ontario is always considered a "have" province with an assured future, but even in a "have" province there are "have-not" regions. In today's economy, no one's future is assured. There are many parts of Ontario that have a lot in common with provinces that have deep concerns about their future in terms of sustained employment and industrial activity. There are many industries in Ontario that look back fondly on a distant past when they were led to believe they had an assured future.

There is no question that our first commitment must be to our own province, but we are not blind to everything that is east of the Ottawa River and west of Lake of the Woods. We recognize that some provinces have ground to make up, but that ground must be made up by helping them to run faster, rather than forcing others to slow down.

These are the principles we will pursue on all national issues, from job training to job creation, from trade arrangements to fiscal arrangements. We will always be prepared to accept a fair deal. We will never offer any other kind.

I look forward to our discussions, and the opportunity they will provide to look from all sides at the problems we are all committed to solve.

NATIVE BUSINESS SUMMIT FOUNDATION CONFERENCE AND TRADE SHOW
Toronto, Ontario, June 24, 1986

This first Native Business Summit Foundation Conference and Trade Show is truly an idea whose time has come.

This conference gives Native entrepreneurs the chance to find out more about domestic and international markets, and potential investment services. It gives Native and non-Native entrepreneurs the chance to get together and replace barriers to investment with avenues to opportunity.

Like most good ideas, this one became a reality only because there were people with the desire, drive, and determination to make it happen.

No matter how apparent, needs are not answered unless there are people to provide the answer—to push, to prod, to organize.

I congratulate the organizers on their vision, and on making it come to life.

I'm delighted that the Ontario government has the opportunity to participate. Throughout the five days of this summit, 14 ministries will be represented, with staffers on hand to provide advice and explain the range of Ontario government programs and services available to Native communities and business people.

While we recognize that development of Native entrepreneurship is only one step to Native self-reliance, it is an important one. So it is encouraging to see a first-hand demonstration of the growing trend among Canadian Native people to make the most of the private sector as an effective route to their economic goals.

Bien sûr, quand on laisse les principaux intéressés en dehors des politiques, celles-ci s'avèrent automatiquement malcontent. Quand l'on ignore tout le potentiel du leadership autochtone, on se rapproche inévitablement de l'échec.

This conference is a boon to all who are participating—Natives and non-Natives alike. Opportunities for investment lead to opportunities for jobs—which lead to opportunities for further investment. What you are working on this week is a virtuous cycle.

While I am offering congratulations, I should also congratulate you on choosing Toronto as the site. As its name implies, Toronto is an excellent meeting place. It has proven to be a city of opportunity for many, and I'm sure it will be for you this week.

Certainly the timing could not be any better. It appears that changing conditions and attitudes are finally beginning to allow full use of entrepreneurial skills that seem to come naturally to North America's first fur traders.

Trust companies, sportswear, trucking, and shopping malls. What do these fields of commerce have in common? They're among the many in which Native people across this country own and operate profitable enterprises.

The organizers of this conference have done such a good job of communicating the facts about Native entrepreneurship, it seems redundant to go over them. But they bear a bit of repetition, because of what they tell us about the potential for growth.

Across Canada, there are more than 5,000 businesses owned and operated by Natives.

Native people and the enterprises they own and run contribute more than $1 billion to our economy every year.

Indian entrepreneurs alone are expected to create more than 36,000 jobs over the next five years. Clearly, the time for Native entrepreneurship is now.

The timing of this conference is excellent in other respects as well. Canadians are finally becoming aware of the strengths that can be drawn from Native cultures, traditions and values.

Moreover, this conference falls in the midst of a historic constitutional debate that will determine the relationship between Native and non-Native Canadians for many years to come.

Il s'agit d'un débat constitutionnel sur lequel toute notre énergie devra se porter. Sur ses résultats vont dépendre toutes nos relations pour les décennies à venir.

Clearly, that relationship must be based on mutual respect, and across-the-board rights and freedoms.

The essence of freedom is that each of us shares in shaping our destiny. That is the challenge we must meet.

That challenge is at the same time simple and complex.

In Ontario, we have approved a policy framework that will provide substantial guidance in our efforts to meet that challenge.

The policy framework is based on five key principles:

1. continued commitment to the ultimate constitutional entrenchment of aboriginal people's rights to self-government;
2. efforts to secure agreements with the federal government and Native organizations respecting aboriginal self-government in the province;
3. encouragement of increased self-determination and self-reliance by Native peoples;
4. emphasis on programs and services specifically geared to meeting the particular needs of Native peoples, and protect Native cultures; and,
5. full consultation with Native communities in the development of policies and programs that primarily affect them.

In making these principles a reality, the Native Business Summit Foundation can be a very effective tool.

I will remind you that the call for Native self-determination has been made not just on the basis of a purely abstract principle. Rather, it is based on a diagnosis of the problems that have hampered Native development.

Native leaders have looked at the programs that were supposed to alleviate problems in their communities, looked at the results and found them wanting.

Why have these programs not met with greater success? Certainly not for lack of desire, or lack of effort, either on the part of those who have developed them, or those who were supposed to benefit from them.

And that is the problem right there. The programs have not been developed by the people they were supposed to benefit. They have not been developed by Native people. They have been developed by non-Natives, based on non-Native assumptions.

It is not surprising that such programs have not been more successful. The non-Native majority was trying to provide leadership. When it comes to Native affairs, leadership is something that must come from Natives themselves.

We are experiencing a remarkable shift. We are seeing the twilight of an era of benevolence, and the dawn of a new era of independence.

We are saying goodbye to a period when non-Natives tried to set Natives' course, and welcoming a new period when Natives set their own course.

New trails tend to be alarming and formidable. But they are also exciting and illuminating. And more importantly, they can lead to new horizons.

Over the past few months we have seen this new approach in Ontario. We have already seen several initiatives to increase self-reliance in Native communities.

We've seen increased self-reliance in the area of child welfare. Three Native corporations have been set up to provide child welfare services in Native communities in the north. In other provinces it has been found that when child welfare services are delivered by Natives, the result can be greater harmony and less disruption.

We've seen increased self-reliance in the area of education. Ontario has now introduced a "Native as a second language" program. The study of Native languages will be integrated into the school day. Again, experience in other provinces has shown that Native children do much better in an educational environment that sustains and reinforces their culture and languages.

In the area of law enforcement, the Ontario government has worked with Indian organizations to set up an Indian Police Commission. The Commission will provide advice on the operation of the band constable program, to improve relations between police and Indian communities, and develop preventive programs on reserves.

The principles that have shown so much promise in child welfare, education and law enforcement—the principles of self-reliance and mutual respect—also have tremendous potential in economic development.

I am as delighted as you are by the promising economic statistics and forecasts I cited earlier. But I am as disappointed as you are that more of the fruits of economic prosperity have not found their way to Native communities. It is disappointing, for example, that for most Natives, income, employment and education levels still fall well below average.

Again, if Natives have been unable to build the foundation for economic prosperity, it may be because non-Natives have been selecting the tools and choosing the construction site. That's why the Province of Ontario has set up the Ontario Native Economic Support Program. This program has been established to provide financial support for the development of Native community facilities.

My government is also developing a Native economic participation program to widen the opportunities available to Native entrepreneurs.

And we have set in motion the development of a Native economic development strategy for Ontario.

All of these efforts have one thing in common—they are designed to support Native enterprise, not supplant it. Because the fact is, that is the only way any government effort can be truly helpful.

Take the Native people's goose-and-duck hunting camps, seven of them from Fort Severn to Moosonee.

The Ontario government transferred the camps to Native control several years ago. They employ more than 200 Indians, mostly from the Swampy Cree nation. They operate the camps, run transportation networks, independent booking agencies, and all related service facilities.

Or take the Windigo fish packing plant, just west of Lake Nipigon.

The plant is operated by the northern Native fisherman's co-operative. It makes a profit from fish-packing, and the sale of supplies, and has for years.

I look forward to the social and economic projects that will result from the agreement to compensate the Grassy Narrows and Islington Indian bands for the mercury pollution that forced the English-Wabigoon River system to be closed 16 years ago.

Finally, I would like to bring to your attention the initiatives the Ontario government has taken in our recent budget and throne speech to assist small business entrepreneurs, because they can be especially helpful to Native small business entrepreneurs.

I hope you will take advantage of these programs, which offer access to information, expertise and venture capital. The new ventures program, for example, provides guarantees of loans up to $15,000.

The fact that Native enterprise can be extremely successful will certainly not come as news to you. But I hope the fact that Natives are being encouraged to run their own enterprises will come as good news to you because constitutional, economic, and social progress are not isolated compartments.

The ultimate goal of self-government can only be achieved part and parcel with progress in economic development. Progress on one front advances progress on the other. That is why Native entrepreneurs like yourselves can unlock the door to self-determination, because you are turning the key of self-reliance.

Il est toujours préférable de savoir pêcher plutôt que de se faire donner du poisson. Les autochtones l'ont toujours su. Il est heureux que des gens comme vous se servent d'un tel exemple avec succès.

I'm proud to have this opportunity to address the first Native Business Conference. I look forward to the second, and the fifth, and the tenth.

Because I see a bright day for Native self-determination.

Instead of paternalism, we see self-determination; instead of assimilation, we see cultural enhancement; instead of destitution, we see bright prospects for community well-being.

And the best part is, you're accomplishing it for yourselves and your people.

FIRST MINISTERS' CONFERENCE
Vancouver, BC, November 20, 1986

All of us sitting at this table have much in common. So do the regions we come from. As Canadians, we share a unique set of values.

Different provinces may prefer different paths. But we all seek the same destination—a Canada with the vision to anticipate its people's needs, and the ability to meet them.

We have developed a common way of doing things, a Canadian way that contributes to a distinct cultural and political identity.

It has always been the Canadian way for our people to support each other—regardless of where they live—through such measures as regional development programs and Equalization payments, Medicare and Unemployment Insurance, student assistance and the Canada Pension Plan.

That same spirit of fairness must be summoned to meet new needs, such as specialized health care for an aging population, and services for single mothers and working parents.

That is why we're pleased that this conference has followed up on the prime minister's suggestion to make women's issues a full agenda item for the first time at a First Ministers' Conference.

We're especially pleased that the importance of child care as a national issue has been recognized.

We welcome a partnership that sees this as a national concern. Federal financial leadership and cost-sharing arrangements are necessary to allow the provinces to assume their role in ensuring that quality child care is available to all who need it.

Tomorrow, Ontario will put forward a proposal for a national conference of all ministers responsible for women's issues, ministers of finance, and ministers of social services to develop a comprehensive framework for federal-provincial cost-sharing for child care.

Today, I would like to focus on how we can create the wealth necessary to meet the future needs of Canadians.

We can do that only by improving our ability to compete on a global scale.

We must compete by putting the most advanced technology in the hands of the best educated and best trained workforce. We must compete by becoming more aggressive and skilful at marketing our goods and services to the world. We must compete by encouraging new investment.

Our immediate economic outlook gives us some reason for confidence, but considerable reason for concern.

The current recovery has not benefited all Canadians equally.

Despite pockets of buoyancy, economic development is not uniformly strong in all provinces, including Ontario. Northern Ontario and Eastern Ontario need to diversify and revitalize their economies. Rising US protectionism threatens vital manufacturing and resource sectors.

Like their counterparts elsewhere, Ontario farmers have yet to fully recover from the 1982 recession. Just last year, Ontario farmers saw their income fall significantly.

Ontarians realize we must do our share to generate economic growth for Canada.

Our ability to create jobs depends on our capacity to produce goods and services, and sell them to the world.

But Canada's share of world trade has decreased, and our range has narrowed. Since 1968, Canada has improved its market share in only four out of 70 manufacturing sectors. Our share has actually declined in 21 sectors.

World markets have grown; we have to catch up.

We have enormous room for growth in the Asia-Pacific market. In 1985 they imported $497 billion worth of goods, more than the United States.

For every $100 that Latin-America spent on imports in 1985, only two dollars came to Canada. For every $100 that Europe spent, only one dollar came to Canada.

Last year, Canada sent only 10 percent of its merchandise exports to developing nations. The United States and Japan export proportionately about four times as much to developing countries. Western Europe exports five times as much.

Through trade negotiations, we are attempting to secure access to US markets in the future. But that will not solve the problem of US protectionism now.

Ironically, in the last six months—since Canada and the United States formally initiated free trade talks—US countervail and legislative protectionist actions have affected roughly a billion dollars' worth of Canadian trade with the United States.

Every indication we have seen demonstrates that the pursuit of a free trade agreement offers no relief from current US protectionist fever. Three weeks ago today, the chief US trade ambassador reiterated that the United States government would not drop its tools of trade retaliation—such as the countervail clause that was invoked against softwood lumber—even if a bilateral trade deal is struck.

The reversal of their 1983 determination on softwood lumber demonstrates that US officials will change the rules of the game if they don't like the score.

Just last week, it was again suggested that the Auto Pact be re-examined.

The provisions in the Auto Pact that safeguard Canada's auto industry also safeguard Ontario's ability to contribute to Canadian economic growth. That is why it is vital that the conditions, which have provided thousands of jobs and billions of dollars of production, be left in place.

We have to work to preserve access to the US market for all our goods and services, while strengthening our ability to sell to the entire world.

It was a Canadian who first recognized that the world has become a global village. Canadians must now master the global marketplace.

We're shifting from an economy that is evolutionary to one that is revolutionary. Change is sudden and continuous.

Goods, services, and capital are moving more freely and more swiftly. Competition used to come from around the block; now it comes from around the world. Many countries are now exporting goods they once imported from us. Businesses are finding it is no longer enough to be national leaders in their fields—they must be international leaders as well.

That is why Canadians must develop a strategy to target the areas in which we can excel. And we must be flexible enough to develop new strengths on short notice.

Nations like Japan have shown that a well-educated, enterprising people, backed by a commitment to research and development, can prosper even without a resource base.

Canada can gain a valuable edge by combining our wealth in natural resources with our wealth of human resources—the knowledge, skills and ingenuity of the Canadian people.

Our ability to compete depends on our ability to produce.

But an OECD study found that between 1975 and 1984, Canada posted one of the smallest increases in productivity among industrialized nations. Our rate of growth in productivity was 0.6 percent—compared to 3.5 percent for Japan, 2.2 percent for France, and 1.8 percent for Italy.

We have the potential to improve our ability to compete. The question is whether we have the will.

We will have to make up ground on the basis of our brainpower.

We must take the lead in developing new technologies and applying them to forestry, agriculture, fishing and mining—as well as manufacturing.

We must encourage Canadians to develop their entrepreneurial abilities. Half of the jobs that will exist in 15 years will be provided by small businesses that aren't even born yet—especially in the growing service sector.

We must export not just our goods, but also our knowledge and skills, in order to eliminate a $4 billion international deficit in trade in services. We must improve our ability to market services in health care, education, culture, environmental technology, and finance.

To reach our goals, we must focus on research and development, higher education, and skills training.

Our major industrialized competitors spend more than 2.5 percent of their GDP on research and development. Canada spends about half that.

In 1984, the Canadian private sector funded about $2 billion of R & D activity. At least two individual American firms alone spent more.

In terms of the percentage of our population engaged in R & D, Canada places between Iceland and Ireland.

Shoestring budgets lead to shoestring results. Last year, Canada suffered a high-technology deficit of $12.6 billion—about three times larger than ten years ago.

The Canadian Independent Computer Services Association estimates that we could have created about 180,000 more jobs if not for our high-tech deficit, and half-a-million more jobs could be at stake by 1990.

Canada has achieved some success in a few technological specialties—such as telecommunications, remote sensing, and computer software.

But we lag behind in critical areas such as bio-technology, advanced industrial materials, robotics, and microelectronics.

Canada is the only country in the OECD that suffers a deficit in high-tech trade in drugs, scientific instruments, electrical transmission equipment, communications equipment and components, office machines and computers, aircraft, and automobiles.

We must recognize that a national strategy to strengthen Canada's capacity in science and technology will not result from the simple expression of good intentions.

All governments must work together to increase industry commitment to R & D, and use public resources to lever private-sector investment.

We need to improve technology transfer across Canada—in all regions—and target R & D investment to maximize trade opportunities and job creation.

We must reduce overlap and duplication, match strengths across provincial boundaries, and best apply the resources we have to the opportunities we seek.

Canada's strongest asset is its people. In a global economy centred on knowledge and innovation, education is an essential raw material.

But Canada's per capita investment in post-secondary education is less than it was five years ago.

Federal cuts in established program financing payments stand to cost all provinces $1.6 billion in funding for post-secondary education by 1990. Those funding cuts equal the total budgets of the University of British Columbia, the University of Alberta, University of Toronto, McGill University, and Dalhousie University.

No one at this table can bear all of the blame for these problems. But all of us must share responsibility for solving them. All of us must work to make Canada—and all of its regions—more competitive.

I realize that we cannot address all of Canada's challenges at this conference. Nevertheless, there are priorities that call for our immediate attention.

As a first priority toward building a national strategy on competition, we believe Canada must set out to double its spending on research and development within ten years.

The federal and provincial ministers responsible for science and technology will meet next month. Ontario would suggest they be mandated to produce within six months an action plan to match the university spending of our major industrial competitors—2.5 percent of the gross domestic product.

Ontario believes that this action plan should be brought to a special meeting of first ministers, focussed on the development of a coordinated national science and technology strategy.

Canada cannot march to the music of ten different bands. We have to move in harmony.

If we are to compete in world markets, we will also need a tax system that encourages investment, technology, and job creation, while ensuring equal treatment for women, and fairness for all.

For that reason, Ontario believes that any major proposed change in the tax system must be accompanied by a detailed analysis of its potential impact on Canada's ability to compete, and create jobs.

These are some of the ways we can improve our long-term ability to compete. But we must also deal with the immediate threats to our access to the US market.

No province can afford to ignore these protectionist threats. The recent US actions concerning softwood lumber stand to jeopardize one of Canada's leading economic sectors. What is more, it could set a dangerous precedent that could be applied against other parts of the lumber industry, and other natural resource industries.

Using the softwood lumber precedent today, the Americans could attack us on potash tomorrow, fish the next day, uranium the day after that—followed by oil and gas, wheat, hydro-electricity and other resource sectors.

Let us not forget that we have a totally different system of land ownership and resource management than the United States.

What's at stake in the softwood lumber issue is nothing less than whether Canadian resource policies should be dictated by US interests, or decided by the Canadian people.

In light of the fact that US protectionist pressure has grown since free trade talks got underway, I believe we must recognize it is an immediate problem that calls for an immediate response—above and beyond the current negotiations.

The recent US congressional elections leave Canada with a limited window of opportunity to combat protectionism. We must act now to point out to Americans the negative consequences of protectionism—to themselves, to their best trading partners, and to the world.

We must point out to them that a new round of protectionism could bring on the same dire worldwide consequences as the disastrous beggar-thy-neighbour policies of the 1930s.

If we all share a sense of urgency about this problem, I hope that over the next two days we can jointly work out a plan to counter US protectionism. Ontario would like to see a national partnership in which all of us can work against protectionist actions in a planned and coordinated way.

I would like to propose some initial building blocks for that strategy:

1. We must recognize growing US protectionism is an immediate problem, quite apart from any effort to obtain a long-term free trade agreement.
2. We must remind Americans that we are their best customer. We must remind Americans that trade with Canada provides them with two million jobs. We must remind them that protectionist measures add to their own manufacturing costs, and their own cost of living.
3. We must work with our friends and allies in the United

States on trade issues. Canadian businesses can marshal their US customers and suppliers. They have as much interest as we do in keeping trade open.

4. Provincial governments can take advantage of their relations with nearby states—their governors, senators and congressmen. Our close relations and common interests can help in this issue.

5. We must pool our resources as governments and work together with industry to establish better early warning systems to prevent trade irritants from becoming trade wars.

6. Mr. Prime Minister, your close relationship with President Reagan is an essential element of any strategy to combat US protectionism. You can use your good offices—as you see most appropriate—to work with the president and strengthen his resolve to stand firm against protectionist pressures.

We must harness the energies of every government represented in this room in new and creative ways in order to eliminate this protectionist threat.

All of us seek the best for ourselves and our fellow Canadians—in all regions, and all walks of life. To reach that goal we must defend established markets, and compete for new ones.

More than four decades ago, Stephen Leacock observed that "those who dream most, do most." As Canada approaches the next century, we must summon the vision to dream, and the will to turn our vision into reality.

EDMONTON CHAMBER OF COMMERCE
Edmonton, Alberta, April 7, 1987

I'm delighted to be in Edmonton for my first official visit to Alberta. In fact, it's the first official visit to this province by an Ontario premier in more than a decade. I'm grateful for the opportunity to discuss issues of concern to both our provinces, and for the warm and friendly reception I've received.

It's particularly encouraging when one considers the history of the relationship between our provinces, and the differences that often led to bitterness in the past.

We still have differences. But they have not prevented us from working well together—because we have dealt with each other openly and fairly.

I recall very well my first Premiers' Conference. I was the only Grit in the room, and to tell you the truth I was a little worried I might be thrown out of the place. But I was greeted with open arms by Peter Lougheed, and I will always appreciate the courtesy and warmth he showed me.

That tradition is alive and well in your province. Don Getty has been chairman of the Conference of Premiers during a most difficult period— in the midst of free trade negotiations, the softwood lumber dispute, and the fish treaty. Yet he has managed to put forward Alberta's point of view with force, and listen to other provinces with sensitivity.

That is exactly the kind of leadership that Canada needs.

We are seeing the emergence of a new generation of political leadership in this country—a generation that seeks to tone down the rhetoric, not exacerbate it; one that works to strengthen the ties between us, rather than weaken them.

The economic diversity of our regions sometimes has perverse results. When one region is enjoying an economic resurgence, it is possible for another to be in economic stagnation.

We have to take advantage of our strengths and find ways of cutting each other's losses because Confederation works only to the extent that we treat each other's problems as our own.

When Brian Peckford has a problem with codfish, all Canadians have a problem.

When Alberta has a problem with oil and gas, all Canadians have a problem.

When British Columbia and Quebec, Alberta and Ontario have a problem with softwood lumber, all Canadians have a problem.

And we all *must* work on solving them.

I don't know much about codfish, and Don Getty may know even less about it than I do, but we both know about building better relations between Canada's regions. A stronger Confederation is built with the bricks of consensus and the mortar of compromise.

I came to Alberta mainly to listen to what you have to say, and learn more about your concerns. I'm learning that while our provinces are different, they also have a great deal in common.

Both of us depend on the energy industry—Ontario as a consumer, and supplier of equipment and steel; Alberta as Canada's leading oil and gas producer.

Both of us depend on a healthy agriculture sector. In fact, last year Ontario accounted for the largest share of farm cash receipts in Canada. Alberta accounted for the third largest.

Both of us face intensified global competition that requires us to diversify our economies, improve our technology and develop more advanced products and services.

Both of us realize that we can accomplish those objectives only by cultivating our greatest assets—the knowledge, skills, and ingenuity of our people. That is why we are both acting on the need to examine and improve our education and skills training systems.

Both of us have many disagreements with federal government policies that affect our provinces. One should not overestimate Ontario's clout in Ottawa—we share many of your frustrations.

Both of us have recent experience with economic transition and instability. A few years ago, Ontario was dead last among the provinces in the rate of economic growth. Alberta is going through some tough times, but you also possess strengths that ensure your ability to surmount them.

In fact, *both of us* are among the economically better off provinces in Canada. Last year, Ontario had the highest per capita personal income in Canada, and Albertans had the second-highest. Alberta had the highest per capita gross domestic product, and Ontario had the second highest.

Ontario is currently enjoying a period of economic buoyancy, but its benefits are uneven.

Northern Ontario faces a particular need to diversify and revitalize its economy. The resource industries on which its livelihood is based are in serious difficulty in terms of international competition, as you well know.

Like their counterparts here in Alberta and in other provinces, Ontario farmers have yet to fully recover from the 1982 recession.

So we have many areas of mutual concern. Today, I would like to discuss two of them—trade and energy.

The trade negotiations in which we are currently engaged with the United States are as important to Ontario as they are to any province.

We supported the original goals of the negotiations—to secure and enhance our access to the American market.

Those goals are in the interests of all provinces.

You send 75 percent of your exports to the United States.

Ontario sends about 90 percent of its exports to the United States.

The jobs of two million Canadians depend on Canada's exports to the American market.

Ontario takes a very pragmatic view on free trade. We would favour any agreement that benefited all regions of the country—and oppose any that failed to.

Obviously, we would all like to shield Canada from US countervail protection measures—the range of laws and regulations used to block trade practices the Americans dislike.

The softwood lumber dispute demonstrated that resource industries are particular targets of US measures. Like Alberta and every other province, we have reason to be concerned about that—the mining and forest industries account directly for 170,000 jobs in Ontario.

But if security of access is our prime objective in the talks, what would we have to give up to achieve it?

The United States has targeted Canada's subsidy system as a trade irritant. They would undoubtedly demand limitations on government assistance to industry.

Both Ontario and Alberta would have considerable reason to be alarmed about any agreement that limited our scope for resource management.

Like Albertans, we were seriously affected by the softwood lumber dispute. We would be delighted if a trade agreement could change the result. But would the US lumber lobby accept a rollback so soon after their victory on that issue?

Like you, we wish to secure and enhance access for beef exports to the United States. But the US farm belt is extremely protectionist, and could vigorously oppose any measure that would create new competition for them, through such means as revising health and public inspection standards.

Would the Americans insist that any agreement restrict transportation subsidies such as those provided through the *Western Grain Transportation Act*?

We support the effort to overturn the US federal Energy Regulatory Commission's decision to restrict access to Canadian gas—a move that could cost Canadian producers as much as $400 million.

But major US producers form a strong lobby, and they believe the current penalty is justified in order to ensure a level playing field. The spokesman for US independent producers reaffirmed that last week.

Would a protectionist US Congress be prepared to approve a free trade agreement that eliminated such restrictions?

These are concerns that we all share.

Sometimes, and in some quarters, there is an unfortunate tendency to present the free trade issue as one of province-against-province. The fact is that every province stands to gain under an agreement that takes Canada's true needs into account, and every province stands to lose under any agreement that fails to.

Anyone who attempts to pit province against province over this issue displays a fundamental lack of understanding of the integrated nature of the Canadian economy, and the goodwill of the Canadian people.

Moreover, anyone who sees this issue as one in which they can reap short-term political gain at the expense of long-term national needs is fooling only themselves.

Another area in which we must work together in the future is one that sometimes pulled us apart in the past—energy policy.

On the energy issues, we must start from the basis of our common objectives: We both have a strong, long-run interest in secure supply at a fair price.

For that reason, both producers and consumers have a common interest in energy prices that provide a reasonable reward for the risks taken.

When deregulation was agreed to under the Western Accord and the Natural Gas Agreement in 1985, it was expected that oil and gas prices would remain reasonably firm. But the collapse of oil prices in January of last year, and tight competition in the US gas market drove prices down—with substantial losses to industry and governments.

Abrupt changes in the world energy market reversed these expectations.

We are all affected by the result—cutbacks in exploration and production.

Exploration and production in Canada's oil and gas sector fell from $8.6 billion in 1985 to $5.4 billion last year. It has been reported that less than 40 percent of drilling rigs in Western Canada are currently active.

That downturn cost thousands of oil industry jobs, endangered long-term security of supply, and sent ripple effects that were felt in many other industries, such as steel.

Alberta's reduction of royalties and the federal government's removal of the petroleum and gas revenue tax, combined with some world price stabilization, have helped to alleviate the situation.

The recently announced Canadian Exploration and Development Incentive Program will also help.

Ontario supports this combined effort—in your interest and our own.

There is considerable room for us to work together. Our recent co-operative efforts in promoting the use of Western Canadian coal serves as a good example.

In 1985, Ontario Hydro consumed 3.1 million tonnes of Canadian coal—and 7.3 million tonnes from the United States.

Ontario industries purchased 43,000 tonnes of metallurgical coal from the West, and 6.2 million tonnes from other sources.

We are working towards improving Western coal sales to Ontario.

We've established a committee under the chairmanship of Don Mazankowski to identify ways to make Western Canadian coal more competitive in Ontario markets. I'm delighted to work on that committee, along with premiers Getty, Vander Zalm, and Devine.

Ontario Hydro has already announced it will take all of its coal downsizing over the next five years from US sources. By 1992, Western Canadian supplies will make up 50 percent of Ontario Hydro's annual coal purchases—despite declining requirements and the fact that western coal is still 47 percent more expensive.

Ontario will contribute to a program to develop technologies to increase the uses of Western Canadian coal. We are prepared to commit ourselves to substantial funding for similar projects.

And we will take steps to encourage Ontario's steel industry to purchase metallurgical coal from Western Canada. To that end, we will be convening a conference of major coal purchasers in Ontario to work out ways to make greater use of the domestic product.

We must apply this co-operative spirit to other sectors of the energy industry—such as natural gas.

From Ontario's point of view, the problem in energy pricing is not the absolute cost but the relative cost. I'm sure you could understand the reaction many Ontarians would have to a wholesale price in Detroit that is lower than the price in Windsor—especially if that lower rate was the result of low-cost Canadian gas exported into the American market.

At the same time, I can understand the need of natural gas producers to expand their share of US markets—especially when there is a healthy surplus of natural gas supply, and the producing industry is in need of cash flow.

That is why last month, for the first time in history, the Ontario government urged the National Energy Board to give natural gas producers greater freedom to expand their share of US markets.

We continue to support the principle that Canadian requirements should be given priority before foreign customers are served. But to improve access for Canadian natural gas to US markets, senior officials from the Ontario Ministry of Energy will next week be urging the National Energy Board to adopt the following proposals:

- The current protection test should be relaxed in a manner that permits substantial additional volumes for export.
- The current regulatory framework should be revised to allow greater flexibility by relying on actual market demand and natural gas production, not forecasts.
- Gas exports would not be restricted in the future if new supplies are found to replace reserves and meet growth in domestic markets.

Obviously, there are still many points to resolve before we achieve a national consensus on all energy pricing issues.

I realize that many of you disagreed strongly with the Ontario Energy Board's report on contract carriage two weeks ago, when they took the position that all gas users should have access to direct-purchase supplies.

In fact, at this point I don't think the board chairman, Bob Macaulay, could be elected dogcatcher in Alberta—and he's a long-time Tory.

But I can understand the reasoning behind his opinion.

It's a direct extension of the mandate for deregulation in the natural gas agreement—an agreement which Ontario was denied a role in shaping.

In fact, at the time the agreement was announced, the then-federal minister of energy, Pat Carney, said, and I quote:

"The customers, these are the municipalities, the hospitals, the big industrial users, will be able to make their own deals with producers right away in this transition year."

Consequently, Bob Macaulay was only implementing that interpretation of the agreement.

That being said, I can understand the objections that the report has aroused.

Things have changed in the 18 months since the gas agreement was signed.

Brutal competition in the US market has resulted in lost sales to the Canadian industry. The federal Energy Regulatory Commission's ruling put pressure on producers to undercut their competitors.

This has hurt the industry, discouraged re-investment, hit Alberta taxpayers in the pocketbook and raised concerns that some people may take unfair advantage of the current difficulties of the producers.

Obviously, that has negative impact on long-term security of supply—a prime concern for all of us, and one that we realize must be *carefully considered*.

I'm certain that the Ontario Energy Board view was based on its best interpretation of its mandate.

But my government's mandate is to weigh the needs of consumers *and* producers, and consider the *national* interest.

Moreover, we have a particular responsibility to encourage long-term security of supply, based on incentives for replacement investment.

The Ontario Energy Board will be considering the first applications in *that* context.

As well, I would like to suggest four additional ways that we can help meet these many needs:

1. We will follow the principle that energy price deregulation is not a one-way street. If consumers are to have the benefit of lower prices in today's markets, we must recognize that when prices start to rise, it would be unfair to turn around and insist on a return to administered prices.

2. We should consider means to ensure that the National Energy Board is able to meet its mandate in a spirit of balance and conciliation. Too often, the structure of the NEB process tends to pit one province against another. For example, we might want to charge the federal and provincial energy ministers with the responsibility to set goals and guidelines for the NEB. The success in January of the first Conference of Energy Ministers, under the excellent co-chairmanship of Mr. Masse and Dr. Webber, encourages me that this forum

would be an excellent one to ensure full and equal representation across the country in reconciling national energy interests.

3. Perhaps we should consider establishing an action committee to come up with ways to expand natural gas markets—similar to the working committee on coal. In particular, we could take steps to encourage wider use of natural gas as a transportation fuel, and for co-generation. Ontario industry currently uses 12 billion cubic feet of natural gas a year to generate electricity. Industrial co-generation of electricity and steam could raise the use of natural gas by almost 40 billion cubic feet. If natural gas use for vehicles could increase by 5 percent of the natural gas market by the year 2000, it could lead to the additional sale of up to 30 billion cubic feet.

4. The Ontario government is interested in exploring ways in which we can co-operate with major oil and gas development projects. We realize if we spread the risks, we all stand to benefit. We know the province and the industry have a number of projects in the planning stage, and we will watch them with interest because we believe they're potentially important to security of supply.

Looking at some of the long-term issues on the national stage—such as trade and energy—I think it's clear we have much in common.

We can make sure our differences remain a thing of the past, and our partnership a legacy for the future. So long as we remember an overriding truth: The things that unite us are far greater than the things that divide us.

First Ministers' Conference on the Economy
Toronto, Ontario, November 26, 1987

On this, Ontario's first opportunity to host a First Ministers' Conference on the Economy, I would like to congratulate Prime Minister Mulroney on having the foresight to establish these meetings on an annual basis.

By meeting every year, we are recognizing the fact that Canadians from coast to coast have a great deal in common. We face the same challenges; we seek the same opportunities.

These conferences are about nation building. They are about reforming and restructuring our economy to benefit not only the private commercial interests of Canadians, but also the public interest in the strength, independence, and unity of our nation.

But for national dialogue to be productive, it must be positive. It must be filled with goodwill, and free of acrimony.

That is the spirit we must summon in considering the proposed Canada-US trade pact. This issue must not be a tug of war between regions. It must be an honest, wholesome debate among Canadians.

We must share our perspectives. I invite all first ministers to come to Ontario to give the people of my province the benefit of your views.

In every province, there are Canadians who support this agreement and those who oppose it.

The trade debate is not a debate between regional interests—it is a debate about what is in the national interest.

We all stand to gain under a good trade agreement, but we all stand to lose if we settle for a bad one. From either standpoint, it is one of the most important issues Canadians have faced in many years.

But we must keep this issue in perspective. This trade agreement would produce neither instant prosperity nor instant disaster. The question is, would it advance our goal of economic development or set us back?

Canada sought a trade agreement with the United States to secure access to the US market for our goods and services. Ontario shares that goal.

So far we have only seen a preliminary agreement. But it is apparent that the agreement as tabled does not achieve our goal.

Under this deal, our access to the US market would not be appreciably more secure than it was the day negotiations got underway.

Under this deal, Canadian firms would still be vulnerable to harassment under US countervail and anti-dumping law. The new bilateral panel to review anti-dumping and countervail disputes would only be able to determine whether trade actions are consistent with the same US laws and regulations that are being used to harass Canadian exporters now.

In these negotiations, we gained very little that we sought to gain. And worse, we gave up much that we could not afford to give up.

This deal gives away our ability to pursue an independent energy policy—an important instrument of regional economic development.

It gives away safeguards which have ensured the existence of a dynamic auto industry.

It gives away most of our ability to ensure that Canadians benefit from US investment and proposed foreign takeovers of Canadian-owned firms.

This deal can seriously weaken governments' ability to help our people meet their goals.

Under this deal, Canada would give away too much and gain too little.

For that reason, I strongly believe this deal should be rejected.

Some say rejection of this deal would mean that we would be ignoring the problem of US protectionism. The fact is, we would be recognizing that the solution does not lie in a policy of fear and insecurity.

There are those who argue that our nation has no option but to accept the proposed agreement; that no matter what the costs, any agreement is better than no agreement; that if we do not accept the deal as written, a protectionist Congress will continue to harass Canadian exporters.

This is obviously not an argument for a strong, bold and outward-looking Canada. We cannot accept a bad deal in a desperate attempt to buy some goodwill south of the border. Refusal of this bilateral deal would not lead our trading relationship to anarchy—it would leave it under the protection of the GATT rules and procedures to which both the Americans and ourselves would still be bound.

Some say rejection of this deal would mean that Canada was embracing protectionism. The fact is, liberalized trade is everyone's goal. The real question is how to achieve it.

Ontario believes that the GATT process, despite its imperfections, offers the best prospects for progress in opening world trade. Our commitment to that process was demonstrated by our decision to seek an accommodation with the EEC over access to our market for European wine.

Compared to the United States, Canada is a small player in the world economy. But even a small player need not be a pawn.

In the multilateral forum, many of the issues on which Canada has made concessions would not even be on the table. The GATT process provides us with the leverage that comes from sharing interests and goals with many other nations. We can use that leverage to open markets without sacrificing the essential rights and responsibilities of a sovereign nation.

Some say that rejection of this deal would mean that we believe Canada is unable to compete. The fact is Canada can compete anywhere in the world—not only in North America. We have the resources, the industrial base and the talent. We must use our assets to become a stronger international trading nation, not an economic dependent huddling under the American umbrella.

Some say rejection of this deal would deny disadvantaged regions an opportunity to catch up. The fact is, at best this deal would do little to reduce regional disparities.

I agree with those who feel it is counter to all of our interests when unemployment rates in one province are twice as high as unemployment rates in another.

But how would this deal affect that?

Even under the best-case scenario in the Economic Council of Canada study which recommended a bilateral agreement, in eight years free trade would reduce the gap between the highest and lowest provincial unemployment rates by less than three-tenths of 1 percent.

Fixating on a US trade agreement will not make up for a historic failure to devise adequate regional development programs.

Some say Ontario is seeking to deny to other provinces the benefits it has received under the Auto Pact. But the fact is, the Auto Pact has worked as well as it has because it is managed trade. It includes production guarantees and investment commitments. The US-Canada trade deal does not.

Some say rejection of this deal would be a rejection of the need for change. The fact is, we all recognize that change is necessary. The only question is, what kind of change?

We all recognize that Canada cannot just hope to preserve the status quo or return to a bygone era. We all recognize that the economic approaches that worked in the 1960s and the 1970s will no longer serve our needs—but neither will this trade pact.

The US-Canada trade pact was a vision for the mid-1980s, when trade with the United States grew dramatically. What Canada needs now is a vision for the future.

The United States will unquestionably continue to be our most important trading partner. Efforts to stabilize particular aspects of our trading relationship in a truly balanced manner should continue.

But just as we are considering this deal to be our last and only chance, the world around us is changing dramatically.

Just as Canadian trade policy is being totally geared to gaining greater access to the US market, that market may be about to see a decline in its rate of growth. In the wake of the crash of world stock markets, Americans are talking about slowing down the tremendous rate of domestic consumption financed by massive borrowing over the past six years.

The dominant forces of economic change are now global in scope—not just North American.

The volatility of exchange rates demonstrates why we cannot tie ourselves to any single market.

Since 1985, the Japanese yen and the West German mark have appreciated almost 80 percent against the US and Canadian dollars. The current shift in exchange rates can open new opportunities not only in Japanese and European markets, but in other markets where Canadian goods are in competition with Japanese and European goods.

Europe and Asia have already become strong pacesetters in technology. Japan and West Germany are passing the United States in non-military technology—and the competition is getting stiffer.

A comprehensive vision for Canada's future must encompass increased trade with the entire world.

And it must also encompass increased trade within Canada. I find it ironic that we are considering a deal to reduce trade barriers between Canada and the United States, while so little has been done to reduce them between provinces.

A comprehensive vision for Canada's future must also encompass the building blocks that will strengthen our nation and improve our ability to produce and compete. We must address the need for increasing technological development, improving education and skills training, reducing regional disparities, developing a more favourable tax climate, and improving our infrastructure base.

The proposed trade deal does not address these goals. Indeed, it has detracted attention from many of Canada's most serious problems and caused our nation to delay or set aside many of the solutions—including training programs and the establishment of research and development targets.

Canada's ability to compete and create jobs is increasingly dependent on our ability to use our heads rather than just our hands.

We must combine our strengths in natural resources with our strengths in human resources—the knowledge, skills, and entrepreneurial abilities of the Canadian people.

The industries of tomorrow will emerge in those countries which have the vision to pursue them today. Canada has many unique strengths—such as expertise in food production, energy, steel, large-scale construction, telecommunications, transportation, fish and ocean industries, and wood products. We must build upon these strengths by developing and applying technologies and expertise—now.

One of the keys to technological advancement is excellence in the performance of research and development.

While we've been talking about R & D, more and more countries have been excelling at it. The race is on and Canada is barely out of the starting blocks.

Of the 12 largest economies among OECD nations, Canada ranks 10th in R & D spending as a percentage of gross domestic product. In 1986, our R & D spending was 1.35 percent of our GDP, less than half as much as in the United States, Japan, Sweden, and West Germany. That isn't good enough.

The rate of R & D spending by private industry in Canada was about a third as much as in those four countries. That isn't good enough.

We need to encourage Canadian industry to invest more in R & D. But if firms lack confidence in government's commitment to R & D, they will be reluctant to make a commitment themselves.

For that reason, I would question proposed changes in the white paper on tax reform which would reduce the value of federal R & D tax incentives, and eliminate support for 40 percent of the R & D performed by Canada's high-tech companies.

We must pursue technological advances by improving linkages between industries, universities, and government—and between provinces.

Like the federal government, Ontario and several other provinces have established boards and councils to foster close co-operation among various sectors and improve our technological capacity and our ability to compete. But we must begin to work together. Wasted effort is a luxury Canada cannot afford in this high-technology race.

If Canada is to move into the forefront of technological leadership, we must develop new strengths in all regions. We must identify targets for the future among industries which offer potential for regional specialization right across Canada. There is considerable growth potential, for example, in health-related industries.

Public healthcare spending in Canada already constitutes 6.6 percent of our GNP, roughly the equivalent of US military spending, the leading development tool in the United States. By coordinating provincial healthcare expenditures, we can foster new industries in many slow-growth areas.

Any investments we make in technology will yield the results we seek only if they are matched by investments in people.

And as more women than ever before enter the labour force, we must rise to the challenge of tapping the great vitality and energy they bring. If we are to compete in the world economy, we must utilize the talent and skills of all Canadians.

The participation of more than half our potential workforce has been hampered by the lack of support systems to hasten economic equality, such as a national child-care strategy and support programs to help workers harmonize their dual responsibilities at home and at work.

But since the first annual meeting of first ministers in Regina in 1985, the federal government's budget for labour market development and training has been cut in real terms by one-third—$900 million. This is especially ironic in light of the shortages Canada is facing in many skilled trades. In Ontario, for example, we have identified shortages in 98 occupations.

Even while we invest in our human resources and technological infrastructure, we also face a need to shore up our physical infrastructure.

In 1986, it was estimated that $14 billion was needed over the next five years to upgrade or replace an aging network of roads, highways, bridges, sewers, and water mains.

We must also recognize that no matter what measures we take to improve our ability to compete, regionally based economic cycles will continue to beset our nation.

Economic cycles can have widely different effects on regional economies.

Existing national economic tools cannot always serve the economic interests of all regions. There is a need to develop new mechanisms to cushion the regional impact of economic slowdowns.

Clearly, we have a great deal to do if we want to ensure jobs and opportunity across Canada now and in the future. We cannot build the kind of nation we want with free trade as our only brick.

I would like to put forward for discussion some ways in which I believe we can help forge the competitive edge we need for the 1990s:

1. Canada should seek within the next ten years to roughly double our R & D spending to 2.5 percent of GDP—about the same rate as our leading industrialized competitors.

   In order to reach that goal, we need to review the proposed changes to the R & D tax incentives in the white paper on tax reform. And we must bring together the federal and provincial science and technology advisory bodies, so we can jointly work out plans to develop new national industry-university links, and identify fields in which slow-growth regions can develop new technological strengths.

   Ontario would be interested in hosting a meeting of these bodies.

   Later today, Ontario will be releasing a discussion paper that describes how we can best reach our R & D goal.

2. The federal government and the provinces must work together to ensure that the two out of three young people who enter the workforce directly from high school get more opportunity to train for job skills, including expanding and revitalizing the apprenticeship training model. As well, we must enable adult workers and employers to upgrade the skills vital to their competitiveness.

   A solid training strategy must also include a viable and straightforward system of income support for trainees.
   Later in this conference, Ontario will be releasing a discussion paper on how we can meet these needs.
   In our view, a training strategy must be accompanied by a national child-care strategy in order that Canada can take full advantage of the talents of its people. I am looking forward to the federal proposals when they are released.

3. The federal and provincial ministers of finance should be mandated to devise investment instruments to increase our national savings, and finance capital development and the growth of small and medium-sized Canadian corporations across the nation.

4. We must together develop a plan to upgrade our physical infrastructure.

5. We must commit ourselves fully to the elimination of trade barriers between provinces.

6. We must increase our efforts to improve access for our goods and services, in the United States and other markets, through the GATT process.

I look forward to hearing the ideas of everyone at this table, so that together Canadians can begin to shape a blueprint for economic development.

But we cannot allow our vision for the future to be pre-empted by a trade deal that may reduce our options and weaken us as a nation.

Canadians must have the opportunity to make up their minds about whether the proposed US-Canada trade deal has a place in their vision of Canada.

It is now almost two months since we were told a deal had been struck. In a little more than one month, the federal government intends to sign it. But the Canadian people have yet to see a complete text of an agreement that may be as important as any in our history. How can Canadians decide if the deal is worthwhile, until they have seen the hidden costs?

The negotiators have yet to produce a complete agreement after talking for two years. Can we expect the Canadian people to make their judgment on it in less than two weeks?

The US Congress will not even seriously consider the issue for months. But Canadians are being asked to approve the agreement before it is even submitted to them.

The fast-track process slows to a crawl for the US Congress, but it leaves Canadians with little time to even peek at the agreement.

Why should we allow a US deadline to restrict our opportunity to give this agreement the serious and extended attention it deserves? We must follow our own timetable just as the Americans must follow theirs.

We must not be stampeded into accepting a deal before Canadians can determine if it meets our needs.

What Canada needs is an economic development policy. This trade agreement is no substitute. It will not move us in the direction of eliminating regional disparities, developing new technologies, or mastering the skills of the future.

Before we sign any trade agreement, we must ensure that it is consistent with our needs into the next century.

FIRST MINISTERS' CONFERENCE ON THE ECONOMY
Ottawa, Ontario, November 9, 1989

Prime minister, fellow premiers, it is a great pleasure to join you again at the first ministers' table.

It's a particular pleasure to welcome those who are joining us for the first time at a first ministers' conference on the economy.

Premier Filmon, Premier Wells, I look forward to your participation in this uniquely Canadian approach to nation building.

This forum is in many ways reflective of the Canadian character itself. It embodies a commitment to consensus, a spirit of compromise, and a determination to accomplish together those things that we could not achieve on our own.

Canadian history is the story of the triumph of collective will. Once again it is vital that we summon that will.

Canada faces a test—one that I believe is as demanding as any in our history. We face challenges from beyond our borders, and pressures within them.

Canadians can master the challenges from outside—but only if we are able to overcome the pressures within.

We begin with many assets—assets that flow directly from the kind of country we have and the kind of people we are.

Our federal system of government is an asset. It provides us with cohesion and flexibility. It helps us to create wealth, and allows us to share it. The Europeans are trying to construct a similar system for themselves, and even the Soviets have been studying Canada to learn how we make federalism work for us. They are learning, as we did, the truth of Lord Acton's advice: "a great democracy must either sacrifice self-government to unity or preserve it by federalism."

Our multicultural heritage is an asset. It provides us with things that few nations have—a chance to share in the greatness of many cultures, an opportunity to encompass many perspectives.

In the new global economy, it also provides an economic strength that should not be underestimated.

In order to sell to the entire world, you have to know the entire world. Canadians know the entire world, because every corner of it is represented here. That makes Canada very special.

So does our linguistic legacy.

Let there be no question that bilingualism is an asset—for all of us. Every time we advance bilingualism, we open a door to opportunity. We make it that much easier for a Canadian to feel at home in another part of our country, to bring their own individual talents to another part of Canada.

There are countries around the world that can only envy what we have.

Canadians have accomplished what we have for a simple reason—we have always been willing to work with each other, to learn from each other, to respect each other.

We have used diversity as a tool to build a nation; we must not allow it now to be turned into a wedge to drive us apart.

That is exactly what I fear may be happening to our country. I have never been more concerned about Canada's future than I am now.

Our unity as a nation has been at stake before—but never in an atmosphere so fraught with tension and mistrust, and never without a firm response from men and women of good will.

I can recall vividly the way the people of Canada responded less than ten years ago, when our unity as a nation was directly on the line. We rose to the occasion—we fought for Canada, in every part of this country, with every tool at our command.

Now, it seems, many have become tired of fighting. Many have become passive. Some have even come to question their faith in Canada.

This is no way to end a decade that began with a dramatic vote of confidence in Confederation.

The earlier fervent debates over federalism provided the momentum for two great constitutional achievements—patriation, and the 1987 agreement at Meech Lake.

I believed in 1987 and I believe today that the Meech Lake Accord is an essential second step in constitutional reform.

The patriation of our Constitution with a charter of rights was a great historic achievement. But it did not deal with Quebec's place in Confederation, and it did not secure Quebec's assent to the Constitution.

It did not address the very concerns that had provided the prime impetus to constitutional reform for more than a quarter of a century—concerns that the "yes" forces in the referendum had vowed to resolve.

For that reason, I do not regard the Meech Lake agreement as simply a Quebec round. Rather, it is an essential round to make Canada whole—to complete what was achieved in 1982, and set the stage for future constitutional reform.

What has been lost in much of the recent debate over Meech Lake is that the Accord is itself a compromise. Quebec came to the bargaining table with the most moderate set of proposals it has ever put forward. Many historic conditions, such as changes in the division of powers, were put aside at the outset.

Once negotiations got underway, there was further compromise. For example, Meech Lake recognizes, as Quebec proposed, the distinctiveness of Quebec. But it also recognizes, as other provinces proposed, that the English language minority in Quebec is a fundamental characteristic of Canada. Moreover, that same clause obligates all governments in Canada to protect minority rights. And it explicitly states that it does not provide any new powers to any government.

None of us came away from Meech Lake with everything we wanted—but we all came away with what we needed to continue the process of building a nation.

What has changed since the eleven first ministers endorsed the Accord is the atmosphere that surrounds it. Many base their view of the agreement on the symbolic issues associated with it. In English Canada, it is seen by many as an opportunity to protest language policies or the use of the notwithstanding clause—a clause that was already in place before we even sat down at Meech Lake.

But in Quebec, the Accord symbolizes the difference between being fully and truly at home in Canada—or being a grudging participant in Confederation. It is seen as a symbol of appartenance—a feeling of belonging. In my view, that symbol is absolutely vital.

Meech Lake is more than just a deal; it is a covenant of faith—an extension of hands across the chasms that too often separate us. It is an opportunity that will be extremely difficult to recreate. We have come too far, we have come too close, to let it slip away now. None of us wants our children to look back at this moment and say we let them down.

Obviously, we will not be able to leap our constitutional hurdles in the hour-and-a-half that has been set aside tomorrow. But we can—and must—devise a process that will allow us to break the impasse in the months ahead.

In the meantime, let us not make the task more difficult. Let none of us do anything that deepens the wounds or widens the divisions.

I understand the difficulties that everyone in this room is confronted with over this issue. But they pale in comparison with the difficulties that will confront us if we let this opportunity go by.

There is an enormous temptation to use Meech Lake as a bargaining chip for every outstanding grievance. That is a temptation we have to resist. We can redress regional grievances—but not from the midst of a constitutional quagmire.

Make no mistake about it, such a quagmire will exact a heavy price from Canadians—a price that we will have to pay for many years to come.

The future does not belong to nations locked in dispute—it belongs to those able to summon a spirit of co-operation.

The Japanese do not mire themselves endlessly in constitutional deadlock. The Europeans do not allow language differences to prevent them from talking to each other and working with each other, throughout their continent.

Only by ensuring a place for all of us in Canada, can we ensure Canada's place in the world.

There are many issues on which we in Ontario strongly disagree with the federal government—including the proposed Goods and Services Tax, and interest rate policy. There are many issues on which provinces disagree with each other. But there are a great many things we can and must do together.

Frank Underhill once described a nation as a body of people who have done great things together in the past, and who hope to do great things together in the future.

Canadians have done great things together in the past, and there are great things for us to do together now.

First and foremost, we can do great things together to provide Canadians with the educational and training opportunities they need now more than ever.

In that regard, prime minister, I congratulate you on your statement about Canada's need to prepare our children for the knowledge revolution.

Developing a nationally credible system of education is too important to our future not to welcome participation at all levels. All we ask is that every level bring something substantive to the process.

Ontario, like many provinces, is developing and implementing a wide range of initiatives to support excellence in education, to provide full opportunity for all, including the disadvantaged, and to promote lifelong learning.

We believe that the federal government has a vital role to play—including long-term training and income support to help people maintain their participation in the labour market in times of economic transition.

There are ways in which we can pool our efforts. At this conference Ontario will be tabling a proposal, developed by our premiers' council on technology, to shift responsibility for the strategic direction of industrial training programs out of the hands of government and into the hands of the people who are truly familiar with the needs.

Responsibility for directing skills training initiatives would be given to a board composed of the representatives of the partners in the workplace—business and labour. Responsibility for managing the delivery of training would also be given to management and labour through sectoral and regional committees.

We believe training can best be pursued through partnership—and we intend to pursue federal participation.

Second, we can do great things together to ensure Canada's ability to compete in the information age.

The recent report of the Economic Council of Canada is the latest in a series of studies to conclude that Canada's performance in science and technology is weak in every measure that can be applied—from the amount of research and development conducted to the performance of high-tech industries.

All ten provinces have now endorsed a set of strategic goals to begin to address that weakness, including a commitment to a national target of R & D spending of 2.5 percent of our GDP by the turn of the century, just to bring us to the threshold of international standards.

Prime minister, you have a unique opportunity to seal this national consensus today.

If we can leave this meeting with a firm commitment to a national R & D target, endorsed by every government at the table, we will have taken the critical first step in building a new economic future for our country.

Third, we can do great things to create a unified market across Canada.

If we can have a free trade agreement with our neighbour, surely we can have one with each other. If the European Community can integrate its markets through "Europe 1992," Canadians should be able to do the same through "Canada 1990."

That is why Ontario supports the agreement we have before us to reduce barriers in government procurement. And we will support any agreement that will reduce barriers in an equitable manner.

Removing the barriers between us is nothing less than a statement of confidence in our country.

Fourth, we can do great things together to build the new high-technology infrastructure we will need for the 21st century.

Meeting here, in a former railway station, we should keep in mind the important part that the rail lines have played in Canada's development, and the important part they must play in the future.

Instead of tearing down what we have, we should be building it up, using advanced technology to construct high-speed corridors of transportation, like our competitors are doing. Ontario and Quebec are exploring a joint initiative to do this, and we plan to pursue the participation of the federal government.

Fifth, we can do great things together to create a national energy grid, so we can sell to each other, instead of focusing solely on markets south of the border.

Ontario is pleased to be involved in discussions with a number of provinces aimed at tangible arrangements for the exchange of electricity, natural gas, and coal.

There is a role for the federal government to play in marrying our technological expertise with our natural resources so that Canadians can fortify ourselves, instead of our competitors.

Sixth, we can do great things together to ensure a clean environment for our children. There is a public consensus on the need for tough standards—in areas like vehicle emissions and product packaging. Now, we must ensure that the standards are in sync from coast to coast, so that we are all playing by the same rules.

We can do all this and more.

But only if we foster a renewed commitment to work together—to build rather than destroy, to unite rather than divide, to create a climate of trust and respect rather than one of suspicion and intolerance.

We can achieve our goals. We can realize our dreams. We can do it by summoning the Canadian spirit—we can do it by working together.

DAVID PETERSON AND THE MEECH LAKE ACCORD

First Ministers' Meeting
Ottawa, Ontario, June 2, 1987

The agreement which we have signed today, like the Constitutional Accord of 1981, is not so much an act of constitutional reform as an act of constitutional expansion.

We are not undoing, narrowing or overturning our fundamental beliefs. To the contrary, we are extending in the formal language of the Constitution our collective commitment to practices and values which have become broadly accepted.

As with Canada's long history of constitution-making, this act today is one more progressive step of affirming *explicitly* what we have long believed *implicitly*. Much like the making or renewing of vows, we are affirming our mutual respect, understanding and commitment to one another.

On the world's stage, this is a rather unique act. Countries the world over are faced with division and rancor over old grievances and new demands. Yet Canadians continue to demonstrate a capacity to fuse differences into a purposeful nation of many cultures and varied hopes.

By this act, we have enlarged the circle of claims to which we are willing to respond collectively. We have enriched our life experiences rather than forcing ourselves to choose between them. Let me suggest two ways in which this is so.

1. We have reaffirmed what we have always known to be true: that Canada is composed of two distinct linguistic societies. At the same time, we remain committed to the multicultural character of this country.

    We have not chosen one over the other. We have merely

Without Walls or Barriers: The Speeches of Premier David Peterson, Library of Political Leadership Series, by Arthur Milnes and Ryan Zade, Editors. Montreal and Kingston: McGill-Queen's University Press,

stated in fundamental law what we know from our experience: that Canada, as a mosaic of cultures and languages,
can embrace both its bilingual origins and its multicultural
evolution with stability, prosperity, and security.

The Constitution pays tribute to all Canadians as a generous people, for only a generous and tolerant people can
make the complexity of a federal system a constructive and
positive reality.

2. By this act, moreover, we state that both the Canadian nation and all of its parts can be strengthened simultaneously.
Some would say we must choose one or the other. Such is
the counsel of a poverty-stricken imagination. It is not the
Canadian way; it has never been the Canadian way.

Repeatedly in our history, starting with the Fathers of Confederation,
we recognized we are a people of sufficient vision and purpose to embrace both diversity and unity.

Over the years, first ministers have reaffirmed this, and have retained
the confidence of the Canadian people. Our Constitution as approved
in 1981 also balances national and provincial needs. The actions that
we are taking today—on the spending power, on the Supreme Court of
Canada, on the Senate, and indeed on the very character of Canada's
distinctness—all balance national and provincial strength.

This constitutional amendment signals the emergence of a confident,
mature, and stronger Canada in which the federal and provincial governments can work together to respond to the future needs of our citizens.

Our vision of Canada does not encompass a rigid, confrontationist,
bureaucratic system of politics.

Rather, it is a Canada in which the two orders of government can respond to both the predictable and the unpredictable needs of our citizens. It is a Canada in which governments can both co-operate and
compete, in a productive way, to serve all Canadians more effectively,
while avoiding a country torn apart as politicians score debating points
about arcane legal and constitutional questions.

As George Brown told the 1865 Parliament in speaking on behalf of
Confederation: "let not honourable gentlemen approach this measure as
a sharp critic deals with an abstract question, striving to point out blem-
ishes and display his ingenuity; but let us approach it as men having but
one consideration before us—the establishment of the future peace and
prosperity of our country."

This package of amendments does not alter the federal government's
direct contact with all citizens of Canada. It does not detract from a
strong, activist central government introducing a national child-care
program or guaranteed annual income scheme.

Yet it enables provincial governments to freely participate in such pro-grams, and tailor them to the needs of their citizens, provided they do so in a way that meets the national objectives set down by Parliament.

Today's agreement signals the fact that Canada's 11 first ministers have come together in a long-awaited act of national consensus to launch a new era in the public affairs of our country. We did not look at this agreement from the point of view of the interests of the federal government or the provincial governments, as has sometimes been the case in the past; we looked at this agreement from the point of view of the interests of the Canadian people as a whole, and how they can best be served in the future.

We have deliberately affirmed, for the first time, the powers of the Parliament of Canada to spend money on matters of federal *or* provincial jurisdiction.

We have built upon the work of our predecessors who gave Canadians a Charter of Rights and Freedoms, and who established for the first time in Canadian history the power of the courts to review the protection of individual rights of citizens.

Moreover, we have succeeded in bringing Quebec into the Canadian constitutional family. We have thus fulfilled in 1987 the promise our predecessors made to the people of Quebec during the referendum of 1980.

Plainly, we cannot meet our needs without working together; patently this must include the government and people of Quebec. By our actions today we have renewed our collective spirit for the challenges of the century to come. Canada has lifted a millstone from its neck.

I believe this achievement was possible today because Canadians trust each other more than they have at times in the past.

For in the final analysis it will be men and women of goodwill who will fashion the Canada of the 21st century, not any single constitutional document or fiat that goes against the nature of our nation and its people.

However much we may wish our life to be more simple, our politics less complex, our options clearer, or our successes more assured, there is no reason to retreat into a mentality that excludes the uncertain and insists that every imaginable contingency be provided for in every detail.

It is possible to accept a broad national consensus if there is a political will on all sides, and goodwill among all participants.

Because trust and goodwill in Canada are stronger than they have been in recent years, our talks have been characterized by a debate over principles, not personality; and by an exchange of ideas, not insults.

In discussions among our governments, acrimony has become a thing of the past—and the past is where it belongs.

Canadians understand that to be strong, leadership must be constructive. Canadians recognize that reconciliation is not weakness, and divisiveness is not a strength.

Mr. Prime Minister, as you are well aware, it takes strength to be conciliatory.

I am proud to be sitting at this table with colleagues who recognize the need for that strength, and command the will to summon it.

One of Canada's greatest strengths is the ability to find common ground. We found common ground at Meech Lake five weeks ago. We built upon it today. I'm confident it will serve Canadians well in the future.

REKINDLING THE NATIONAL DREAM
Toronto, Ontario, November 6, 1989

As we approach the end of another year, and the beginning of a new decade, we find our country facing a number of difficult issues and critical choices.

The issues are in many ways complex, but the choice is in some ways a simple and fundamental one: We can either continue following the Canadian tradition of building on the basis of the things that unite us, or we can succumb to the more recent trend of tearing ourselves apart over the things that divide us.

At the moment, Canada is confronted by both challenges from beyond our borders and pressures from within.

From beyond, we're feeling the stresses and tensions of adjusting to a global economy in extraordinary transition.

Canada, as much as any other country, is being buffeted by the forces of globalization—pulled south by a bilateral trade agreement, east by the desire to capitalize on European economic integration, and west by the magnet of Asian growth.

At the same time, there are pressures from within.

As I look across our country, I see the emergence of a new spirit of divisiveness and intolerance.

In many ways the anger and animosity that I've seen over the past six months are greater than any that I have witnessed during the course of my political career.

I say very candidly that I have never been more worried about the future of our country than I am at the present time.

I see things that tell me that some of us have abandoned the dreams and ideals that helped make this country great.

I see majorities in many regions less comfortable with minorities—far less willing to let them speak out and enjoy their legitimate rights.

I see a hardening of attitudes and a closing of minds toward the legitimate aspirations of many Canadians.

I also see a broad national vision breaking down into a series of narrow, more parochial perspectives.

I fear that Canada may be fragmenting into a country of solitudes—linguistic solitudes, regional solitudes, cultural solitudes, economic solitudes.

I worry that in many ways we are becoming a house divided against ourselves—each of us retrenching into our own comfortable little cocoon.

Suddenly as a nation we seem so much better at finding the things that divide us than those that unite us.

Suddenly, our diversity—so long a source of strength—is being used to drive a wedge among us.

I look across the country and I see separatism within Quebec and alienation in the west—each feeding on the other's destructive energies, combining in a divisive whirlwind that threatens to tear Canada apart.

I look to Quebec, and I see the invoking of the notwithstanding clause and a restriction of the rights of English-speaking minorities—a move that has very much embittered the atmosphere in this country.

In turn I see a backlash in other parts of the country and a desire to slam the door in the face of Quebec's legitimate aspirations.

As someone who takes great pride in his province and his country, it embarrassed and it angered me to see a small group of narrow-minded Ontarians burning the official flag of Quebec.

It embarrasses and it angers me to see to a growing momentum to limit the rights of francophones outside of Quebec—as if the diminution of rights in one part of the country justly compensates for the diminution of rights in another.

I tell you that I do not understand a logic that says that moral wrongs can make up for the abrogation of constitutional rights.

I find it very difficult to comprehend how these people can come to me and say, "You shouldn't be advancing French rights in Ontario because you know that in Quebec they're punishing Anglophones." I recognize the message they're giving me. They're saying, "If they take a hostage, we take a hostage."

But the fact is, this country wasn't built on vindictiveness and retribution. It was built on tolerance and respect.

And even if other provinces take actions to which we object, we must never compromise on our dreams and our ideals and our desires to advance all minorities in our province.

So I feel a profound sense of unease as I see Canadians being pitted against other Canadians.

That unease grows as I hear people saying that the dream that built this country—respect for minorities and equal rights for all—is no longer the national dream.

What particularly disturbs me is the sight of some of our country's leaders fanning the flames of divisiveness for partisan gain.

I see leaders playing region against region, majority against minority, focusing on short-term expediencies instead of on the things we collectively value.

I say to those who seek to exploit divisions rather than to heal them, to those who seek to play the ends against the middle by driving people apart instead of bringing them together, that they do so at great peril to our country.

I say to them you can't build a strong and united country by making side deals on minority rights or compromising with separatists.

The fact is that in some situations there can be no compromise. We can never compromise on the Canadian ideals of respect for minorities and equal rights everywhere in the country.

We must return to that first premise of Confederation and recognize that if any one minority group is threatened in this country, then all minority groups are threatened.

And so we have to say loudly and clearly that there will be no compromise with the forces that want to tear us apart. The anger in our country and the exploitation of that anger serve as a real threat to the future of Canada.

But there is another threat—and that threat is apathy.

As a nation, we are suffering from what I believe is a "crisis of the spirit."

There is a growing malaise—a sapping of our national will.

At the beginning of this decade, when our unity as a nation was visibly at stake, the people of Canada rose to the occasion—in every province, in every region, in both official languages.

People cared and they showed they cared—fighting for Canada in communities in every province.

People were trying to learn the other language. Parents were pressing immersion classes to create space for their children.

Many were engaged in a wrenching effort for national unity. The debate over federalism—that was reflected in the 1980 referendum in Quebec and in the 1982 patriation of our Constitution—was filled with emotion.

There was a passion in our hearts and a fire in our souls when we spoke of Canada.

But now it seems that many have become tired and passive. There are too many people on the sidelines and not enough on the front lines.

There are too many tired federalists saying "we've fought the good fight before, now it's someone else's turn."

Sadly, a decade that began with Canadians affirming their faith in Canada is now coming to an end with many questioning that faith.

Saddest of all, more people than ever seem to be saying, "If Quebec wants to leave—so be it."

The anger, and the apathy, is compounded by another problem—an absence of national leadership and a strong central vision.

I look at the federal government and I see an abandonment of the role that federal governments have always played as the repository of our collective goals and vision—of our national dream.

I see a government that is unwilling—or unable—to serve as the centripetal force that binds us together, and instead opts to feed and pander to the forces pulling us apart.

I see a government that seems determined to shatter the symbols of our unity.

I see a government that has forgotten that this country was put together on the strength of a national railway system, a national telecommunications system, and a national broadcasting system.

I see a government that instead of helping to create a sense of shared purpose among Canadians is locked into a course of eroding the real and symbolic things that have helped build our nation.

And so we see the selling off of our national assets under the nodding head of Investment Canada—an agency that has rubber-stamped 650 foreign takeovers in just four years.

We see the starving of vital institutions like the CBC, a truncation of our national railway links, and the weakening of important social programs that embody the caring and compassionate values of the Canadian people.

We see a failure to recognize that we must use advanced technology to build new symbols of unity—a new core around which we can coalesce and move into the future.

Instead of dismantling VIA Rail, we should be examining the use of new technologies to build high-speed corridors of transportation—like our competitors are doing, like Ontario and Quebec are co-operatively exploring.

Instead of just selling our energy to the south, we should be putting together a national power grid—marrying our technological expertise with our natural resources for the betterment of all of us—fortifying ourselves instead of our competitors.

Instead of using mass communications systems as a means of extending opportunities for the growth of American culture within our own borders, we should be using those systems to find new ways of communicating with our fellow Canadians.

Ladies and gentleman, I believe that we must find a means of recapturing our passion for Canada.

We have to find a new will and a new way of making Canada work.

We have to find a way of forging a broad national vision that transcends parochial interests.

We have to find a new way of building bridges of understanding, because if we cannot build bridges of understanding, then we have little hope of building a nation.

I believe that a major bridge stands before us in the form of the Meech Lake Accord.

This agreement was put together in the same spirit as our original Confederation.

It came about as a result of people of good will sitting down together in a spirit of tolerance and understanding, advancing the goal of nation building by one more step, rekindling the fires of our national dream.

The Accord itself was a compromise—an attempt to find a common ground between competing visions of our country.

Not everyone got what they wanted—I know I didn't—neither did Premier Getty, Premier Peckford or Premier Bourassa.

In fact Quebec came to the bargaining table with the most moderate set of proposals that it has ever placed before the Canadian people—and went on to compromise further from there.

So I repeat, none of us got everything we wanted—but we all achieved what we needed to continue the process of building a nation.

The Meech Lake Accord recognizes the distinctiveness of Quebec—but it also recognizes that the English language minority in Quebec and the French language minorities in other provinces are fundamental characteristics of the national fabric.

The Accord obligates all governments in Canada—including the Province of Quebec—to protect minority rights.

I know that many have said that the Meech Lake Accord is in some ways flawed.

I say in all candor, as one of its most ardent supporters, that it is indeed not perfect.

But if we waited for perfection, we would still be waiting for a patriated Constitution and a charter of rights *without* a notwithstanding clause. Indeed, if we waited for perfection, we'd still be a handful of colonies seeking a basis on which to found a nation.

That's why some of the recent debate surrounding the Accord gives me great cause for concern.

In the search for perfection, that debate has in many ways shed a great deal more heat than light.

A number of objections have been raised to the agreement, but the main focus has been on two basic concerns.

The first is a fear that the "distinct society" clause confers some undefined new powers on Quebec—powers that will allow it to move further and further away from Canada.

If you look closely, you will find that this fear is not based on a reading, but rather a *mis*-reading of the clause and the current situation.

The fact is that the clause—an interpretive clause—confers no new powers on Quebec. Indeed the clause explicitly states that it does not affect the division of powers between the federal government and the provinces.

The distinct nature of Quebec's society—a reality that every school child in this country recognizes—is already a factor being used by the Supreme Court in constitutional interpretation.

If we were to go along with the Manitoba Task Force's recommendation that the Accord be amended to state that nothing in this clause affects the Canadian Charter of Rights and Freedoms, we would in fact, as our attorney general pointed out in his analysis tabled last week, be leaving Quebec with less legal recognition of its distinct society than it enjoys today.

Another concern expressed with respect to this clause, is that when it describes the "fundamental characteristics" of Canada, it does not provide an exhaustive list of those characteristics, leaving out minorities and Aboriginal people.

Meech Lake pointed out—that from a symbolic point of view, it would have been better if a more thorough list of characteristics had been included.

But you have to take into account two critical factors.

The first is that the purpose of this particular clause was not to list all of the fundamental characteristics of Canada, but merely to give constitutional recognition to two characteristics that were not previously included in the Constitution as interpretive principles.

The second point is that the multicultural character of Canada, and existing Aboriginal rights and treaties are already enshrined in the Constitution.

The other major criticism of the Accord is that it entails an unacceptable weakening of Canadian federalism by limiting the powers of the federal government.

Again, this is based on a misinterpretation rather than a correct reading of the Accord.

This Accord does not in any way limit federal legislative powers in areas of *federal* jurisdiction such as the economy or tax policy.

The Accord, had it been in place 20 or 30 years ago, would not have prevented the federal government from introducing the Canada pension plan or the unemployment insurance program.

What the clause does is limit federal spending powers in areas of exclusive *provincial* jurisdiction.

Even that limitation is done in an even-handed way. It begins with recognition that the federal government has the right to set *national* objectives and initiate cost-sharing programs in areas of *provincial* jurisdiction.

It then balances that recognition with the right of a province not only to opt out, but also to receive federal compensation if it provides a program of its own that is "compatible with national objectives."

In fairness, there are a number of valid concerns that have been expressed with respect to the Accord. Some have been expressed by our select committee in Ontario, others by the committee in New Brunswick.

But in our considered judgment, none of them finds a "fatal flaw" in the Accord, or gives good reason why those concerns could not be addressed in a new round of constitutional negotiations following the ratification of the Accord.

In short, none of the objections provides a sound reason for scuttling the Accord.

Let me now give one further reason why I believe the Accord must be ratified.

The Meech Lake Accord is more than just a legal contract—it's also a social contract.

The Accord gives us a means of embracing Quebec as a full and willing participant in the Canadian constitutional family.

The symbolic value of Quebec's signature—or the failure to obtain that signature—on our Constitution is, I know, sometimes difficult to fully comprehend in English Canada.

But in Quebec, it means the difference between feeling fully and truly at home in Canada—or being a grudging participant in Confederation.

In French, there is a word "appartenance." It means "a feeling of belonging."

Everyone needs to have a feeling of belonging. I need it—you need it—Quebec needs it.

Now, perhaps more than at any other time in our history, we have the opportunity to provide it.

We have a historic opportunity in front of us—a chance to renew the bonds of Confederation. If we fail to grasp it, that opportunity may never present itself again in our lifetime.

And if our loss of will—or our loss of nerve—prevents us from embracing Quebec, where else will that failure take us?

How will we ever summon the will to alleviate western alienation, to bring prosperity to Eastern Canada, to reform our national institutions, or to address the many challenges that demand our attention?

If we lose our will, I truly believe that our children and grandchildren will look back at this point in our history and say "that is the moment they let Canada slip away."

In a few days, the Meech Lake Accord will be on the agenda of the first ministers' meeting in Ottawa.

As a politician, I am an idealist. But I am also enough of a realist to understand that we must sail through some stormy waters before we see the final ratification of the Meech Lake Accord.

But just because the going has gotten tougher, just because the atmosphere has become a little more bitter, there is no reason to give up on the ideals that we believe in and hold dear.

I don't expect any magic solutions to present themselves at the conference. But I am hopeful that it will lead to a more productive dialogue on the agreement and ratification before the summer deadline.

As the discussions in Ottawa approach, I think it's useful to reflect on how our Confederation first came about.

It was people with a broad national vision and a sense of values putting forward both a practical and an idealistic dream.

It was French Canadians and English Canadians, Catholics and Protestants sitting down and making a deal. And had they not been able to make that deal they would not have been able to put this country together against the backdrop of the United States of America.

And the deal was this—they said "look, I will respect your religion and you will respect mine. I will respect your language and you will respect mine. And together we will respect all minorities who will come to make Canada their home."

That was the essence of Confederation. That was the start of the spirit of tolerance and understanding, caring and compassion that our ancestors sought to instill in our bones and root into our flesh.

That deal set the course of an experiment that was unprecedented in the history of the world—an experiment that in many respects has made Canada the envy of the world.

People look at our country and say "what a remarkable achievement."

We've been able to take people in from all walks of life and all lands—people of all colours, all races and all creeds—and put them together in a country that is second to none in tolerance and compassion.

We have an opportunity to further that process through the final ratification of the Meech Lake Accord.

As we approach that opportunity, we must do so mindful of the fact that national reconciliation is not just a symbolic end unto itself, but a means of moving forward together to address the many challenges that await us in the 21st century.

The fact is that if we allow ourselves to be bogged down in a constitutional quagmire, we will sit and stagnate while other countries pass us by.

Because the Japanese do not pause to mire themselves in an endless constitutional deadlock. The Europeans do not allow language differences to prevent them from talking to each other and working with each other, throughout their continent.

If they can achieve Europe 1992, there is no reason why we cannot bring about Canada 1990.

Frank Underhill once wrote that a nation is a body of people who have done great things together in the past, and who hope to do great things together in the future.

We Canadians *have* done great things together, and there are great things for us to do together now.

As a nation we must strengthen and diversify our economy. We must rebuild our roads and our rails and the rest of our physical infrastructure.

We must find new ways of meeting our energy needs and strengthening our communications systems.

We must attain new summits of educational excellence in a knowledge intensive world.

We must make new strides in social programs to combat poverty and inequality.

We can do all that—and more. But first we have to rediscover our faith in Canada.

The time has come to remind ourselves that we have more cause for pride than anger—that the frustrations that divide us are trivial compared to the accomplishments and opportunities that unite us—that to cease caring passionately about Canada is to cease caring not only about each other but about the birthright of our children.

Throughout our history, each generation of Canadians has summoned the will to forge a new consensus, to build on the spirit of tolerance and understanding, to build a nation—and fight to keep it together.

Make no mistake about it, maintaining the kind of Canada that we want to pass on to our children will take a fight—but I hope that you will all share with me in the belief that Canada is worth fighting for.

Address to the Quebec City Chamber of Commerce
Quebec City, Quebec, February 5, 1990

Ladies and gentlemen, it's a great pleasure to join you this afternoon.

Though I must admit I was somewhat reluctant to accept an invitation to speak in Quebec during the first week of February—familiar as I am with some of the events that have taken place here during this time of year.

I'm aware, for example, that on this day in 1663, a major earthquake shook the province.

I'm aware that during this week in 1854 a fire destroyed the Quebec parliament buildings.

And I'm aware that on this day in 1972, Quebec's prison guards went on strike.

I trust that in issuing your invitation it was in anticipation that my speech would match those events in terms of dramatic impact, rather than disastrous effect.

But in one respect I'm very grateful for the timing, because it allows me an opportunity to follow a long parade of Ontarians who are joining you in celebrating the world's biggest winter carnival.

Unfortunately, my visit to the carnival comes at a time when Premier Bourassa is in Europe—but there is a positive side to that as well.

You see, my good friend Robert may be a great leader and a wonderful person—but a party animal he isn't.

There's nothing worse than having to watch Robert sip another glass of milk and plow through another government file—while you're trying to bend over backwards and suck back that last drop of "caribou" from your plastic cane.

So I want to thank Robert for removing the guilt factor from my visit.

I also want to thank the Quebec City Chamber of Commerce for the opportunity to share some thoughts with you on the mood of our country, on the direction in which I see us headed, and on the challenges that lie ahead of us.

As I look across this country—from the perspective of one who loves and believes in the concept of Canada—from the perspective of one who loves Quebec and very much shares your goals and aspirations—I feel a great sense of sadness about some of the things that are taking place.

We are in the midst of very difficult and troubling times in this country—times that measure the depths of our souls as a people, and times that measure the depth of our commitment to Canada as a country.

Suddenly it seems as if every problem has become more complex, every discussion more loaded with anger and venom, and every national issue more polarizing and divisive.

Suddenly as a nation we seem so much better at finding and magnifying the things that divide us, instead of fortifying and building on the things that unite us.

A few weeks ago, a national political analyst observed that the "demons of disunity are lurking everywhere below the surface of our national life, making this a time of national distemper..."

The change of mood taking place is very evident outside of Quebec in the form of an erosion of support for the Meech Lake Accord.

A couple of years ago, if you had asked me what the Meech Lake Accord meant to this country, I would have described it as a great symbol of our unity as a people.

It stood as a sign of our willingness to sit down together and reason, to put aside our differences, and to take one step further along the path charted by our forbearers—a path constructed on a bedrock of tolerance, respect for minorities, and equal rights for all.

I still believe that that is what the Accord represents.

As one of the authors and one of the signatories of that Accord, I am very proud of that agreement.

I am proud, not only of the five principles on which the Accord is based—but of the specific language as well—language that is in keeping with our long-standing Canadian tradition of understanding, accommodation and compromise.

But I also recognize that there are many outside of Quebec who have hardened their hearts against the Accord, and I think it's important to understand why that very regrettable backtracking has taken place.

People often ask me what has changed so dramatically over the past couple of years to reverse the enthusiasm with which the Accord was heralded just two-and-a-half years ago.

Certainly the Accord hasn't changed. But the mood of our country has very definitely changed.

One factor that has contributed to that change and had a very unsettling effect upon our country has been the federal government's determination to shatter many of our national symbols—or sit by idly while others destroy them for us.

Over the last few years we have seen a truncation of our national railway system—a system that has great symbolic value in our collective consciousness—a system without which we would not have been able to build this nation.

We have also seen a weakening of the social programs that embody the caring and compassionate values of the Canadian people; and, a selling off of many of our most promising high technology industries.

Another factor has been an apparently reduced commitment to minority-language rights. Too many side deals and compromises have been made on French-language rights outside Quebec. And, increasingly, militant English-rights groups are getting a sympathetic hearing, as was the case recently in Sault Ste. Marie, a situation which I deplore.

You recognize, too, I'm sure, that the passage of Bill 178 and the invoking of the notwithstanding clause has very much changed and embittered the mood of this country.

I understand the pressures that gave birth to those actions. But I also ask you to understand how those actions have alienated many people who are sympathetic to the goals and aspirations of Quebec.

The alienation and the compromises have been compounded by the failure of the federal government to adequately promote the Accord outside of Quebec—an approach that has created the very mistaken impression that Meech Lake is good only for Quebec, and not for the rest of Canada.

This impression has not been helped by some people who are promoting the Accord on the basis of fear, threats and apocalyptic scenarios.

To me that represents a tremendous perversion of Meech Lake—because Meech Lake doesn't stand for fears, it stands for dreams.

The passage of the Accord will stand as a great and historic achievement.

For Quebec—as many of my friends in this province have told me—it will symbolize an acceptance by the rest of Canada of its hopes and dreams—an acceptance that must be there if we are to move forward as a nation.

For Canada, it will symbolize our ability to tackle and resolve complex national issues, and gives us hope that we will be able to succeed in addressing other difficult issues such as Senate reform, regional disparity and Aboriginal rights.

For the world, it will symbolize Canada's resolve to move beyond constitutional paralysis and tackle the economic challenges that await all advanced countries.

Believe me, those challenges are there.

As you know, we are moving into an era of unprecedented global competition.

In Europe, a rapid-fire series of economic and political changes are setting the stage for the creation of a dynamic integrated market of more than one billion people—with all of the power and economic clout that number would suggest.

This is a move, which I note is taking place in spite of differences in language, culture, and history that are much broader and deeper than those we have ever encountered here in Canada.

In Asia, Japan continues to move forward as the world's brightest economic superstar, followed by a group of countries developing at breakneck speed.

Not only must we face those international challenges, but there is also the domestic challenge of rebuilding and refocusing a Canadian economy that has not changed in substance in more than 50 years.

We must begin to address that challenge by using advanced technology to rebuild our physical infrastructure and renew our national bonds.

Instead of dismantling VIA Rail, we should be using new technologies to build high speed corridors of transportation—something that I am very pleased that Ontario and Quebec are currently exploring together.

We should be creating a national power grid, marrying the resources and expertise of Hydro Quebec, Ontario Hydro, Newfoundland and Manitoba—fortifying ourselves instead of our competitors.

We should be rebuilding our science infrastructure—improving not only the quality of innovation, but the quantity.

We should be working together to dismantle a system of interprovincial trade barriers that stand like miniature Berlin walls dividing our provincial economies.

Canada is much too small a country to afford the luxury of provinces competing with each other. We should be building together and taking on the world, instead of competing with each other while the world passes us by.

We should be strengthening our intellectual infrastructure. Working together to develop our human resources may very well be our single most effective strategic weapon for success.

Ladies and gentlemen, these are just some of the challenges that Canada is facing. As I look around this room at the very healthy state of entrepreneurship in Quebec, I am confident that we can rise to the occasion.

But first we must accept that, in a world where economic integration is taking place at lightning speed, we have a much better chance of succeeding by competing as a large and united economic power, than as a series of small and disparate groups. I think we all appreciate that none of us, as an individual entity, would be accepted as a member of the G7.

We have a much better chance of attracting investment and co-operative ventures to a country with its constitutional house in order, than to a country that is permanently bogged down in a constitutional quagmire.

We have a much better chance of promoting growth and prosperity in an atmosphere of stability and cohesion, than in an atmosphere of volatility and hostility.

To me, an honourable way to create that atmosphere, solve our constitutional problems and make federalism work, is to pass the Meech Lake Accord.

I know that the Accord is not perfect—constitutional arrangements never are—in this country, or any other.

There is no such thing as perfection—in life—in human relationships—in constitutional arrangements.

But the important thing is that Meech Lake is a step forward. It's not a final chapter in our constitutional history, but it's a stepping stone upon which we can build a solid future. It represents a chance to keep moving ahead instead of endlessly quarrelling over the past.

Let's not delude ourselves into thinking that if we scrap the Accord, a better idea will come along. We're not suffering from a shortage of ideas in this country—we're suffering from a shortage of political will.

My friends, when all is said and done, I have great faith that we can find that political will, and resolve the difficult issues that we are facing in this country. That has always been the history of Canada.

I think it's important at times like this that we maintain a sense of perspective about the issues that confront us, and a sense of history as well.

The fact is this is not the first time that we have felt stresses and tensions in our country. There have always been problems to address and tensions to resolve in a nation as big and diverse as Canada.

But we have never encountered a problem or tension that we couldn't overcome, because we have always found the will to do so. I believe that we can summon that will again.

I believe it, because I believe that there is something good and decent about this country, something worth preserving and building upon—regardless of the hurdles that currently stand before us.

This country did not come about as a result of an accident of geography or a fluke of history. It came about because of people who shared a common vision—a vision of a country built on understanding and accommodation, a vision of a country built on respect for diversity, a vision of a country based on a collective responsibility for the welfare of all of its citizens.

I believe that when you scratch beneath the surface of the cloud of doom and gloom that hangs over our country today, you will find that the commitment to those values is still there.

Over the past few months I've had the opportunity to visit Atlantic Canada, Western Canada, and Quebec. I know that people in this country still care about each other, still share a desire to reach out and understand each other, and still share each other's joys and sorrows.

When that tragic massacre of young women took place in Montreal, not only Quebec grieved, but an entire nation mourned.

On a daily basis I see new signs of people in both our major linguistic groups demonstrating a willingness to understand each other's cultures, share each other's aspirations, respect each other's rights, and build together.

I see those signs in the way people have banded together across the country in nonpartisan groups to support the Meech Lake Accord.

I see those signs here in Quebec City where your Chamber of Commerce has taken the initiative to establish a dialogue with its counterpart in Toronto. I welcome this step forward, and you have my full personal support.

I see those signs in Ontario—everywhere from the long lineups to see *Jesus de Montreal*, to the support for our *French Languages Services Act*, to the explosive growth of interest in French language immersion programs.

Over the last four years, the number of Ontario elementary school students enrolled in French immersion programs has increased by nearly 40 percent.

We're raising a whole new generation of Ontarians with a personal commitment to Canada's French heritage and recognition of Quebec's status as a distinct society.

We can see that reflected in the fact that support for Meech Lake is greatest among the young people in this country.

So I see many reasons to feel optimistic about the future of our country, many foundations upon which we can build a more co-operative future.

All we need to do is to remind ourselves that as a country we have more cause for pride than anger—that the frustrations that divide us do not measure up to the accomplishments that unite us—that to cease caring passionately about Canada is to cease caring not only about each other, but about the legacy of our ancestors and the birthright of our children.

As a divided country torn apart in opposite directions, there is little that we can accomplish separately. But as a united country, with a national consensus, there is little that we cannot accomplish together.

ADDRESS TO THE SPECIAL COMMITTEE OF THE HOUSE OF COMMONS TO STUDY A PROPOSED COMPANION RESOLUTION TO THE MEECH LAKE ACCORD

Ottawa, Ontario, May 5, 1990

Mr. Chairman, ladies and gentlemen, I know that everyone in this room is familiar with Wilfrid Laurier's statement that the 20th century will belong to Canada. If the past year has served any purpose, it was to indelibly imprint that quotation onto the mind of every Canadian.

When Laurier made that statement, he wasn't putting it forth as a precise economic prediction. He offered it as a statement of faith—a belief that no matter what the future held, Canadians would be able to deal with it and emerge stronger and more united for the experience.

I think it says a great deal about the state of our country today, that you don't hear anybody predicting that the twenty-first century will belong to Canada.

When people talk about Canada and the twenty-first century, it isn't in terms of whether Canada will flourish, but rather, in terms of in what diminished capacity Canada will survive—or whether indeed it will exist at all.

We're bombarded on almost a daily basis with one apocalyptic scenario after another—political collapse, economic chaos, union with the United States.

We've come dangerously close to a fatalistic acceptance of an inevitable breakup of a country that has in many respects served as a model to the world for more than 120 years.

It's as if our national soul has been put through a wringer and come out the other end in a series of little strips that are only precariously connected.

We've lost the ability to focus on the broad swath of things that connect us. As a country, we've become fixated on the narrow range of things that divide us.

I think there's something fundamentally wrong about this streak of pessimism and historical inevitability that's blinding our vision.

You see, I don't believe that the future of our country lies in a Hobson's choice between going out with a bang or going out with a whimper.

I don't believe that our future lies in deciding which provinces will be included in a diminished Canada. I do believe that our future lies in a stronger, more united Canada—if we can summon the will to bring that about.

That isn't just an abstract hope or wishful dream. It's based on a very realistic belief that our commitment to the values that first gave birth to this country are as strong and real today as they were at any point in the past 123 years.

I know in my heart that the vast majority of Canadians are still a tolerant and understanding people who respect diversity—who believe in a country that embraces differences in language, religion, and culture.

I know in my heart that we still believe in a country that extends opportunity to people in all regions. We have never accepted the concept of economic Darwinism—the survival of the richest regions—and I do not believe that we accept that concept today.

We still believe that a child growing up in Bathurst, New Brunswick, or Summerside, PEI, should share in the same opportunities as a child growing up in Toronto, Montreal, or Vancouver—and that Canada is the best vehicle to bring this about.

And, in my heart I know that we're still committed to the creation of a caring and compassionate society. We believe that there is a standard of living below which no one should be allowed to fall.

These are the ideals that first gave birth to this country. These are the ideals without which we would not have been able to defy geography, climate and the pull of the great nation to the south.

These are the ideals which each generation has taken and expanded upon in order to build a nation.

This committee, which has met with Canadians in all regions of the country, now has an opportunity to help our generations of Canadians to add to that historical process.

I believe that the Meech Lake Accord represents one step further in that ongoing process of nation building.

It was an agreement that was conceived in the very spirit of Confederation. It was people of good will sitting down together in an atmosphere of understanding and *compromise*.

I emphasize compromise, because the fact that the Meech Lake Accord is itself a compromise seems to have been forgotten over the past year.

No one got everything they wanted at Meech Lake, I didn't, the prime minister didn't, and neither did Premier Bourassa.

Indeed when Premier Bourassa first presented his list of proposals for adding Quebec's signature to the Constitution, the proposals themselves were a compromise.

They represented the most modest set of conditions that Quebec had ever put forward—and Premier Bourassa, in the spirit of give and take that characterized those discussions, went on to compromise further from there.

So when I hear people describing the Meech Lake Accord as giving in to Quebec, I have to say: that isn't history, it's historical fiction.

And that historical fiction has been shrouded in a further cloak of myth that surrounds the Accord. I believe that if we could clear away that cloud of smoke and let people understand what's really in the Accord, then the majority of Canadians would conclude that it's a document worthy of their support

I don't want to discuss the Accord clause by clause, but I do want to mention two areas where the myths have overshadowed the realities.

The first area is the "distinct society" clause. There is a fear that this clause confers some undefined new powers on Quebec—powers that will allow it to move further and further away from the rest of Canada.

The reality is that the clause—an interpretive clause—confers no new powers on Quebec. The distinct nature of Quebec's society—a reality that every school child in this country recognizes—is already being used by the Supreme Court in constitutional interpretation.

Everyone—even those who are opposed to the Accord—agrees that Quebec is a distinct society. Do we really want to see this country torn apart over whether that recognition is in the preamble or body of our Constitution?

A second myth about the Accord is that it entails an unacceptable weakening of Canadian federalism by limiting the powers of the federal government.

Again, the reality is that it does not in any way limit federal powers in areas of *federal* jurisdiction. Had the Accord been in place 20 or 30 years ago, it would not have prevented the federal government from introducing Medicare or the Canada Assistance Plan.

What the Accord does do is limit spending powers in areas of exclusive provincial jurisdiction—while recognizing the role of the federal government to set the national objectives of those programs.

I would be the first to admit that the Accord is not a perfect document. But the fact is, constitutional agreements never are—that's the nature of the beast.

If we were looking for perfection in a constitutional instrument, we'd still be a handful of colonies arguing over the proper basis on which to found a nation.

Perfection is not the goal of a constitutional document—nor is it even possible—because constitutions are by their very nature compromises. The fact is, the agreement in 1867 wasn't perfect—but it set the stage for the birth of a nation. The agreement in 1982 wasn't perfect—but it set the stage for the dialogue that is taking place today.

Meech Lake isn't perfect—but it is a significant step forward—and it sets the stage for building future bridges of understanding in areas such as Senate reform and Aboriginal rights.

I want to state today for the record that I am personally committed to a reformed Senate that will better represent the interests of Eastern and Western Canada. I support Senate reform because it is in the national interest—it will build stronger national institutions and a stronger Canada. That's why our legislature in Ontario has established a select committee to hold hearings on Senate reform.

But I think we are kidding ourselves if we believe that Senate reform can be achieved without Quebec's signature on the Constitution.

I support Meech Lake today, as I supported it three years ago.

I support it, not because I believe that Canada will fall apart without it—you can't build a nation or keep it together on the basis of fear. Fear and loathing are not the bricks of Confederation.

I support it because after three years of close scrutiny, it still stands up as the best vehicle we have for bringing about national reconciliation.

I support Meech Lake because it is about what Canada is about—creating a national dream and finding the will to go out and make that dream come true.

Like most dreams, the dream of greater national strength through a new constitutional understanding has great symbolism attached to it.

To the people of Quebec, the passage of the Accord would symbolize an acceptance by the rest of Canada of their hopes and dreams—an acceptance that must be there if we are to move forward as a nation.

To the people of Canada, it would symbolize our ability to tackle and resolve complex national issues, and gives us hope that we will be able to succeed in addressing other difficult issues such as Senate reform, regional disparity and Aboriginal rights.

To the people of the world it would symbolize Canada's resolve to move beyond constitutional paralysis and tackle the economic challenges that await all industrialized countries.

Believe me, the world is growing a little impatient at Canada's inability to escape from its constitutional quagmire.

They are asking: How is it that twelve very different European nations can move forward so quickly toward not only economic integration but political integration as well, yet thirteen Canadian governments cannot agree on a vehicle for creating greater understanding?

They are asking why is it that when the Soviet Union can erase the supremacy of the Communist Party from its constitution with a stroke of a pen, Canada cannot find the right pen or the right strokes to alter its own Constitution?

As I said earlier, I support the Meech Lake Accord. But I am also open to any modifications that will add to the Accord, while retaining the Accord's essential characteristics and achieving the same broad consensus that we first achieved at Meech Lake.

My friend, Premier McKenna, raised a very relevant point when he stated to this committee that it would be futile to scrap the Accord and begin a new round of constitutional negotiations.

At the same time, the companion resolution that he has placed before you represents a very useful contribution to our national dialogue, and has provided this committee with a good starting point for discussions that could end our constitutional impasse.

I'm also very hopeful that next week's meeting of Western premiers will further add to this process.

Canadians want our constitutional impasse to end, and I believe that the will now exists to make it come to an end.

Our country has, for too long, had its eyes fixated on the abyss that stands before us. The time has come to step back from the brink and find the vehicle for achieving national reconciliation.

I urge the committee to reach a unanimous consensus in its deliberations. A unanimous report, endorsed by members of all political parties, will be an important symbol and instrument of national reconciliation. It would provide a sound basis for a meeting of first ministers to bring the current impasse to an end.

I am confident that we can find a means of breaking the logjam. It may be true that conflict has always been a part of our national character. But it is even more true that conflict resolution has been a greater part.

At the same time, I think we all recognize that constitutional reform will not by itself bring about national reconciliation.

National unity involves more than just constitutional arrangements. It involves the love and goodwill extended by the people brought together under the umbrella of a nation.

We are, at the moment, down a few pints in that goodwill. The greatest deficit facing our country is not our budget deficit—serious as it may be, but the deficit in our will to make Canada work.

I believe that we can find that will. I believe that if we look deeply into our souls, we will find that the values that gave birth to this country are values that we still cherish—values that give real meaning to the concept of Canadian nationhood.

I believe that we are still willing to reach out to each other, to share each other's dreams and aspirations, and to make this country a place that will continue to be the envy of the world.

I believe that we are still willing to work together—to accommodate diversity—to improve regional opportunity—to build a caring and compassionate society.

I believe that deep down inside all of us, is the will to work together to meet the challenges facing our nation.

Those challenges are many. While we have been encumbered by constitutional paralysis, other countries haven't been standing still. We have a great deal of catching up to do.

As a nation, we must strengthen and diversify our economy. We must rebuild our roads and rails and the rest of our physical infrastructure.

We must find new ways of meeting our energy needs and strengthening our communications systems.

We must attain new summits of educational excellence in a knowledge-intensive world.

We must make new strides in social programs to combat poverty and inequality.

We must lead by example in the global effort to protect our planet's environment.

We can do all this—and more. But first we must rediscover our faith in Canada.

My friends, a number of years ago, a great nation builder by the name of Mackenzie King observed that Canada's problems stemmed from the fact it has too much geography and not enough history.

We will, over the course of the next few months, be making a great deal of history. Let us make sure that it is the type of history of which our children and grandchildren will be proud.

ADDRESS TO THE NEWFOUNDLAND LEGISLATURE

General Assembly of Newfoundland, St. John's, Newfoundland June 20, 1990

Mr. Speaker and members of the Legislative Assembly, should I say at the outset that I am delighted, personally, to have accepted your invitation, your personal invitation, to attend on this historic opportunity to share my views with members of the Assembly. I recognize this is a rare privilege, if not a unique honour, and I also know how dangerous it is on an occasion like this, when unanimous consent is required, for someone like me to speak here, and I thank you all for the privilege you have accorded me. I was here, I think in November last, and I received a very warm greeting in your House from you, Mr. Speaker. I was delighted to attend, and you reminded me on that occasion that after the *Act of Union, 1949*, Ontario donated the chair in which you sit, and may I tell you how handsome you look in that chair. And, sir, regardless of the outcome of this discussion, you can keep that chair, Mr. Speaker. I would like you to know that.

This is, indeed, a historic occasion and probably, I would suggest, as important an issue as any to which we have applied our collective minds as a nation. There are lots of difficult issues in politics, lots of pressures, issues come and go, as all of us know who have practiced in the crucible of a legislature in our lives.

And it is not as if this will affect an unemployed fish worker or an unemployed auto worker tomorrow morning or next week but, I would argue, that it will have as profound consequences for the future of our country as, perhaps, any discussion that we have ever had. And I know that this legislature and all the members herein are approaching it with solemnity and seriousness, and I am proud to be part of those discussions.

I phoned my wife this morning and she wished me well. She said, "David, this is probably the most important speech you will ever make in your whole life." I thanked her very much for taking the pressure off me, and I am proud to participate.

I come not to lecture, not to cajole, not to threaten, not to plead, but to share my views of this debate as someone who has been intimately involved in this discussion, really, for the last four years, but even beyond that. I was one of those as a student—as I know many of you were—who followed the developments of Quebec since the beginning of the Révolution tranquille in the 1960s. As we, as a country, Quebec as a province, all of us, were trying to work out the problems there in that community, and as we went through a number of difficulties, crises if you will, referendums, elections of separatist governments, all trying to address our minds to that problem and the great question was always asked, Well, what does Quebec want? How do we work out a confederation that accommodates their needs and hopes and aspirations as well as contributing to the greater unity and to the greater whole?

I come, not really in a position to speak for all of Canada, because I would never be so presumptuous, and I cannot even stand in front of you and say I speak for all of Ontario, because there are many people in my province who disagree with me. This has been an issue that is beyond partisanship. It is as difficult, as I said, as any issue that we have ever faced; it has caused many splits in my party and other parties, as well, right across this nation. People of conscience, people of judgment wrestle with this most fundamental question.

But I do come to you as one who cares passionately about this country, as one who believes that we can make it whole and make it better for the future, that we have far more things in common than we do that separate us. And, at the same time, we can recognize and understand the uniqueness and specialness of various areas and accommodate their special needs as we have always done historically, and will do in the future as well, and go on together and build a stronger confederation and more unity of purpose.

I believe, Mr. Speaker, it is important in this discussion to review, if I may, just a little of the history. Many of you know that the most important change probably in our Constitution occurred just in this last decade, in 1982, and you remember the discussions leading up to that. In my view, it was a heroic achievement, an achievement of historical proportions, to take men and women at that time who had dramatically different views on the country. You will remember the debates with Mr. Trudeau and Sterling Lyon and some of the Western premiers, they were all there, and it looked like it was an absolutely intractable position. Yet, through a process of compromise and a process of accommodation, the Constitution was brought home for the first time in over a hundred years. We now had the power to amend our own Constitution, brought in a Charter of Rights, which has had a dramatic effect on this country in the last eight years, and we now had power over our own future.

But there was a price paid, and it was not perfect. That is not to in any way denigrate what the leadership of the country at that time did. But there were two omissions, or, if you like, one omission and one massive compromise. The notwithstanding clause was a massive compromise. It was far more devastating in its consequences than anything that we are discussing today at Meech Lake. And we have seen the use of that notwithstanding clause in Quebec and in other provinces, for that matter, and we know that the use of that has poisoned the debate in this country and there is a great tendency to relate the two. But in fact and in law, the notwithstanding clause and Meech Lake have nothing to do with each other. And one of the points I believe I have in agreement with your premier is that we would both like to get rid of that clause. There is not unanimity on that question, there is not even a general consensus on that question, but I hope someday in the future we will be able to get rid of that. But that was a price paid at the time, because without it, we would not have what we have today. But I also say that had I been there in 1982, and I was not, but had I been there, I would have been proud to sign on, and I would have said at the time it was a price worth paying.

But there is another price that was paid, and that was the price of patriating the Constitution without Quebec's signature. Now, in fairness, Quebec would not have signed anything at that time. Quebec was headed by a separatist government whose sole object was to destroy the Confederation. Someone in our recent discussions quoted one of the premiers as saying, "Well, Mr. Parizeau's sole object is to destroy the nation." When Mr. Parizeau was asked about that he said, "He is absolutely correct. That is my object, to destroy the nation." But then the question became, well, how do we bring Quebec to the table? How do we get them participating in the other discussions about Senate reform, Aboriginal self-government, and other things?

The political leadership of the day rightly, in my view, made the judgment to go ahead without Quebec, They felt, and again I think rightly, that there were strong Francophone spokesmen in Ottawa representing Quebec who had every bit as legitimate a voice to speak for Quebec as did the provincial government of the day, and then we as federalists and as Canadians were blessed, in my view, by an election in Quebec that brought a federalist government after ten years. Mr. Bourassa came, and he had had a thorough discussion with his party and with his province about joining Confederation, signing on, becoming a willing partner, and he reduced all of these proposals to five. It started originally about six years ago, in a document called *Maîtriser l'Avenir*. It went through a document called the Beige Paper that was submitted for public discussion. Those who were interested are familiar with it. He brought that to an election in 1985 and had a mandate to negotiate his way into full partnership in Confederation. There was nothing secret about that. It was not a private discussion. It was a thorough and total public discussion. Admittedly, it did not have the attention that some of our other discussions have, but it was all there for everyone to see.

Four years ago, the premiers gathered—the prime minister was not there—the premiers gathered at one of our annual conferences in Edmonton, and all of us together signed a document called the Edmonton Declaration. We agreed then, together, that our first priority was to bring Quebec into full partnership in the Constitution. It was an initiative right across this country from coast to coast.

So we went on from there to the Meech discussions, and those had all been discussed publicly. Admittedly, again, it did not have a high degree of public attention. I remember, personally, walking up the road to Meech Lake, where I had never been in my life, and, with any luck, will never go back again, and I remember people asking me, "Well, are you optimistic? Do you think this thing can be put together?" Because nobody thought this could be put together. This problem has bedeviled this country for a 123 years, and if you want to look beyond that, since the Plains of Abraham in 1759. This is not a new or unique problem; it is a problem that has always been there. And the history of our constitutional debates in this country, the history of the great debates in Parliament, is filled with this discussion. So you, ladies and gentlemen, are part of a major historical debate, not just one that is subject to the pressures of today.

We went to Meech Lake and put together the principles of a partnership with Quebec, for Quebec to become a full member. We were not trying to solve all the world's problems. We were not trying to deal with all the problems of aboriginal self-government or Senate reform or fisheries, or whatever, but we were trying to bring Quebec to the table so they could participate in the future, recognizing that our Constitution, in Canadian terms, was very, very new. It was only since 1982. We did not, at that point, invent the amending procedure, or the three-year time period required under it—that came out of 1982. And had we unilaterally taken it upon ourselves to change that process, you can imagine the criticism that would have come forward. We did the best we could, perhaps, and I think we have all learned a lot about some of the inadequacies of that process.

So we put it together at Meech Lake and we subsequently went on to Langevin, where the legal niceties were all put together. That was seen, at the time, to be a historic achievement. People across this country—and there were dissenters, no question—but, by and large, it enjoyed a very high degree of popular support. People thought it was wonderful. You know how rare it is to get agreement on anything in this country, but to have eleven governments sign on was seen as absolutely an amazing achievement. Little did we know then some of the changes that would develop in our country over the subsequent three years. There were changes of provincial governments, no question about that, including in this Province of Newfoundland and Labrador.

There were changes in mood. There have been many hurtful things done and said in this country, including many in my own province, which I deeply regret. Many things have been transmitted back and forth to each other, and we have seen a sensitive nation react in many ways to these things. Bill 178 that I referred to—English Canada has changed dramatically the support for Meech Lake, even though it is not legally related in any way. And we have seen, at the same time, a very high degree of symbolism overtake this debate. In many ways, in Quebec, Meech Lake, today—forget the legal niceties for a moment, I will talk about those in a moment—is seen as a symbol of belonging. It is a question of, in French the word is *appartenance*, the symbol of acceptance, just as, outside of Quebec, many people have used Meech Lake as a way to express frustration about Quebec, about the fact that they are *demandeurs* and too noisy and always, they think, whining about something or have special status, getting something we are not getting, a way to express their hostility.

So we have seen all of these dimensions to this debate and it's forced a much wider discussion as well into the very essence of our Canadianism. What are we? What kind of federation? How do we put together this diverse population? How do we reconcile the distinctiveness of Newfoundland and Labrador with the distinctiveness of British Columbia or Ontario, Quebec, or Manitoba? And how do we put all of that together in a federation? Because it is not easy as you know. Some populations, some provinces, are dramatically different than others. Look at the linguistic component today of New Brunswick—and you will be graced by the presence of the premier of New Brunswick this afternoon—who can talk from a unique perspective of the only bilingual province in this country. Newfoundland and Labrador tends to be more homogeneous than other provinces. Toronto today: over 50 percent of the people in Toronto are not native-born French or English. We teach in our schools in Toronto over 80 different languages today, not just the obvious ones like Italian, and Greek, but Chinese, Cambodian, Vietnamese. There is recognition of all of our people, new and old, and we have historically been very, very good at dealing with diversity and respecting diversity and understanding that is an important part of the Canadian characteristic. And in spite of all of our problems I would argue that we have been better than any other country in the world probably, in reconciling those differences, putting them together, respecting them, yet finding a common good at the same time

So we have had, as I said, probably the most discussed, worked over, analyzed little piece of paper, Meech Lake, in the history of this country. This is quite different than 1982. In 1982 this did not go to provincial legislatures. As you recall, it did not have provincial hearing. Then it had to go to the mother of all parliaments, the Parliament in Westminster in order to patriate our Constitution. So in many respects a far, far more significant piece of paper, the patriation and Charter of Rights in 1982 had far less attention and far fewer discussions than did this Meech Lake discussion we are having at the present time.

I want to, if I may, take the time, Mr. Speaker, to address some of the issues that have been raised, and I heard part of the attorney general's speech as I was sitting in the Speaker's office waiting to come and share my thoughts with you. And the question is: What is a "distinct society"? Does it give some special status? Are Quebecers different than us? Do they have more rights or less rights or fewer privileges? What does it really mean for us today? What does it mean for someone working in a gas station in St. John's or in a mine in Sault Ste. Marie? What does that really mean?

Let me back up a little bit before I come to that. Our Constitution in 1867, the *BNA Act*, is a very interesting document. It is not filled with the heroic language of the Constitution of the United States, and there is no "We, the people" kind of clause to summon everybody around common principles. It is in rather sparse prose, Balzacian prose, if you like. It defines not only our governing institutions and the distribution of power, but it also recognizes the differences. It was created by people with dramatically different views of our federation. John A. Macdonald wanted a unitary state, a very strong federalist. Cartier had a totally different view; …[he] wanted a strong federalism to protect the rights of Quebecers. Again they were almost like Sterling Lyon and Pierre Trudeau in terms of their differences of opinion, but they were able to put them together in 1867 and it was a heroic act of statesmanship, irreconcilable views penned together again. And what, I would argue, is more important than the governing institutions that were created in 1867, was that that document is a monument to toleration, and to respect, and to minority. Here you have a completely different Province of Quebec with a unique legal system.

In 1774, in the *Quebec Act*, it was granted its distinct status, at that point. They still have a different legal system than the rest of Canada. They obviously spoke a different language, the majority had a different religion, and they had a different school system. And the Catholics and Protestants in Upper Canada were worried about their particular school systems, run as they were by the churches in those days, all of these differences were accommodated and given constitutional protection in 1867. And what it really said is, "Look, I can have my religion and you can have yours. You can educate your kid the way you want to educate him and I will educate mine. You can have your legal system and I will have mine, and we can all put it together underneath the umbrella of Canada." That is what they said to each other. And it is my view, because of the toleration and understanding shown at that time, we created the underpinnings—the intellectual and emotional underpinnings—for the most tolerant society in the world today. And now we have an advanced multicultural society which allows us, based on those principals, to bring in people from lands from all corners of this globe and make them feel comfortable and wanted here, and full and true Canadians. I think that is the most important achievement in 1867. And along the way accommodations were made. When BC came in there were special provisions to build a railroad—part of the constitutional provisions. There were special language provisions for Manitoba in 1870. And when Newfoundland came in in 1949 there were special provisions for the protection of the parochial school system here, special provisions with respect to the sale and distribution of margarine. Now putting margarine in a constitution is not exactly the most heroic thing I have ever heard of, but it was a recognition of a reality here, and people were not so fixed in their mind that they could not adjust to a reality, and so they fixed it. And frankly, who gives a damn? It was a reasonable accommodation to a reality of the situation. Heroic, maybe no, but it sure was sensible and has stood up to the test of history.

So we have gone on to that, to the question or, well, what this distinct society means. How do we put all of this together in the context of our constitutional history of the past? I will just give you a little quote from Sir John A.—an anecdote of life of Sir John A. Macdonald—and he was talking about Confederation at the time. He said, "Certainly Confederation was the product of politicians of all stripes from five colonies." And certainly the idea did not originate with Macdonald. To Brown's original concept were added the financial expertise of A.T. Gait and Cartier's insistence on minimum essential guarantees of provincial rights. There was no pride of authorship; they all shared in the authorship of a document that is the underpinnings of our great country.

So the question now becomes, well, is the distinct society clause out of character with that? Does it give special powers, special status to Quebec? Does it give them things that Newfoundlanders or Ontarians do not have? Is it out of character with the kind of decisions that we have made historically to accommodate new provinces coming into Confederation? We solicited legal opinions on this, because frankly it was a question that worried us, of Meech and the Langevin discussions. I have an opinion, and I recognize that lawyers… you get three lawyers in the room, you get three different opinions. And I am sure the premier will tell you if you had 100 lawyers in the room as we did, you would get 100 different opinions as well.

But I quote only from Peter Hogg, QC. I think Peter Hogg is probably recognized as the leading constitutional lawyer in Canada today, the most quoted in the Supreme Court. And he was asked his legal opinion. Does the Meech Lake Accord confer special status on Quebec? Something everybody wants to know. I will table, Mr. Speaker, this opinion with you if it would be helpful in your deliberations, but, he said, in opening his opinions, he said it's important to notice that the Constitution of Canada does not treat all provinces equally, and as a result there are now minor differences in the constitutional status of each province, including differences in each province's power. That is what I said in my brief exposition of our Canadian Constitutional history. But let me quote to you his conclusion: he says, "since there is general agreement that the Constitution does not now confer special status on any province, despite minor variations in their powers, it follows that the distinct society clause does not confer special status on the Province of Quebec." I recognize there are other opinions on this question, but I think I can say with candor that the majority of constitutional lawyers in this country share that view. It was also part of a document tabled with the new agreement that was signed a week or so ago, signed by a number of leading constitutional lawyers, and I commend this opinion to you. Its weight in court will be a subject of some discussion although, as you know, in the last ten years particularly, the Supreme Court has taken into account a variety of different views in a variety of different cases. I just leave with you, for example, in the famous referendum on wage and price controls, one of the documents quoted, indeed in the judgment and in the argument, was a speech from the then governor of the Bank of Canada to a service club in Saskatchewan with respect to anti-inflation policy, so I believe it will have weight. This document says the following—and I will not read the whole thing—the rights and freedoms guaranteed thereunder are not infringed, or denied, by the application of the clause. They are not denied by the application of the clause, and continue to be guaranteed subject only to such reasonable limits prescribed by law as can be demonstratively justified in a free and democratic society. That is the opinion of the experts. Now nothing in that clause creates new legislative authority for Parliament or any of the provincial legislatures, or derogates from any of their legislative authority. It may be considered in determining whether a particular law fits within the legislative authority of Parliament or any of the legislatures. Those opinions are a matter of record and I am sure you will take them into consideration.

I am confident, and I am one of those who had worries about this issue, that we are not creating a special legislative status for Quebec, or giving special powers in those circumstances. In fact the distinct society, by definition, describes Quebec as a majority of French-speaking Canadians and a minority of English-speaking Canadians. In other words it does give the minority now, for the first time, constitutional status in Quebec, and I think one could even make the argument it gives the minority more power. But let us just say for a moment I am wrong. Supposing my opinion is wrong, and some lawyer somewhere argues, well, yes, but maybe someday on the margins—out 20, 30, or 50 years—some judge interprets it differently than I do, and says there is a little special power inherent in the distinct society clause. I do not believe that will be the case, based on legal opinion, but if it does, *if* that is the case, it would not affect one Newfoundlander's rights, or one Ontarian's rights. It would only affect rights, if it were operable, in the Province of Quebec, and Quebecers want Meech Lake. When you think about it, here we are, non-Quebecers, all of us, passing judgment on them. Do we have the right to tell them that they cannot have something that they want and that they think is important to their cultural identity, to developing their constitutional future? Even at the margin, and I do not believe there is any risk, should we hold up this document because of an outside infinitesimal remote possibility that somebody's rights in a province that we do not live in, that wants this document, [that] we do not think they should have it? That is a question that has to be addressed by all Canadians. That question was, I think, along with the Senate question, the major subject of discussion during the last week in Ottawa.

The second question to be dealt with in great depth was a question of the Senate. It was not the intention of the original authors of Meech Lake to try to solve the question of Senate reform. Even though it was high on the agenda of the Western provinces at that time, particularly Alberta led by Premier Getty. He was insistent at that point on the unanimous veto. Interestingly enough, there have been lots of discussions on that question, but the chief author and the chief architect and the chief proponent of Senate reform was in favour of the unanimous veto.

I think it is important to note, because most people I think who have not read Meech carefully, think that the unanimous veto applies to everything in the Constitution, that is not correct. It just applies to Section 41, to institutional change on the Senate, on Parliament, the Supreme Court and new provinces. The general amending formula still stands, of seven provinces with 50 percent of the population.

Your premier has very strong views about Senate reform, and feels that perhaps Meech Lake... not perhaps—and I am very, very careful because I would never want to speak for another premier—said this could jeopardize the prospects for Senate reform in the future. There is no question through his eloquence and his great knowledge and passion on the subject that he has dramatically advanced the agenda on Senate reform. It is something I would support, because I believe that we have to continue to build our institutions in this country, to give real voice to all Canadians, to make sure that every Canadian feels they are participating in building this country.

I understand, coming from central Canada, some of those cries from the less populous regions, and I want every single Canadian to feel that they have not only a right but a responsibility to participate in the governing of their country. I believe that Senate reform is one of the ways to do that. The question is have we advanced the cause or have we set it back? I think probably at this point the premier and I have different views. We agreed in the last go around that we would immediately set up a commission of equal representatives from all provinces to look at the question of Senate reform along certain defined principles: elected Senate, better representation from the less populous regions, and an effective Senate without interfering with the powers of the House of Commons. Should that not take place over the next five years, we have agreed, Ontario, New Brunswick, and Nova Scotia as well, to a redistribution of Senate seats to assist the less populous regions, the West and Newfoundland particularly, in having a greater say at the centre.

At the very worst, if we cannot get Senate reform in the next five years, and I believe that we can because I believe there is a great deal of momentum when we have all agreed it is the priority, at the very worst there will be guaranteed, as Ron Watts says, partial Senate reform.

It does not conform to everybody's views on the matter, just as nothing else we did does, but I would argue it is a major step forward. We have set the course. If we were forced to deal with that issue today, and we would not be capable of doing that because Quebec is not at the table, then it would probably stalemate itself and we would see any momentum, any advances, come to a grinding halt. So I would argue that the process has been served and we are making progress.

There were many other improvements that were agreed upon in the last week or so, as many of you know, and they were the result of very wide hearings across this country, in many different provinces and a great deal of discussion. We have improved the sexual equality provisions, we have improved the provisions with respect to appointments from the Territories, and we have agreed on a process to try to develop that Canada Clause which was very important to Manitoba. And I understand that, and I would like to see a Canada Clause. We don't have a Canada Clause but, let us be frank, it has bedeviled legislatures for the past 123 years. It is not an easy question; the philosophy is easy, the specifics are difficult.

There are a number of suggestions on the table from a number of provinces, but we are now going to deal with that question and try to put into our Constitution the basic and fundamental characteristics.

Someone said during the discussion that the fundamental characteristic of Canada is constant constitutional change. It might be the one thing on which we all agree. But we have also, I think, all agreed collectively that we have to address the question of Aboriginal self-government. I participated in a conference on Aboriginal self-government in 1987. We were dealing with an enormously complex set of issues, and we then had nine provinces at the table. Quebec was not there. Quebec historically has been enormously sympathetic to the questions of our first peoples, and has been very progressive in a number of regards. But we had five out of nine provinces at that time. The provinces which turned down the proposals on the table were the three Western provinces and Newfoundland. But there have been changes in Newfoundland, as well, and it may be with a new and fresh approach and with Quebec at the table and a guaranteed constitutional conference, that we can make progress in that regard as well. We have not changed the amending formula with respect to Aboriginal self-government, and I am one of those who believe that major progress has been made in that regard.

We have agreed, as I said, all of us, that the process was not adequate. None of us enjoyed the way it developed, even though we got to know each other extraordinarily well in that week, and there were some enormously heroic moments and emotional moments. And I consider it to be one of the most interesting and deeply rewarding experiences of my life, because I saw acts of statesmanship and generosity that I wish all Canadians could have seen. But we know we have to change that. We know we have to develop the Constitution in partnership with the people, and not many of us have many ideas on how to do that. That is a subject we will be discussing, and I think we can make improvements.

But lest we be too hard on ourselves in that regard, let me say that it was not a process we invented; we inherited it in 1982. We were working to a deadline that none of us liked, and I think in the future it can be more relaxed with far more pre-discussions going on. But, it is also fair to say, like any other big discussion in this country, there will not always be unanimity on these questions. There are many, many people who looked at this whole Meech Lake discussion and said, "Ah, if just those horrible politicians could just get out of this, we, the people, could sit down and solve all these problems." So you remember the media would gather them up, they would all go away and sit in a lodge for a weekend and they would solve all the problems, and at the end of the weekend they were all fighting.

You see, we are elected. We do have a democratic responsibility and an obligation to make decisions, as difficult as they are, from time to time, and all of us are used to taking the consequences of that, be they good or be they bad. And we all recognize whatever we do, there will be the critics, as there should be in a free and democratic society.

The question then becomes, and I heard the attorney general speak about this this morning, what will happen if Meech fails? The so-called fear mongers, the scaremongers, are we being threatened or cajoled into signing this bitter pill? And what are our responsibilities to the nation? And is Quebec always going to be demanding something? Is this just the beginning of separation? Are they going to go anyway, with or without Meech Lake? And what about the nationalists in Quebec? And maybe they are headed that way anyway, and there is nothing you and I can do to salvage that situation. It is part of the debate. And the answer to the question is "C": do not know the answer. And nobody knows for sure. I cannot predict the next hundred years.

I believe the Meech Lake Accord will give us a period of stability in which we can work out other problems, but we all recognize that. Quebec only has two major parties. One is a federalist party and one is a separatist party whose ambitions and aims are very clear, and we all remember the referendum of 1980. And do you know what the score was? It was 60–40. And if you take the Anglophones out, it was 50–50 amongst the Francophones. So make your own judgment about whether this is important in Quebec or not.

And the other question asked was, will this keep Quebec quiet for a while? Will they stop demanding all these things? Well, the answer to that is probably no. Because that is the nature of our federation. Will grain payments out west stop the farmers for asking for more? No. Will support for the fisheries here help fishermen to stop asking for more? No. Will help for Ontario get me to stop asking for more? The answer is no. That is the nature of our federation. Everybody is a *demandeur*. And what is the matter with that? And sure they will ask for more, and Newfoundland will ask for more, and Alberta will ask for more, and British Columbia will want help with their gas pipeline projects, and Alberta will want help with their upgraders. And what is the matter with that? We have lived with that for 123 years; we will live with it for another 123 years. Just as you have every right to stand up on every occasion and put forward the case of your province, so do I have that right for my province, as well, and so does the government of Quebec.

So I believe you have listened to the testimony of many people before the Select Committee. You have heard the chairman of Burns Fry saying interest rates would go up two percentage points, and you know the effect of that if Meech Lake is not signed. You have others saying the country will fall apart. You have read about the pressure that Mr. Bourassa is under from the Separatists, but you also read about the pressure that Mr. Getty is under, Mr. Devine is under and that I am under, that we are all under. We all recognize this is not the most popular document in the country today, but I do not believe that you can keep a country together on the basis of threats or fear. And if that is your only reason for supporting Meech Lake, do not support it. You support it because it is part of the great and generous tradition of this country of accommodating its regions, there is nothing dramatic or unique or out of character with our constitutional history, either now or in the future.

You see, I do not believe you can keep a country together on the basis of threats. You can keep it together on the basis of love and respect and accommodation and tolerance—the kind of principles which are articulated in our *BNA Act, 1867*. And you have to recognize, as I said, it is part of our honourable tradition and it is not going to stop with Meech Lake; it is going to continue. And there are going to be a lot more strains on this country. It is not the fact that we have had strains in this country that is unique, because we always have had and we always will have in the future. What makes us unique as Canadians is we have always been able to solve our problems in the past. And, look, read the Confederation debates, read about the discussions over conscription, read about the Statute of Westminster, and all the tough negotiations that have gone on. The issues pale into insignificance in the clear light of history, because of the glory of the thing we have created together. You know, Frank Scott, in his essay on the Constitution, *Aspects of Canadian Law and Politics*, said this: "Changing a Constitution confronts a society with the most important choices, for in the Constitution will be found the philosophical principles and rules which largely determine the relations of the individual and of cultural groups to one another and to the state. If human rights and harmonious relations between cultures are forms of the beautiful, then the state is a work of art that is never finished."

We are, ladies and gentlemen, in historical terms, a mere adolescent on the world stage. We are only 123 years old. We are wrestling constantly with our own identity, wrestling for new ways to put ourselves together, recognizing there is much unfinished business to complete. Much of it is part of the agenda articulated forcefully and eloquently by your premier, and I share his views in that regard.

Meech Lake was not a document written by one person. There was the blood of twenty-five million Canadians in that, and eleven governments. The agreement signed a week ago is the same way. No one person in Canada could have sat down and written that document at the beginning of the discussion. It took a week to evolve, as difficult as that was. And there was part of Clyde Wells in that, there was part of Robert Bourassa in that, part of Grant Devine in it, part of Joe Ghiz in and part of David Peterson in it, and I am proud to have participated in that exercise.

There is, as many of you know, a famous painting of our Fathers of Confederation. It was painted by Robert Harris, and it hangs in many of our legislatures. It has, as some of you know, three large windows in the background, behind the Fathers of Confederation, and those are the windows of the Legislative Assembly in Charlottetown. But behind that the scene that is drawn in is the harbour as it looks out on Quebec City. And, interestingly enough, in that fictional painting of the Fathers of Confederation, there are two representatives of Newfoundland, Ambrose Shea and F. B. T. Carter, and everybody knows that Newfoundland did not join Confederation for another eighty-two years. But there was something prescient about that, and something very, very Canadian about that portrait that takes the best from across this country and puts it together in the common good, and glorifies those things that we have in common, but celebrates our diversity at the same time.

Lord Acton once said a country can either sacrifice self-government to unity or preserve it through federalism. I would argue that this country is too large and too diverse to govern without recognizing some of those differences, the uniqueness of Newfoundland, the uniqueness of Ontario, the uniqueness of British Columbia, and put it all together.

Ladies and gentlemen, let me just offer one final note. I know of the intensity of the debate in this province; I know of your discussions with your constituents in the last several weeks. And I know and you know that the eyes of the nation are upon you, and Manitoba, as well. And you are going to make as important a decision as you have made, as I have said I believe, in your political lives. And you have the power to kill Meech Lake. You have that democratic right, and no one denies you that. I know, as you know, that Meech Lake and these discussions, both from a process side and from substance side, is not the most popular document this country has ever seen. And I know, and you know, of the pressure that has been brought to bear on all of us, some informed, some not so informed, some to the issue and some on other issues that are bedeviling our province and our country at the same time. I also know that public support has gone up and down. It has been a roller coaster ride. If you look at one poll one day and they say they support it, and you listen to somebody else and they do not support it, in this poll and the other. Frankly, I would like to define as a fundamental characteristic of Canada getting rid of pollsters, but that is another story for another day.

I do not believe that any of us in making a decision of this nature can just ride the crest of the moment. No, we cannot be oblivious to public opinion, because that would be arrogant and rude and insensitive. But, at the same time, we cannot be dragged down into the lowest level, either. As Edmund Burke said, our responsibility is to speak our conscience and not just to take the lowest common denominator on every issue. I believe in politics that there are only two real tests. The one test is the test of conscience, which all of you have, and I believe that will be exercised in all of you in the benefits of how you see the interests of this great country. The other test, I think, is the test of history. How will this judgment bear up to the scrutiny of your kids, and your grandchildren, and your great-grandchildren? Will they say you seized the moment, that you responded to the occasion, that you served the national interest? Or will they say you did not? Because they are going to say, daddy and mommy you were there. You had a voice.

I thank you for inviting me today. As I said at the beginning, I know it is a historic occasion. This certainly is for me, and I consider it, personally, to be a rare privilege to address such a distinguished group.

I will leave you with one quotation from Norman Angell in June 1913. He said, "God has made Canada one of those nations which cannot be conquered, and cannot be destroyed except by itself." I know of your generosity, I know of your love for your country, and may God grant you wisdom in your deliberations.

ADDRESS TO THE LEGISLATURE OF ONTARIO ON THE FAILURE OF THE MEECH LAKE ACCORD

Queen's Park, June 25, 1990

I want to take this opportunity to comment on the failure to secure the passage of the Meech Lake Accord and to inform the members of the legislature of the course of action that Ontario will proceed with in light of the current situation.

Today I believe all Ontarians, and indeed all Canadians, look back at the events of the past few weeks with a mixture of both sadness and frustration: Sadness because we were unable to reach down and draw upon a spirit of accommodation and compromise in order to build something in which we could all take pride—we had a historic opportunity to take a major step forward in building a stronger and more united Canada, but that step was not taken—and frustration because we came so very close to doing just that.

Three years ago the first ministers unanimously endorsed a formula and framework for unity and co-operation. We did not at that time anticipate a need for further discussions but, when those discussions became necessary, we again secured the agreement of all first ministers to pass the Meech Lake Accord as well as a companion resolution. Even as late as Friday afternoon, we had eight provinces and the federal government that had ratified the Accord and a ninth province that had signalled an intention to do so.

Il est important de comprendre qu'au cours des trois années de discussions, jamais la province de Québec n'a été isolée.

Adding to our frustration is the knowledge that the Accord drifted into history in such an ignoble manner. It did not die on a matter of principle or substance or vote; it died as a result of misunderstandings, miscalculations and technical manoeuvring.

I will not attempt to minimize or trivialize what has happened. We are in for some difficult times in the days ahead. There is a challenge to which we must all rise. Accordingly, Ontario will be proceeding with the following course of action.

First, we will act to build a strong and united Canada. The people of Ontario want Canada to stay together. I want Canada to stay together and to grow strong. The Constitution is just one tie that binds our country together, but there are many, many other ties. We are bound together by more than 250 years of history, a history that predates our Confederation by more than a century. We are bound together by geography, by economic links and by emotional and personal ties that transcend political boundaries.

Ontario worked to strengthen those ties. It is extremely important that our province continue to build bridges of understanding and to keep the lines of communication open to all regions in this country. To this end, I will be meeting with Premier Bourassa tomorrow in Montreal.

Second, we all understand that a strong Canada requires a strong Ontario. As Canada's largest and most industrialized province and the engine driving Canada's growth, Ontario has a special role to play in ensuring the overall prosperity and standard of living in this country. Canada's economic dynamism is very much dependent on Ontario's economic dynamism. Ontario counts for 38 percent of Canada's gross national product and the largest portion of federal government revenue. Ontario will continue to fulfill its economic responsibilities and obligations to Canada.

We will continue to move forward with an aggressive economic agenda of attracting new investment, modernizing our industries, creating new jobs, expanding opportunities for job training and improving our level of research and development. Today, for example, and throughout this week I am meeting here in Toronto with the leaders of the most industrially advanced areas in West Germany, France, Italy and Spain to establish new and close economic links and to pave the way for relations with Europe of 1992. It may not be politics as usual for Canada, but it will be business as usual for Ontario.

Faisant partie du processus visant à doter l'Ontario d'une économie forte, nous allons continuer à former des lignes économiques solides avec la province de Québec et les autres provinces aussi. Le Québec est une province que nous respectons et que nous reconnaissons en tant que société distincte.

Il est important d'avoir un Québec fort et dynamique si nous voulons avoir un Canada fort et dynamique. Je ne laisserais rien de ce qui est arrivé au cours des dernières semaines diminuer d'aucune façon les liens historiques, émotionnels, économiques, et personnels qui se sont tissés entre nos deux provinces.

Third, we will continue to pursue joint actions with all of our fellow provinces in areas of common interest. When the discussions at Meech Lake first took place, each of the first ministers knew that it was not an end but the beginning of an ongoing process of building a stronger nation. We must now turn our attention to other acts of nation building, such as building a more competitive economy in order to create jobs, expanding opportunities for job training, establishing a caring and tolerant society and protecting our environment for ourselves and our children. By pursuing these goals together, I hope we can build a new foundation of trust and respect among all the provinces, a foundation that could one day lead, perhaps, to the resumption of constitutional discussions.

Fourth, with the death of the Meech Lake Accord it is obvious that the process of constitutional reform has for the foreseeable future come to an end. Unfortunately, we will not be able to proceed with initiatives in areas that we supported, such as Senate reform and Aboriginal rights. There is no longer any reason for the Select Committee on constitutional reform to continue its hearings on the Senate reform issue. However, as the Select Committee indicated last week, there is universal agreement that whenever we do return to the constitutional table we will need a new, more open and consultative process.

Therefore, I want to indicate my continued support for the Select Committee's recommendation that the Committee proceed to hold hearings on the future process of constitutional reform so that improvements can be made in advance of any further discussions, should they take place. I hope to discuss this with the government house leader in the very near future.

The task ahead of us is not an easy one. There is a great feeling of disappointment and a recognition that the process of nation building has been set back. We are embarking on times that will measure the breadth of our national soul and the depth of our commitment to Canada. I say to members and to all Ontarians that I—and I am sure I speak for all my colleagues—will never give up on Canada. We have in the course of our history been tested on many occasions. Had we succumbed, had we given in, we would not have been able to build one of the wealthiest, most dynamic and compassionate societies in the world. It would be a mistake of historic proportions to now let Canada drift into historical obscurity.

It is said that the last spirit to escape Pandora's Box was hope. We have in this country seen a number of spirits escape over the past couple of years, but I believe that the spirit of hope is still very much with us. More than hope, we still have the means and the will to build a stronger and more united Canada.

I know that I speak for each and every member of this House when I say that we share a great love for this country, that we are passionately committed to making it stronger and more united, and that we are determined to learn from, and rise above, the failure of the Meech Lake Accord process.

May I also just say to my colleagues opposite that I apologize because I have been in meetings all day and will continue to be, so I will not be able to stay to hear my honourable colleagues' responses, although I am very interested. I humbly apologize to them in advance. I will be attending their remarks and I will get an immediate report on them. I thank members for their forbearance.

ONTARIO AND THE WORLD: 1985–1990

CONSULAR CORPS LUNCHEON
Toronto, Ontario, December 19, 1989

I suppose I would be making the understatement of the century if I began by observing that the year since your last Christmas luncheon has been one of unprecedented change.

Indeed, it's been the type of year that has given new meaning to the old saying that "the one unchangeable certainty, is that nothing is certain or unchangeable."

There have been moments when it seemed as if someone has pressed the fast forward button on history. Events which one might have thought would unfold over the course of decades have, in fact, transpired almost overnight.

Entire epochs of history have been rewritten in the course of a weekend.

And an army of intergovernmental officials have had nervous breakdowns trying to keep the briefing books up to date.

Many of these events have been truly joyous occasions. As we've watched the Cold War thaw, and the walls—both real and symbolic—come tumbling down, we've had new reason to believe in the Christmas spirit of peace on earth and goodwill toward all people.

Certainly anyone who has watched the events taking place in East Germany, Czechoslovakia, and across Eastern Europe has seen new testimony to the strength of the democratic will, a will that can be suppressed—but not deterred, trod upon—but not buried, turned back—but not turned away.

No one is more affected by these events than the men and women who serve their countries through the Consular Corps. It's your job to

Without Walls or Barriers: The Speeches of Premier David Peterson, Library of Political Leadership Series, by Arthur Milnes and Ryan Zade, Editors. Montreal and Kingston: McGill-Queen's University Press,

monitor these events, to help interpret them for us, and to assist us in adjusting to the changing realities of a world racing forward at break-neck speed.

No one appreciates your efforts more than those of us in government. It's through your advice and assistance that we are able to reach out and establish links with people around the world—to build on existing friendships and to forge new ones. That's something that we in Ontario have been very actively pursuing over the course of the past year.

I've been very pleased to personally lead trade and investment missions to Italy, France, West Germany, Boston, and Los Angeles. Our minister of Industry, Trade and Technology, Monte Kwinter, has also led a number of important missions, including ones to the Soviet Union, the Netherlands, Denmark, and Scandinavia.

These initiatives have resulted in a number of very positive benefits for Ontario, including agreements with the Ukrainian Soviet Republic, Lombardy, and Baden-Württemberg—agreements that will lead to co-operative industrial, educational, and cultural ventures.

In the future, we're going to become even more energetic in reaching out to the world. We recognize that in this era of intensified global competition, we cannot afford to seek shelter in our own corners.

At the same time, we recognize that the world is taking a greater interest in Canada. Over the course of the past year, Ontario has been pleased to host visits from a number of world leaders, including King Hussein, Princess Chulabhorn, President Aquino, and the governors of the Great Lakes states. And of course we're laying the foundation to play host to the ultimate international gatherings—the Olympics in 1996 and the World Fair in the year 2000.

I want to take this opportunity to thank all of you—for making both our missions abroad, and the missions that have visited us from abroad, the successes that they have been; for promoting Ontario around the world and making us more aware of developments within your own country; and, for helping us to chart a smooth course through the sometimes choppy diplomatic seas. Yours is a difficult and often a thankless job, and so I would like to take advantage of this opportunity to express, on behalf of all the people of Ontario, our heartfelt thanks for your good work.

And in keeping with the spirit of the season, I would also like to wish each of you a healthy and happy holiday season.

ADDRESS TO THE AMERICAS SOCIETY
New York, New York, November 6, 1986

I'm delighted to have this opportunity to address the Americas Society. I admire your commitment to increased understanding and communication among all people in our hemisphere, and with all the people of the world.

The timing of this gathering could not be better: just two days after your congressional elections. I'm anxious to learn more about the new Congress, and the impact it will have on relations between our countries.

And in light of recent political developments, I'm eager to express Canadian concerns about the apparent shift in the historic US commitment to expanded world trade.

Over the years, our trade relationship grew and prospered with only a few minor hiccups along the way. It's ironic that since bilateral free trade talks between our countries got underway, we have seen the opening of a Pandora's Box of trade irritants.

First let's put these differences in perspective: our countries enjoy the largest trading relationship the world has ever seen.

Canada is by far your biggest trading partner. This year, the value of trade in goods and services between us will approach $150 billion.

In fact, other than Canada as a whole, the Province of Ontario is your biggest customer.

The United States exports more to the nine million people of Ontario than it does to the 120 million people of Japan.

You export more to the nine million people of Ontario than to the 200 million people of Britain, Germany, Holland, France, and Belgium— your five largest European trading partners. Two-way trade between Canada and the United States provides jobs for two million Canadians and for two million Americans.

Not only are we your best market, we are also your fastest-growing market—and your most dependable one.

Between 1981 and 1985, US exports to Ontario increased by more than 50 percent—while your exports to the rest of the world were falling.

Currently, Canada enjoys a surplus in *merchandise trade* with the United States. But that goes to paying off our deficit in *service transactions*.

Even in merchandise trade, you enjoy a surplus in several pivotal areas, including high-technology goods.

The goods you sell to Canada generally have greater value added, allowing you to create more jobs, more high-skill jobs, and better-paying jobs.

Our factories are filled with equipment that was made in the United

States. We're selling you today's goods, and you're selling us tomorrow's technology.

Sometimes trade between our countries has benefited Canada more. Sometimes it has benefited the United States more. But it has always benefited both of us.

It's obvious that the best thing either of our countries has going for us in trade is the business we do with each other. Both of us suffer trade deficits with every industrialized country outside North America.

It's clear that rapid technological advances will continue to alter the way all of us do business.

Suddenly, new markets are opening up, just as developing nations are acquiring the manufacturing capacity to meet their needs.

Suddenly, our customers have become our competitors. And suddenly, we have to develop more advanced products and services.

We realize that we can surmount these hurdles only by cultivating our most important resource: our people—their knowledge, skills, and ingenuity.

Neither of us can afford to ignore the challenges and opportunities of an expanding and more competitive global market.

In Ontario, the thrust of our public policies is to build competitiveness in international markets, where we face the same challenges as you.

But there is no question that the United States will always be our most important trading partner.

It is now just over a year since Canada's federal government proposed negotiations to work out a bilateral trade agreement between our countries.

Since negotiations were initiated, Ontario has remained open-minded, fair-minded—and tough-minded.

Obviously, we're anxious to secure and enhance our access to the US market. Certainly, we're determined that any trade agreement must provide mutual improvements in job opportunities and living standards.

But we also recognize that when it comes to strengthening our ability to produce and compete, a bilateral agreement can at most be only part of our effort. There are many other approaches that both of us must consider.

There is one option that I believe we must both reject—a frantic stampede into a new and dangerous round of protectionism.

We are all aware of the consequences incurred when the international trading system collapsed after the adoption of such measures as the Smoot-Hawley tariff of 1930, and the British tariff of 1932.

The sudden surge of protectionism snapped a golden age of trade, cutting down assembly lines and creating soup lines, closing banks and foreclosing farms.

The foundations of those protectionist trade walls bear a remarkable resemblance to trends we see today, more than a half-century later.

The trade wars of the '20s and '30s were sparked by slow growth in demand for traditional goods and services, a sudden spread of technological knowledge which narrowed competitive gaps between nations, an abrupt decline in the need for raw materials, and rapid shifts in the balance of market power.

The similarities to today's conditions remind me of the words of a great philosopher, Yogi Berra: "It's deja vu all over again."

Americans can be proud of your post-war efforts to ensure an era of stability and predictability in international trade.

I'm certainly proud of Canada's role.

Both of us helped to usher in this century's second golden age of trade. And both of us benefited—along with the rest of the industrialized world. It's hard to see how a new round of protectionist measures can help the United States any more than in the 1930s, when Hoovervilles ringed Washington.

As a wise person once observed: "perhaps if we listened to history, it would stop repeating itself."

We seem to be witnessing the birth of a new strain of protectionist fever—a neo-protectionism that attempts to disguise a provocative offense as a justified defence.

The neo-protectionists claim to be only responding to the unfair trade practices of others. What they are really saying is: do unto others before they get a chance to do unto you. They assume that if some US industries are finding it difficult to compete, it must be because other countries are acting unfairly.

In the past few months, neo-protectionism has spawned high US countervail tariffs on a wide range of Canadian products, including hogs and pork, fish and raspberries.

It has threatened the access of a number of goods, from steel to uranium, from cement to telecommunications equipment.

Ironically, in the six months since Canada and the United States formally initiated free trade talks, US countervail and legislative protectionist actions have affected roughly three-quarters of a billion dollars in trade with Canada.

Since 1980, similar actions or threats have affected about $4.5 billion in trade with us.

These actions have harmed Americans as well as Canadians.

The steel dispute offers a good example. The fact is every dollar of Canadian steel exported to the United States generates $1.29 in exports of US goods and services to Canada.

An example of blatantly unjustified actions against Canada was the Commerce Department's preliminary determination, under considerable US industry and political pressure, to apply a 15 percent countervail surcharge against softwood lumber from Canada.

I cannot overemphasize the importance of this issue to Canada, and what serious damage it can do to our relationship.

The Commerce Department is almost literally missing the forest for the trees. The lumber determination was legally flawed, and politically motivated. In 1983, the US Commerce Department ruled there was no basis for countervail. In the three years that have passed, the only thing that has changed is the US political climate.

Domestic political considerations took the place of sound trade considerations.

Officials of the Canadian federal and provincial governments are meeting today in Washington with Commerce Secretary Malcolm Baldrige to protest the lumber tariff in the strongest possible terms.

Ontario fully supports the Canadian federal government's determination to fight this case with every legal means at our disposal.

Many Americans opposed this action, including the National Lumber and Building Material Dealers Association, the National Association of Home Builders, the Lumber Association of Southern California, several US senators, and a number of US newspapers.

The US Federal Trade Commission said a surcharge is not justified.

Because of our economic links, actions directed at Canada's economy cause enormous harm—to both of us. They add to the costs of materials for many US manufacturers, and reduce the buying power of your best customer.

The surcharge would raise the cost of the average American home by $1,000. The National Association of Home Builders has estimated that for every $1,000 cost increase, more than 300,000 American families would be priced out of the housing market.

A study conducted by Wharton Econometrics estimates that the surcharge will eliminate four American jobs for every one it creates. That will do away with more than 13,000 US jobs in less than four years.

As the saying goes: "if you burn your neighbour's house down, it doesn't make your house look better."

The lumber issue could also damage the reputation the United States has earned as a fair trader. US spokesmen described bilateral trade talks as an opportunity to demonstrate a model for the world. Is this the model they want to display?

As a friend and neighbour, I'd like to offer an observer's view: The United States can wipe away its trade deficit only if it concentrates on opening foreign markets to American goods, rather than closing American markets to foreign goods.

Given the historic leadership the United States has shown in promoting world trade, we can understand your frustration with countries that move into open markets while closing their own.

For our part, Canadians have always sought fair trade. The best proof of that is the enormous two-way trade that benefits both of us.

Trade with Canada brings major benefits to this region in particular.

It's responsible for about half a million jobs in the Great Lakes states alone.

These trade figures show how beggar-thy-neighbour policies could easily produce beggar-thyself results.

One of the most disturbing aspects of the trade actions against Canada is the fact that US officials have made it clear they will not drop their methods of trade retaliation—such as the countervail clause that was used against Canadian lumber—even if a bilateral trade deal is struck.

Just a week ago today, Trade Ambassador Clayton Yeutter reiterated that position.

Mr. Yeutter has also charged that Canadian exporters benefit from differences in our political system, and our approach to economic development.

This is the latest in a series of suggestions that Canadians should eliminate many of our unique economic, political and cultural characteristics in order to make North America a level playing field for economic competition.

The problem with the concept of a level playing field is that it is entirely subjective. Whether the playing field appears level depends on which side you view it from.

For example, Canadians have a longstanding commitment to reduce economic disparities among our regions, and to provide for our people's social needs—such as health care and unemployment insurance—in our own way.

We are equally determined to support our cultural industries—not to block the influx of US books, records and magazines, but to preserve Canadian cultural identity in their midst.

US trade officials have said many Canadian federal policies, such as research and development grants that amount to about $135 million, constitute a bump on the level playing field.

The fact is the US government provides far more support to its nation's industries.

In the United States, the federal government spends more than $52 billion a year on research and development. US military spending alone dwarfs the Canadian government's R & D activities. This year, defence spending will provide two out of every three dollars spent on R & D in the United States.

New inventions are researched and paid for by the military until they are taken up by private enterprise. For example, the department of defence funded research into artificial intelligence for 30 years until it became commercially useful. Defence projects allowed the United States to pioneer in such industries as commercial aviation, computers, and semi-conductors.

US government projections indicate that the Strategic Defense Initiative alone will account for 26 percent of US spending on research and development in less than four years.

As well, US municipalities and counties stimulate their economic development through municipal bonds to provide services to new industries. State pension funds are used to build technology centres.

Would Americans be prepared to forego these tools of economic development?

Whether it's military programs or municipal bonds in the United States, or regional development programs in Canada, each of us must be free to determine our own priorities.

Just as we must steer clear of extreme protectionism, we must also avoid taking free trade to an extreme. Some may see a contradiction between those two themes. But I believe they are inextricably linked.

Free trade will achieve nothing for either of us if it prevents us from acting on legitimate regional or sectoral development needs. And it will work against us if it is based on an unrealistic assumption that our economies are identical.

In trade policy it is clear that we need a balanced approach—one based on diversity, flexibility, global co-operation, and fairness.

First, both of our countries must maintain the ability to preserve our unique values, and our unique ways of solving our own problems.

If government programs help our industries to become more competitive, that could benefit all of us. If Canadians earn more money, they can buy more US goods—and vice versa.

We have to distinguish between protectionism to shelter inefficient industries, and legitimate economic development efforts to bolster efficient ones.

We have to find ways to ensure that both our countries can pursue technological innovations, without imposing on each other, approaches for which we are not suited.

Rather than try to prevent the development of new technologies, we should work out an approach that will encourage growth within a framework based on fairness. Otherwise, all of North America will fall behind.

Second, we must leave undisturbed those areas in which we have already developed a flexible approach. A good example of that is the automotive products trade agreement—the Auto Pact.

Since Canada and the United States entered into that agreement 20 years ago, automotive trade between our countries has leapt from $1.2 billion, to $42 billion.

In some years you have enjoyed surpluses, in some years we have. But over the course of the agreement, auto trade has flowed equally between our countries.

In my view, the Auto Pact has been as successful as it has because it's based on neither protectionism nor unfettered free trade. Rather, it's a managed trade approach that is by and large fair to both countries.

We strongly believe that the safeguards in the Auto Pact must remain intact.

Third, we must seek growth on a global basis. The new GATT round that got underway recently in Geneva must be dedicated to international growth, by the fairest and most effective means possible.

While Canada and the United States have a great deal to gain from maintaining and expanding our unique trading relationship, the price for doing so cannot be exclusion from the rest of the world.

Canadians do not want to see the return of Fortress America. The establishment of Fortress North America holds as little appeal.

Our closest links will continue to be southward, but our vision must be worldwide.

Fourth, and finally, Canadians cannot be expected to enter into an agreement that does not include relief from the threat of countervail actions such as the recent softwood lumber surcharge.

If any agreement is to be viable, it must include a fair method for settling disputes, as an alternative to countervail.

If Canadians see no hope of relief from the policies characterized by the recent tariff on softwood lumber, then the value of any trade agreement has to be questioned.

We can grow together, even if we sometimes take different paths. I'm hopeful that we can avoid the trade wars that led to hardship for so many, and resume our mission of prosperity for all.

CANADIAN-AMERICAN PAGEANT: 175TH ANNIVERSARY OF THE WAR OF 1812
Sackets Harbor, New York, July 18, 1987

I'm delighted to join you today for this magnificent 175th anniversary pageant.

Appearing at the same event as the governor of your great state, sharing this stage with one of the most articulate and compassionate leaders of our time, is indeed a great honour.

It's also a humbling experience speaking on the 74th anniversary of an address at Sackets Harbor by Franklin Delano Roosevelt. I believe it was Will Rogers who once observed that "Roosevelt could explain a complex matter like banking so simply, that even bankers could under-stand it."

I mention Roosevelt's address because it's very difficult to stand here at Sackets Harbor and not feel surrounded by a tremendous sense of history.

One can almost hear the booming echoes of the War of 1812, when the control of Lake Ontario was of immense strategic importance, and Sackets Harbor was a hive of shipbuilding activity for Admiral Isaac Chauncey's flotilla.

Canadians recall, with a great sense of nostalgia, that it was from Sackets Harbor that 8,000 American troops under the command of James Wilkinson set forth down the St. Lawrence River where they were defeated near Morrisburg, Ontario.

Americans, on the other hand, may choose to look back with some-what greater nostalgia to an earlier and more successful amphibious as-sault on Toronto, known then as York, by Brigadier General Pike and his 1,700 men.

A great deal has changed since the Treaty of Ghent ended the War of 1812, and the Rush-Bagot Treaty that brought about naval disarmament on the Great Lakes

We now share a border that runs nearly 4,000 miles without a single gun or fort to protect it. It's the most friendly and least visible line of international power in the world. No walls divide us, no armies stand between us.

We are the best of continental neighbours, sharing a land mass divid-ed not by force but by consent.

The ships of war have been replaced by ships of commerce. Indeed, it was fifty-five years ago this very day that our countries agreed to work together on one of the most ambitious and mutually beneficial projects in our continent's history—the construction of the St. Lawrence Seaway.

Today when our two countries do battle it is not with muskets and gunpowder, but with bats and balls, sticks and pucks.

When we are engaged in serious combat it is as allies not adversaries. Three times this century our armies have marched together arm-in-arm to the far shores of the Atlantic and the Pacific to defend freedom and democracy in the world.

Today we are partners in NATO and in NORAD.

When citizens of your country were taken hostage in Iran, we provid-ed a path to freedom to those we could help, and we shared the anguish and the heartache of those we could not.

None of this is to say that our histories and our societies have been identical.

Your country, for example, achieved its independence through revo-lution. Ours came about through evolution.

Your country was engaged in a great civil war. As for ours, in the words of former baseball player Jim Brosnan: "Canada never had a major civil war. After hockey, Canadians would probably have found it quite dull."

Our two countries do not always see eye to eye on every issue. We sometimes view matters of foreign or domestic policy from different perspectives. We sometimes disagree on how best to preserve our national identities, our unique cultural heritages, and our precious natural resources.

In recent months and years we have differed over what constitutes fair and unfair trade subsidy, and over how we might best improve our trading relationship.

But the point is that since the guns of 1812 were quieted, we have been able to listen to each other long enough to discover that the things that unite us are much greater than those that occasionally divide us.

We share the world's longest undefended border, and the largest trading relationship in the history of the world, not because of treaties, or defence agreements, but because we share common interests and a commonality of spirit.

We believe in the same fundamental values for our society. We seek the same unlimited opportunities for our children.

We each believe in a society that is based on what Franklin Roosevelt described as the four fundamental freedoms—freedom of speech and expression, freedom to worship God in our own way, freedom from want, and freedom from fear.

Our constitutions and our forms of government may differ, but we are both devoted to the principle of democratic decision making, open to all people.

We in Ontario, and New York State in particular, share a number of things in common, besides our obsession to sit atop the baseball standings in the American League.

We share a knowledge of the disastrous effects that acid rain can have on our natural resources, our economy and our health. We share a determination to pass on a clear and pure environment as a legacy to our children and grandchildren.

We share something else as well, something Canadians and Americans have shared since 1812—a tendency to take our friendship for granted.

That is why I am so grateful to the organizers of this pageant. You recognize that although friendship between our two countries now comes easily, it has not always come automatically.

You appreciate that the close relationship between our two peoples is unparalleled in the world. Most importantly, you understand that it *is precisely because our relationship is so rare*, that we must celebrate and cherish it—and work to make it grow.

REMARKS TO THE CANADIAN CHAMBER OF COMMERCE IN JAPAN AND THE CANADA-JAPAN SOCIETY

Okura Hotel, Tokyo, Japan, September 29, 1986

It is especially appropriate that one of my first official duties during my four days in Japan is to speak to the Canadian Chamber of Commerce in Japan and the Canada-Japan Society.

Because the members of both organizations can be proud of your tremendous contribution to developing a solid economic and cultural relationship between Canada and Japan.

The working partnership between Canada and Japan owes much to your efforts.

This is a relationship based very much on personal friendships—friendships that have evolved over long periods of time—friendships that lead to better understanding between our two countries.

In discussing friendship and understanding between our countries, I would at this point like to pay my respect to Prince Takamado, who has honoured us with his presence today. An alumnus of Queen's University, in Kingston, Ontario, Prince Takamado is an excellent example of the way in which Canadians and Japanese can learn from each other, and build bridges of friendships that span an ocean.

I am proud that Ontario's Tokyo office team has done so much to strengthen those bridges over the past 16 years.

A spirit of cooperation—a working partnership—also exists between Ontario's Tokyo office and the Canadian embassy.

I thank Ambassador Steers and his staff for their participation in the working partnership—for helping us to extend that spirit of friendship and cooperation.

We are in Tokyo today—on the first leg of a business mission that includes the People's Republic of China and the Republic of Korea—to cement our working relationship with the Japanese business community.

And we are here to strengthen our cultural and business ties with Japan and other countries of the Asia-Pacific region.

Of course, we have made this journey in the midst of some important events that could have tremendous impact on Canada's trading relationships.

As you are aware, Canada and the United States have entered into negotiations aimed at achieving a bilateral trade agreement between our countries.

Certainly, Ontario is as concerned as any province about securing and enhancing our trade opportunities in the US market.

But we also recognize that in order to ensure our future competitiveness we must develop opportunities in other markets as well. Certainly Japan and Canada have much to gain from increased trade and investment with each other.

Japan is already Ontario's second-largest trading partner, and our third-largest market for exports.

Ontario's trade with Japan has grown substantially in recent years. Indeed, trade between Japan and Ontario has almost tripled in the past six years.

Japan's direct investment in Canada more than quadrupled between 1978 and 1984.

And Japanese portfolio investment in Canada represents 30 percent of Japan's foreign holdings.

Seven Japanese banks operate in Canada. All are based in Ontario.

More than 110 Japanese corporations maintain subsidiaries in the province.

And the opportunities for further co-operation and investment are increasing. Just last June, the Ontario government endorsed the principle of opening up our securities industry to more direct participation by foreign investment dealers in our province's marketplace.

This step recognizes the important role played by the major overseas dealers, including the Japanese firms Nomura, Daiwa, Nikko and Yamaichi.

But there is still enormous room for growth in our bilateral trade relationship with Japan—as there is in our trade relationship with all the countries of the Asia-Pacific region.

That is why the Ontario government has adopted a long-term strategy to strengthen our ties with this vital part of the world, and enhance a partnership that can benefit both our peoples.

Ontario is a trading province in a trading nation.

Our economic future depends on our ability to sell our goods and services in an expanding and fiercely competitive global market.

My government unveiled our Asia-Pacific strategy last year, in our first budget. It has always been at the top of our forward-looking trade agenda.

And our Asia-Pacific agenda has been set in motion here in Tokyo.

We have established an Ontario house in Tokyo, and we have appointed a senior and respected public servant, Tim Armstrong as agent general for this region—based in Tokyo.

Mr. Armstrong will do much to raise Ontario's profile in Japan and the rest of the Asia-Pacific region.

I know that many of you have already met Mr. Armstrong—and that many more members of the Canadian business community will come to rely on him for assistance—particularly for his expertise in developing consensus among labour, business and government—something that has been effectively achieved in Japan.

His colleague Ray McCague will head up Ontario's new trade office in Seoul—another important step in our Asia-Pacific initiative.

Many of you will remember Mr. McCague from his service with our Tokyo office from 1980 to 1983.

I will be travelling to Seoul next week to officially open our office there.

Later this week, I will participate in another important Asia-Pacific initiative—the opening of the Ontario-Jiangsu Science and Technology Centre in the People's Republic of China.

I am confident that the Centre will make great advances in the sale of Ontario products through the transfer of technology—and lead to increased trade between the two provinces.

This leads me directly to a point I would like to emphasize. Canada is well-known in Japan as a reliable supplier of resources. But we also have a growing capacity in technology, an area in which Ontario is poised to expand, and lead the way.

Our high-technology products and services are up-to-date and competitive.

But we know that we will have to work even harder to catch up with the rapidly advancing and innovative technology that is in place worldwide.

My government has a commitment to developing technology in our province.

Just a few months ago, Ontario undertook a major new initiative to involve the private sector in decision making to support long-term growth.

We brought together leaders of business, labour, and post-secondary education to form a Premier's Council, which will direct a $1 billion technology fund and guide Ontario's technological development over the next ten years.

I am proud to chair this Council, which will be administered by my colleague, Hugh O'Neil, the minister of industry, trade and technology, who is here today and who spoke to you a year ago.

These two initiatives—the Premier's Council and the Asia-Pacific thrust—complement one another.

While the Premier's Council works to keep Ontario on the leading edge of technology innovation and application, the Asia-Pacific strategy works to find international technology that can be adapted and perfected in Ontario.

As well, the Asia-Pacific strategy will identify new international markets for the full range of Ontario products—including our technology products.

Certainly this 16-day trade and investment mission is an important part of the strategy. While I am in Japan I will meet with government and business leaders—outlining Ontario's commitment to innovative policies, policies to ensure that Ontario is internationally competitive.

And of course, I will be promoting Ontario products and investment opportunities.

This morning I met with Prime Minister Nakasone and the minister of foreign affairs.

I will be meeting with a number of Japanese business leaders.

And tomorrow I will address the 1986 Ontario, Canada investment presentation at the Akasaka Prince Hotel.

At the presentation I will point to a number of recent Japanese investors who have joined the Canadian business community in Ontario.

They include some of the leading names in Japanese industry—Mitsubishi ... Honda ... Toyota ... Suzuki ....

The most recent Japan-Ontario venture—GM-Suzuki—represents a total investment of $500 million.

It also represents a spirit of Japan-Ontario partnership.

Last month, when General Motors and Suzuki announced this investment, they made the commitment that the assembly operation would involve more than just the final assembly of parts and components that are often produced in offshore locations. Both General Motors and Suzuki Motor Company committed themselves to the same minimum level of production that Canada achieves under our Auto Pact with the United States.

We were delighted that both companies had the confidence to make this commitment, which will allow Ontario suppliers to compete for contracts to supply parts and components, and provide the 2,000 employees with opportunities for highly skilled jobs.

This principle—the principle behind the Auto Pact—is one that Ontario believes must be extended to *all* vehicle manufacturers who do business in Canada.

I believe that is an essential element to a Japan-Ontario partnership in the auto industry.

In all areas, I am convinced that we can continue as a co-operative unit—to look for creative avenues for investment on both sides.

On the Ontario side, we look forward to developing transfer technology, joint venture or direct investment in several key sectors: automotive assembly and parts, consumer and industrial electronics, machinery and equipment, and resource-related industries.

By promoting these sectors as co-operative ventures, Ontario will benefit through increased markets, access to new technology and new investment.

From the point of view of our Japanese partners the advantages are clear:

A North American partner, situated right in the middle of a vast manufacturing and distribution centre—with easy access to 120 million consumers.

And that is a message that you—both the Japanese and Canadian members of the two organizations here today—help us to convey.

PACIFIC RIM CONFERENCE
Toronto, Ontario, December 1, 1987

I'm delighted to be here with you this afternoon and to extend a sincere welcome on behalf of the Government of Ontario to this important conference.

This conference is taking place in the midst of a national debate over one of the most important issues Canadians have faced in many years—the proposed Canada-US trade pact.

The proposed deal is itself a response—I believe one that is inadequate at best—to the enormous economic changes that are taking place around us.

In the new post-industrial era which we have entered, the world is becoming a smaller place, and our industries are engaged in a fierce competitive struggle.

We see dramatic advances in science and technology. Decisions about labour and capital can be made more quickly than ever before. Reduced trade barriers, as a result of the Kennedy and Tokyo rounds of GATT, have created new opportunities. Rapid industrialization has given less-developed countries the means to move into markets that were once ours alone. New technologies are creating far-reaching changes in manufacturing and resource-based industries.

Like all industrialized nations, Canada must improve its ability to produce and compete. Our policy on trade relations can be only a part of that. But it is of course a very important part.

Ontario is a trading province in a trading nation. Export earnings constitute 26 percent of Canada's gross national product; they make up 32 percent of Ontario's gross provincial product. This compares to the United States at 5 percent, and Japan at 11 percent.

Canada's economic future is tied to our ability to produce goods and sell them to many markets around the globe.

At the same time, Canada needs foreign investors who have the financial resources and the technological know-how to develop and manufacture products for all of our foreign markets—in North America,

Europe and Asia.

Our ability to attract investment and sell our products and services to the world will determine our capacity to create prosperity and build the kind of society we seek in Canada.

Our ability to compete depends not only on our ability to recognize the need for change, but also on how we respond to it.

We all recognize that Canada cannot just hope to preserve the status quo or return to a bygone era. We all recognize that the economic approaches that worked in the 1960s and the 1970s will no longer serve our needs.

But neither will a policy that ties us exclusively to any single market.

The United States will unquestionably continue to be our most important trading partner. Efforts to stabilize particular aspects of our trading relationship in a truly balanced manner should continue.

But the dominant forces of economic change are now global in scope—not just North American.

Just as Canadian trade policy is being totally geared to gaining greater access to the US market, that market may be about to see a decline in its rate of growth. In the wake of the crash of world stock markets, Americans are talking about slowing down the tremendous rate of domestic consumption financed by massive borrowing over the past six years.

The volatility of exchange rates demonstrates why we cannot tie ourselves to any single market. Since 1985, the Japanese yen and the West German mark have appreciated almost 80 percent against the US and Canadian dollars. The current shift in exchange rates can open new opportunities.

Europe and Asia have already become strong pacesetters in technology. Japan and West Germany are passing the United States in non-military technology—and the competition is getting stiffer.

If you want to get a sense of where new industrial innovations are coming from, consider the fact that between 1966 and 1986, the number of patents granted by the United States to US inventors declined by about 30 percent. During the same period, the number of US patents granted to German inventors increased by about two thirds, and the number granted to Japanese inventors increased more than eleven-fold.

Indeed, the share of US patents granted to non-Americans more than doubled between 1966 and 1986—from 20 percent to just over 40 percent.

It was a Canadian who first recognized that the world has become a global village. Canadians must now master the global marketplace.

An important part of any global trade and investment strategy has to be the Asia-Pacific region—the most dynamic growth area on the face of the globe. The Asia-Pacific region accounts for 30 percent of the world's population and 20 percent of global GDP; it is an area of enormous geopolitical, economic, and cultural importance.

These facts have already been reflected in the Canadian experience.

Since 1984, our trans-Pacific trade has exceeded our trans-Atlantic trade. For the last decade, we have had more immigration from Asia, each year, than from all over Europe.

Over the past year and a half, we have taken many steps to deepen our ties with Japan, Korea, China, and other countries of the Pacific. We expanded Ontario's Tokyo office; created the position of agent general for the Asia-Pacific region; posted an Ontario government representative in Seoul, and opened the Jiangsu-Ontario Science and Technology Centre in Nanjing. These steps, along with vigorous programs of trade and investment promotion and cultural and educational exchanges, represent the first stage of a long-term strategy to strengthen Ontario's ties with the Asia-Pacific nations.

I visited the region one year ago and my meetings in Japan, China and Korea reinforced my personal conviction that renewed efforts are essential to Ontario's future growth and prosperity. I look forward to returning to the area at an early date, to expand the valuable contacts which I made last year.

The significance of the region cannot be overstated. Thirty years ago, Europe and North America were unchallenged as the nucleus of industrial production in our global economy. In terms of industrial development, Asia was considered an underdeveloped periphery.

That is now history.

Japan is the prime example of exponential growth. In three decades, it has gone from a subsistence economy to the world's largest creditor nation, with $180 billion in foreign assets in 1986. In 1960, Japan accounted for 3 percent of the world's gross product and the United States accounted for 33 percent. By 1985, Japan's share had grown to 12 percent and the US portion had dropped to 22 percent. Eight of the ten largest banks in the world are Japanese. The world's largest insurance company—Nippon Life—has $1 trillion worth of policies in force and 70,000 salesmen. Last year, for the first time, Japan's per capita income exceeded that of the United States, by approximately 6 percent.

Nor is this dramatic growth limited to Japan. Four countries—Korea, Taiwan, Singapore and Hong Kong—are aptly termed the "miracle economies" of the Pacific Rim. All underdeveloped in the 1960s, they are now recording astounding growth rates. In 1986, Korea's GNP increased by 12.2 percent, Taiwan's by 10.8 percent, and Hong Kong's by just under 10 percent. Singapore, after two sluggish years, recovered in 1986 to post a growth rate of 7 percent. In this region of the globe, there is now no commodity that cannot be efficiently produced—from TV sets and steel to the ships that carry them to ports all over the world.

The other nations within the Pacific Basin—China, Thailand, Malaysia, Indonesia, and the Philippines—are in various stages of economic evolution. All are positioned for significant growth in the next decades.

Of these, China, with its one billion population—20 percent of the world's population—has perhaps the greatest potential impact, both as a consuming and producing nation. China's greatest potential is for the long term.

Nonetheless, there are, as I perceived during my visit there last year, substantial opportunities now, for those with the determination and ingenuity to persist in the Chinese market. The prospects have been enhanced by continuing trade liberalization, more attractive and equitable investment laws, and the relaxation of limitations on the availability of foreign exchange—especially for those projects which involve technology transfer and the production of goods destined for export markets, which will earn China much-needed foreign exchange.

Some have argued that we should be shielded from Asian imports because of the wide disparity in wage rates, which are only partially offset by our superior productivity. Since the fall of the dollar against many Asian and European currencies, it is becoming increasingly difficult for us to use that particular crutch. Now, in fact, Japanese wages, in real terms, are marginally higher than ours. Wages in Korea, Taiwan and other developing nations are still well below our levels—but the gap is narrowing, and we are at no greater disadvantage vis-à-vis these nations than is Japan, Germany, or the United States.

Although our trade with the Asia-Pacific countries is growing, we remain in a deficit position. And in our trade promotion efforts, there are tough perceptions to be overcome.

For example, Canada is still regarded, in many quarters, principally as a supplier of raw materials—a land of rocks and logs, grain and fish. The scope, variety, and excellence of our secondary manufacturing and service sectors are not fully appreciated in the Asia-Pacific region. Thus, although our manufacturing and trade with the US continues to grow, our deficit in manufactured products with Japan and other Asian countries is mounting.

In 1986, Canada's two-way trade with Japan was approximately $14 billion, with a deficit of $2.1 billion. Ontario's two-way trade was $2.7 billion, with a deficit of $2.2 billion. Regrettably, deficits occurred in most of our other Asian markets as well. Government and industry obviously have a substantial educational, promotional, and marketing job to do.

But perhaps our most important task is to convince ourselves that we have what it takes to penetrate the market.

Ontario and Canada have a great deal to do in order to move into the forefront of technology and improve our ability to produce.

It is for that reason that a year-and-a-half ago we established a Premiers' Council, bringing together men and women from unions, large corporations, small business, universities and colleges, and the provincial Cabinet.

The Council's principal task is to plan for the long term—not next month or next year, but the next decade and beyond.

The emphasis is on science and technology, but the whole realm of government industrial policy is open to review and amendment.

Last June, the Council announced the establishment of seven centres of excellence to stimulate the production of advanced research, and encourage the transfer and diffusion of technology.

The seven centres—each of which pools the resources and expertise of Ontario corporations and post-secondary institutions—will focus on unique areas of strength in our province.

In and of itself, the centres of excellence program will increase research funding in Ontario universities by 10 percent. Private-sector research groups that formerly weren't even aware of each other's existence are now talking and exchanging information.

We have a great deal more to do in this area. But we already have many excellent products to sell: telecommunications, aircraft and aerospace equipment, computers—both hardware and software, road building and heavy construction machinery, electrical generation, transportation, and pollution control equipment. We are leaders in all these fields and many others as well. And I believe there are more things we can and must do to make our trading partners aware of our capabilities and the excellence of our products.

Take Japan—a market I am familiar with from my years of business. I know it's a tough market. Frankly, I think a greater degree of openness in the Japanese market would benefit Japan as well as the nations it trades with.

But some of the negative perceptions about it are exaggerated. Others are simply wrong.

It is said, for example, that Japan is a closed society, economically; that whenever possible, the government regulates to freeze others out; that the Japanese have an unalterable preference for domestic suppliers and domestic goods; that the Japanese distribution system is too complex, the language too difficult.

Like all generalities, there is some justification for these assertions. But the truth is that the Japanese market is far from closed or impenetrable. Many North American firms have proven that. Despite all the negative publicity about the Japan/US trade imbalance, Japan remains the second largest market for US goods after Canada—a market 60 percent larger than the US's entire European market.

There are many firms here, in the United States and Europe, that have proven there is no reason for lethargy or defeatism in selling to the Japanese. Quality, reliability, price, and determined marketing efforts have paid off for countless firms. We must be at least as aggressive, innovative, and persistent as our competitors.

And we must not become one-dimensional in our vision. That, I believe, is one of the gravest dangers in the proposed US-Canada trade deal.

The federal government argues that the proposed trade deal would secure guaranteed, open access to the US market from Canada, and therefore will induce further foreign investment from many sources.

In fact, under this deal, our access to the US market would not be appreciably more secure than it was the day negotiations got underway.

Under this deal, Canadian firms would still be vulnerable to harassment under US countervail and anti-dumping law. The new bilateral panel to review anti-dumping and countervail disputes would only be able to determine whether trade actions are consistent with the same US laws and regulations that are being used to harass Canadian exporters now.

Would potential offshore investors be satisfied that this arrangement meets their needs for secure market access?

Offshore auto assemblers in particular have reason to be concerned. As you know, three leading Japanese automobile assemblers have made major investment commitments in Ontario, on the not-unreasonable assumption that there would be no major changes in the commercial rules in effect when those investment decisions were made. Under the trade agreement, however, they find themselves seriously disadvantaged in a number of ways: They're excluded from eligibility for Auto Pact status, deprived of duty remission and drawback arrangements in force when the decisions were made, and faced with new and uncertain requirements relating to content and rules of origin.

This is not only wrongful discrimination—it is poor economics.

As business people, you are well aware of the dangers of becoming captive to one supplier, especially if it is a supplier of critical goods.

You are also aware of the dangers of becoming captive to one customer, especially if it is a customer much larger than you, with alternative suppliers.

Just as a company must achieve a balance with respect to its suppliers and its customers, so must Canada as a nation achieve a similar balance.

Let me assure you that in seeking to increase international trade and investment ties Ontario will continue to look east and west, as well as south. Regardless of the outcome of the current trade discussion, we will build an even better production base to serve not only the North American markets, but all of the markets of the world.

Canada has a great deal going for it in selling to foreign markets and attracting foreign investment. We have the resources, the know-how, the industrial base, and the talented workforce to compete anywhere in the world—not just in North America.

Canada will achieve equality with its international partners not by looking inward to itself and one trading partner, but by looking outward to the entire world and a multitude of trading partners.

To all of our strengths we must add one more—diversity. The Canadian entrepreneurs who recognize that fact will help to create enormous opportunity and prosperity—not just for yourselves but for all Canadians.

Ontario: A Global Competitor

World Economic Forum, Davos, Switzerland, January 29, 1988

I'm very pleased to have this opportunity to participate in the World Economic Forum. The presence here in Davos of so many business, financial, and political leaders from around the world testifies to the remarkable role this annual conference has come to play as an occasion to exchange ideas and develop or renew personal contacts.

In that sprit, it is very timely for me to bring you up to date this morning on what is happening in Ontario and on our vision of the future.

Ontario is changing rapidly because it is growing rapidly, and it is growing rapidly in a very specific and intended direction—that of international dynamism. Ontario is ready to be recognized as a true international competitor.

I am sure you won't be surprised to hear that Ontario is changing—so is virtually every society on the face of the earth. But what distinguishes the success stories from the tales of woe is the *management* of change. For that reason, our great priority in Ontario for the past several years has been to work with the private sector in seeking to anticipate, focus, and shape the socio-economic changes we must inevitably undergo.

Some of those changes may result from the new Canada-US trade agreement recently negotiated by our current federal government. I support in principle all forms of fair and meaningful trade liberalization, whether multilateral or bilateral. That's because Ontario can compete anywhere in the world. So I would certainly be supportive of a mutually beneficial Canada-US agreement that enhanced our security of access to the American market.

Opinion in Canada is divided on the merits of the actual agreement that was negotiated. I am among those who are strongly critical of the terms of that agreement, because I do not believe that Canada has gained enough to justify the concessions that were made.

We greatly value our close trade and investment relationship with the US, which is—and will remain—by far our largest partner. But we are not prepared to put all our eggs in one basket. For a whole society as much as for an individual company, it is simply bad business to become overly dependent on a single client or supplier. For that reason, this new agreement will only further strengthen our resolve to broaden and diversify Ontario's trade and investment relationships.

Ontario is Canada's industrial and economic heartland, but our horizons are not limited by the borders of Canada nor even of North America. We intend to pursue Ontario's mission as a true global competitor by building further on our province's very considerable existing strengths.

Ontario is positioned at the very centre of the rich North American market, with 164 million consumers living within two days' truck drive of our borders. Ontario's own population of 9.2 million is larger than the population of nearly two-thirds of the world's countries—and we're still growing rapidly. Between 1983 and 1986, Ontario's population grew at an average annual rate of 1.3 percent—faster than any of the leading industrial nations.

Ontario's gross domestic product of $142 billion US is larger than the GDP of such nations as Switzerland, Sweden, Austria, or Denmark. In fact, if Ontario were an independent nation, it would rank as the 11th largest nation in the world in terms of gross domestic product.

Ontario's growth in real GDP since 1983 has outpaced all the major industrial countries. In 1986, for instance, we grew by 4.9 percent, compared to 3.1 percent for Canada as a whole, 2.7 percent for Germany, 2.6 percent for the US, 2.3 percent for the United Kingdom and 2.2 percent for Japan.

Ontario's disposable income per capita is among the highest in the world. In 1986, it was third highest among the industrialized nations.

Ontario is the world's third largest exporter to the US, ranking ahead of every country except Canada as a whole and Japan. And Ontario's total global exports increased by 112 percent between 1980 and 1986, from $29.5 billion to $62.6 billion.

Employment in Ontario grew by more than 630,000 people from 1982 to 1987—an average annual growth rate of almost 3 percent, which is a rate higher than was achieved by any of the seven major industrial countries in the world. In the first 11 months of 1987 alone, the Ontario economy created more than 145,000 jobs.

Our economy is growing so rapidly for the simple reason that Ontario is a very good place to do business.

Between 1981 and 1985, after-tax corporate profits in Canada as a percentage of GDP were consistently higher than in the United States. In 1985, they were almost three times higher. Between 1981 and 1985, Ontario's corporate profits before taxes grew at a rate almost twice that of the United States.

In addition to our ready access to a huge market and to an abundance of natural resources, we in Ontario offer such advantages as dynamic and sophisticated capital markets, a favourably positioned currency, a well-educated workforce, a low cost of living, an exceptionally good quality of life, and mature and stable labour-management relations.

It is no exaggeration, I believe, to say that the Canadian capital market is second only to the US in its breadth, its depth, the quality of its regulation and, most important, its efficiency in terms of the cost of raising capital, and of distribution, and clearance and settlement systems. And Ontario, and particularly our capital city Toronto, is at the centre of Canada's national and international banking and financial system.

Five of Canada's six largest chartered banks have their headquarters functions in Toronto. Together they account for more than 90 percent of all domestic chartered bank assets. As well, 46 of the 59 foreign bank subsidiaries operating in Canada have located their head offices in Toronto.

The Toronto Stock Exchange, for its part, accounts for more than 75 percent of the dollar value of all shares traded on Canadian exchanges. In 1986, the Toronto Stock Exchange was the 7th largest in the world in terms of equity. It traded more than 4.9 billion shares worth more than $63.6 billion in Canadian funds.

Last June, we further strengthened Toronto's role as a major international capital market by removing restrictions on ownership and participation in the Ontario securities industry by foreign dealers and by domestic and foreign banks and other financial institutions. Subject only to some interim transitional rules which expire on June 30 of this year, the Ontario capital market is now, along with London, the most open major market in the world.

This opening up has already been a great success, with 23 of the world's major investment dealers now registered with the Ontario securities commission. Among these firms are the five leading Japanese firms, Nomura, Nikko, Faiwa, Yamaichi and Sanyo Securities. Among the American firms are all the leading firms including Salomon Brothers, Morgan Stanley, Girst Boston, Goldman Sachs, Kidder Peabody, Shearson Lehman and the existing resident firms, Merrill Lynch, Prudential-Bache, and Dean Witter.

Among the international banks that have either purchased Canadian firms or sought registration for wholly owned subsidiaries are Union Bank of Switzerland, Deutschebank, Citicorp, Morgan Guaranty, Bankers Trust, Hong Kong and Shanghai, Security Pacific, and Chase Manhattan, to name just the major players.

In June of this year, Toronto will host the annual economic summit of the heads of government of the seven leading industrial nations. Hosting these crucial deliberations on the future of the international economy is an appropriate and timely honour for this Ontario city that has earned recognition as one of the world's important financial centres.

Ontario's international competitiveness, in terms both of exports and of attracting investment, is further enhanced by the current position of the Canadian dollar. Since September, 1985, the Canadian dollar has depreciated by 36.4 percent against the yen, 33.5 percent against the mark, 27.1 percent against the franc, and 14 percent against the pound. Our dollar is currently trading in the range of 77 cents US.

Ontario's labour pool is young, growing, adaptable, and very well educated. Our systems of elementary, secondary, and post-secondary education are strong and forward-looking by any international standard. We have a total of 40 universities and community colleges.

And Ontario workers are naturally international in their orientation. We are a society of immigrants and their descendants, with a population made up of people from every part of the world and every ethnic group, living together in harmony and tolerance. Virtually every language in the world is spoken in Ontario.

The quality of life in Ontario is excellent. Our universal Medicare system assures the same state-of-the art quality of health care to everyone, regardless of individual income. Our unemployment insurance, old age pension and social welfare systems are among the world's most progressive.

Fully 65 percent of the Ontario government's total spending is devoted to social expenditures—32 percent to health care, 19 percent to education, and 14 percent to social services.

Ontario's cities are modern, well-functioning, and safe. Crime rates are low.

Our cultural scene is lively and enriched by the diversity of our population. Ontario is the home of the National Ballet of Canada, several symphony orchestras, the opera, and a host of other cultural and recreational activities.

The high quality of life in Ontario is accompanied by a comparatively low cost of living and doing business. Toronto's cost of living index is, in fact, the lowest among the major cities of Western Europe, the United States, and Japan.

And total hourly compensation—including both money wages and fringe benefits—for Canadian manufacturing industry as a whole is roughly equivalent to that in Japan and significantly lower than that in the US.

Ontario also enjoys a very positive labour relations climate. There are 230,000 workplaces and 3.6 million workers within the province's jurisdiction. Yet in mid-January, in all of Ontario, there were only 2,410 workers involved in work stoppages. In the five years from 1982 through 1986, between 93 and 96 percent of all collective agreements negotiated each year were negotiated without any form of work stoppage.

To all these other advantages I would add the fact that Ontario has a proud and unbroken tradition as a society of world-class innovators. Breakthroughs as diverse as the telephone, insulin, cardiac pacemakers, the electron microscope, and the use of radioactive cobalt to treat cancer all originated in Ontario.

More recently, Ontario has produced the Canadarm remote manipulator used in the US Space shuttle, digital microwave transmission, domestic communications services via satellite, the Telidon Videotex system used throughout North America, and a host of other pioneering innovations. An Ontarian, Dr. John Polanyi of the University of Toronto, was awarded the 1986 Nobel Prize for chemistry for his work with lasers and light waves.

Together with strength in innovation goes strength in manufacturing. Ontario is an international competitor in today's leading-edge industries such as telecommunications, aerospace, chemicals, advanced transit systems, electronics, and computer software. Between 1983 and 1986, Ontario provided 57 percent of Canadian technology-intensive exports.

And Ontarians are also making their mark on the world in a wide variety of other ways. For instance, a Toronto-based company, Olympia and York, is the world's largest real estate development firm. The Toronto-based Four Seasons hotel chain operates some of the world's finest hotels. An Ontarian, Conrad Black, recently became proprietor of one of Britain's most established newspapers, the Daily Telegraph, and is proceeding to restore its profitability. An Ontario architect, Carlos Ott, was chosen to design the new Paris Opera House.

We are proud of Ontario's accomplishments. But we see them as a point of departure, not as a cause for complacency. We recognize that the future belongs to those who can remain on the leading edge of technological innovation and knowledge-intensive activity, who can quickly translate research breakthroughs into practical and top-quality products, and who can market those new products vigorously and effectively. Success in these crucial endeavours cannot be ensured by relying on day-to-day improvisation.

What ultimately separates the winners from the losers—in the private and the public sectors alike—is strategy: the capacity to look ahead, to think of the future and to plan intelligently for it. Those of us in government especially have a responsibility to do more than just settle for easy, short-term fixes and leave it to our children to deal with the consequences of our short-sightedness. That is why I am determined that the time frame for my government's concerns will always be not just the next quarter but the next quarter-century.

Accordingly, the strategy we are developing and implementing for Ontario has three main elements: First, partnership among government, business, labour, and the academic communities in identifying and addressing our competitive needs and opportunities; second, investment in developing and nurturing our human capital; and, third, diversification of our trade relationships. Let me speak briefly about each element in turn.

Both history and contemporary realities teach us that the most effective competitors are those societies that have a clear sense of common

purpose, a high degree of consensus and a genuine spirit of co-operation. Governments have a vital responsibility to provide leadership in
the pursuit of economic development. But I believe that the best form of
such leadership is to lead in forging a true working partnership among
all the key players.

That is what we are doing in Ontario. In the spring of 1986, my government created a new body, the Premier's Council, with a clear mandate
to steer Ontario into the forefront of economic leadership and technological innovation. The 28 members of this council are a representative
cross-section of dynamic and forward-looking leaders from business,
organized labour and the academic and research communities, together
with four Cabinet ministers. I attend and chair all the Council's meetings. I am personally committed to making it work.

There are many such councils in the world, but what makes ours note-
worthy is that it is in no way just a symbolic or ceremonial body, nor
even just another think-tank. It is an action-tank. We all meet almost
monthly, roll up our sleeves, and get to work as genuine partners in
developing long-term economic development strategies that emphasize
technological advancement and international competitiveness. Working
subcommittees are formed as required to address specific issues in detail and report back to the full council.

The Premier's Council directs a $1 billion technology fund which is
earmarked to stimulate co-operative science and technology research in
the private sector and in post-secondary institutions.

Part of this fund is being used, for instance, to establish centres of
excellence to stimulate advanced research in specific fields by corporations and universities working together. Seven such Ontario centres
of excellence have already been designated: a centre for advanced laser
and light wave research; a centre in space and terrestrial science; a centre
for integrated manufacturing; a centre for groundwater research; a centre in information technology; a centre for materials research; and the
telecommunications research institute of Ontario.

While the Council carries out its vital work, my government is of
course proceeding with a broad range of other economic development
initiatives, such as encouraging and helping Ontario's mature, established industries to meet the challenges of restructuring and modern-
ization.

The second element of our strategy is an emphasis on nurturing and
developing our human capital. In the new knowledge-intensive global
economy, people are the most critical strategic resource. For individual companies and for entire societies alike, it is largely the knowledge,
skills, and motivation of the workforce that sets the winners apart from
the also-rans. I believe, indeed, that excellence in education has become
the single most important key to long-term competitive success.

We are in the process of reviewing and further strengthening the system at all levels—elementary, secondary, post-secondary, and adult training and retraining. Our goal is to ensure that Ontario's young people master the traditional literacy *and* the new literacy—computer skills, advanced mathematics, and science. We must teach not only the three T's but the three I's—innovation, initiative, and ingenuity.

Our strategy also recognizes that economic policy and social policy are complementary and inextricably linked. There could be no lasting competitive success without a high degree of social consensus, and there could be no social consensus without a genuine sense of social justice and a fair sharing of the benefits of prosperity. If we want ordinary people to be committed to the well-being of our economy, they must have reason to believe that our economy is committed to *their* well-being.

With that reality in mind, we will continue to build up Ontario's infrastructure of caring and sharing by addressing new needs, such as specialized health care for an aging population, child care services for single mothers and working parents, and the housing needs of the baby-boom generation.

The third key element of Ontario's strategy is diversification of our trade relationships. We are building stronger links with the Pacific nations, the fastest-growing market in the world. And we are intensifying and renewing our attention to the great European market. Because our mission is to be a true global trader, we are committed to vigorously pursuing mutually beneficial trade and investment relationships with every part of the world.

A noted philosopher once said: "If you don't know where you are going, chances are you'll wind up someplace else."

We in today's Ontario know where we are going: we want to develop further as an effective and dynamic global competitor. We're charting a clear course to get there. And we're taking determined, confident steps in the right direction. To those of you who haven't yet had occasion to do so, I would say: come and visit us, and judge for yourselves.

OPENING OF ONTARIO HOUSE
London, England, February 3, 1988

Your Royal Highness, Agent General Wells, friends:

I would like to thank Her Royal Highness Princess Alexandra for honour us with her presence here today.

In Ontario, we were fortunate to receive a visit from Her Royal Highness just a little over two years ago. Ontarians were pleased to welcome her into our home. Your Highness, today it gives me great pleasure to welcome you to our home away from home.

Given the enormous importance of our province's relationship with Great Britain, and the vital role Ontario House has played in building on that relationship, I am delighted to take part in the official opening of Ontario's new home in London.

I'd like to congratulate our agent general, Tom Wells, on the tremendous effort he has put into ensuring a successful opening, and on the leadership he has provided in strengthening our province's ties with Great Britain. Tom, sitting on the opposite side of the Ontario Legislature for ten years taught me that you're one fellow who always likes to be prepared. You've proven that once again, this time very much to my benefit. I want to thank you for all that you have done to help my first visit productive and enjoyable.

And I want to thank all of our British friends for making us fell so welcome and comfortable here in one of the truly great cities of the world. In doing so, you are following in a British tradition, for Ontarians have always been made to feel welcome here.

We're very proud that Ontario has been represented here since 1869.

Indeed, we can thank an Englishman, the Rev. Horrocks Cocks, for helping to give our representation here an early boost. Back in 1871 he suggested to the Ontario legislature that he be commissioned to give lectures about Ontario in England and Wales. All he asked in return was a small fee of $35.

Certainly, Ontario received more than its money's worth. These lectures helped set the stage for permanent representation that has been co-operative, productive, and at times colourful.

This is Ontario's fourth permanent home here in Great Britain. We've also had a few temporary spots to hang our hat. Back in 1880, our province's office was based in Liverpool, a two-room suite that went for 50 pounds a year and, in the words of Ontario's representative of the day, occupied a "commanding position" on the second floor of a new building.

During the Second World War, the agent general, James Armstrong, set up shop in a building that had no windows, electricity, heating, plumbing, or telephone. Other than that it was perfect. It contained a 100-bed emergency air raid shelter in a cold, damp basement. So Armstrong moved in with a camp cot, bed roll and paraffin heater. Tom, I'm sure you'll be just as comfortable here, but just to make sure of that, I've brought a camp cot, bed roll and paraffin heater. Just as in 1944, nothing is too good for our agent general.

The home for Ontario's representative in London has changed a great deal since 1869, but more importantly so has the role.

Originally, Ontario established headquarters here to encourage emigration, so that our new nation could benefit from the skills and experience found in the British Isles.

As our province's economy grew in the 1880s, the agent for Ontario found himself devoting more of his efforts to widening trade ties between us, primarily exports from Ontario's fruit belt.

The peaches and grapes that Ontario farmers sent to Britain helped set us on a course to becoming a leading exporting jurisdiction. Ontario's total global exports reached $62.6 billion in 1986, a 112 percent increase from 1980. Ontario's gross domestic product of $142 billion US in 1986 was larger than the gross domestic product of such nations as Switzerland, Sweden, Austria, or Denmark. Indeed, if Ontario were an independent nation, it would rank as the eleventh largest nation in the world in terms of gross domestic product. A great deal has changed since 1869. From an agricultural base, Ontario has grown to become a major manufacturing centre and, more recently, a leading financial centre as well.

Last June, we further strengthened Toronto's role as a major international capital market, by removing restrictions on ownership and participation in the Canadian securities industry by foreign dealers and by domestic and foreign banks and other financial institutions. Subject only to some interim transitional rules which expire on June 30 of this year, the Ontario capital market is now, along with London, the most open major market in the world.

But with all that has changed in the past 119 years, one thing has remained very much the same. Our relationship with Great Britain is important to us, and it will always remain so. Over the years, close and strong links have been beneficial—to both of us. Those historic links have established the foundation for the dynamic relationship that exists between our societies today.

Agricultural products are still our leading export to Great Britain. But an economic relationship that was once based on shipments of apples and beans has grown to encompass major trade in aircraft and parts, industrial machinery, communications equipment, and chemicals. There are a great many opportunities for mutual investment.

Forty-five years ago, Winston Churchill said, "The empires of the future are empires of the mind."

More and more, on both sides of the Atlantic, we are learning the farsightedness of that statement. We are both learning that more and more, the most important ingredients of economic success are knowledge, skills, innovation, and entrepreneurship. In developing those strengths, we can help each other.

Britain and Ontario have a common language, a common political and cultural tradition, and a long history of mutually beneficial trade and investment relationships. But I do not believe that we have yet fully developed the potential of our relationship. I am convinced that we can do more, and I am determined to give major new impetus to the effort to do so.

Your Highness, you would honour us by unveiling the plaque commemorating the new location of Ontario House.

ONTARIO: CANADA'S DYNAMIC CENTRE
Heidelberg, West Germany, February 5, 1988

I'm delighted to be here in the state of Baden-Württemberg. Yours is a region that has long justly prided itself on being on the leading edge—whether of royal dynasties, through the Hohenstaufens and the Hohenzollerns in your spending past, or of automotive technology, through Porsche, Mercedes, and Audi in your dynamic present.

My own province of Ontario has a much shorter and certainly less regal history, but in the present there are some remarkable similarities between our province and your state.

We are both the industrial centres of our respective countries. Our populations are the same size. We both have diverse economics in which the automotive sector is the largest. We both have a strong agricultural basis. We both have beautiful lands and vast forests, and therefore share common environmental concerns about acid rain and other forms of pollution.

Baden-Württemberg and Ontario both pride themselves on being technologically-advanced societies of innovators. The bicycle, the motor car and the airship originated in your state. The telephone, insulin, and the electron microscope are among the inventions that originated in Ontario.

Our many similarities provide an exceptional opportunity for co-operation in trade, technological research, and investment. We already enjoy a special relationship signified by the Memorandum of Understanding for Technical Co-operation signed by my government and that of your state in February of last year.

Under that memorandum, we have both undertaken to assist in arranging contacts between companies interested in collaboration such as two-way trade, licensing and joint ventures, to support the arrangement of business delegation trips, and to encourage our respective firms to take part in trade missions and trade fairs.

I am pleased to note that our relationship is flourishing. There are now at least thirty-two companies in Ontario with direct connections in Baden-Württemberg. And I particularly appreciated the fact that last year three members of the Baden-Württemberg management academy spent three months on an exchange visit with the Ontario government.

But we still have only begun to develop the potential of our relationship. We intend to carry on this task with vigor and determination, within the context of our broader commitment to inject new impetus into Ontario's trade and investment relationship with Germany as a whole and indeed with all of Europe.

Ontario has much to offer Europe, not only as a trading partner but as a site for mutually beneficial investment.

We are located at the very centre of the rich North American market, with 164 million consumers living within two days' truck drive of our border. In fact, 120 million of them live within just one day's drive. And Ontario business is served by modern and efficient transportation networks of every kind—air, rail, highways, and shipping.

Ontario is the world's third largest exporter to the US, ranking ahead of every country except Canada as a whole and Japan. Ontario's total global exports increased by 112 percent between 1980 and 1986, from $29.5 billion to $62.6 billion.

We are an international competitor in today's leading edge industries such as telecommunications, aerospace, chemicals, advanced transit systems, electronics, and computer software. Ontario provides more than 57 percent of Canadian technology-intensive exports.

Ontario's growth in real gross domestic product since 1983 has outpaced all the major industrial countries. In 1986, for instance, our GDP grew by 4.9 percent, compared to only 3.1 percent for Canada as a whole, 2.7 percent for Germany, 2.6 percent for the US, and 2.2 percent for Japan.

Our labour force is young, rapidly-growing, diverse, adaptable, and well educated.

Our capital markets are dynamic and sophisticated, and Ontario's capital city, Toronto, is the undisputed domestic and international banking and financial centre of Canada.

Last June, we further strengthened Toronto's role as a major international capital market, by removing restrictions on ownership and participation in the Ontario securities industry by foreign dealers and by domestic and foreign banks and other financial institutions. Subject only to some interim transitional rules which expire on June 30 of this year, the Ontario capital market is now, along with London, the most open major market in the world.

Social stability and social consensus are other vital elements of a successful business climate, and both elements are very much present in Ontario, as they are in Baden-Württemberg—perhaps largely because Ontario, like your state, offers a quality of life that would be difficult to surpass anywhere in the world.

Our universal Medicare system assures the same state-of-the-art quality of health care to everyone, regardless of individual income. Our unemployment insurance, old age pension and social welfare systems are among the most progressive anywhere.

Our cities are modern, flourishing—and safe. Crime rates are low.

Ontario's consensual and co-operative quality of life extends to our labour-management relations. In mid-January, in all of Ontario with its 230,000 workplaces and 3.6 million workers, there were only 2,410 workers involved in work stoppages. In the five years from 1982 through 1986, between 93 and 96 percent of all collective agreements negotiated each year were negotiated without any form of work stoppage.

The high quality of life in Ontario is combined with a comparatively low cost of living and doing business.

Toronto's cost of living index is the lowest among the major cities of Western Europe, the United States and Japan.

Industrial electricity in Ontario costs only half of what it does in many major US cities.

And total hourly compensation—including both wages and fringe benefits—for workers in Canadian manufacturing industry as a whole is significantly lower than in the US and roughly equivalent to that in Japan.

All this helps to make us a very profitable place to do business.

Between 1981 and 1985, after-tax corporate profits in Canada as a percentage of GDP were consistently higher than in the United States. In 1985, they were almost three times higher.

Between 1981 and 1985, Ontario's corporate profits before taxes grew at a rate almost twice that of the United States.

I and my government are proud of Ontario's accomplishments, but we see them not as a cause for complacency but as a point of departure. We are working to further strengthen our capacity for technological innovation, and, as I said earlier, we place high priority on further strengthening our trade and investment relationship with Germany and Europe.

Our links to Europe are strong and deeply rooted in our history as well as in our present. Ontario is a diverse and multicultural society of immigrants and their descendants, and a majority of those immigrants came from Europe. Every language of Europe, along with virtually every language in the world, is spoken in Ontario.

Our trade with Germany is growing steadily, though not entirely in a balanced way. Ontario's exports to your country have increased from $327 million in 1982 to $361 million in 1986. During this same period, our imports from Germany have virtually tripled—from $535 million to $1.5 billion.

The recent development of our trade with Europe as a whole has been even less balanced. Between 1980 and 1986, Ontario's imports from Europe increased by 107 percent—from $3 billion to $6.3 billion. But during this same period, our exports to Europe *decreased* by 7.4 percent, from $3.3 billion to $3.1 billion.

This may be explainable in part by the currency exchange rates that were in effect during that period. But it is worth emphasizing the current position of our Canadian dollar. Since September, 1985, the Canadian dollar has depreciated by 33.5 percent against the mark, 27.1 percent against the franc, and 14 percent against the pound. And it is currently trading in the range of 77 cents US.

I also want to emphasize very clearly that the new Canada-US trade agreement recently negotiated by our current federal government will in no way deflect Ontario from our renewed emphasis on trade and investment links with Europe.

We value our relationship with the US, which is and will remain our largest trading partner, but we are not prepared to limit our horizons or our opportunities. Our horizon is the world, and neither our own self-interest nor the well-being of the international trading system on which we all depend would be well-served by encouraging the emergence of inward-looking continental trading blocs. So you may be assured that this Canada-US agreement will only further strengthen Ontario's resolve to broaden and diversify our trade relationships.

My visit here this week is part of those efforts. Other initiatives are forthcoming.

I am pleased to announce today, for instance, that this fall Ontario will send a top-level economic and scientific development mission to identify specific opportunities and priorities for new linkages between us and the European countries. The findings of this mission will then serve as a basis for a major European-Ontario forum we will host in the spring of 1989 to start translating those opportunities into action.

It was Goethe, I believe, who wrote: "Art is long, life short; judgment difficult, opportunity transient." The opportunity for an expanded and reinvigorated trade and investment relationship between our respective economies is at hand. I hope you will join me in ensuring that it does not pass unfulfilled.

BREAKING DOWN WALLS AND BARRIERS: DAVID PETERSON AS POLICY MAKER

Speech to the Ontario Legislature on the New Liberal Government's Legislative Program
Toronto, Ontario, July 2, 1985

At the outset, let me thank my colleagues for their warm words. I am very mindful of the responsibilities they have in this great chamber and I appreciate their warm wishes for myself and for the new Cabinet, recognizing as they do, and, indeed, as everyone does, that we are inexperienced in our role, having just been sworn into office some six days ago.

I appreciate the consideration demonstrated by the opposition parties and we intend to also demonstrate the same kind of sensitivity. We recognize we are dealing with an inexperienced opposition and I have instructed my ministers to be very gentle in the first couple of weeks, at least until they find their feet.

We are mindful of the very great responsibility we have assumed. It is obvious every opposition member aspires to govern. It is something I have personally worked towards for ten years, and some of my colleagues have been working for it for even longer than that. Taking my place on this side of the House, in this chair, as Ontario's 20th premier, is personally a very humbling experience indeed.

We have much work to do for the people of Ontario. That is why we decided to reconvene this House so quickly after being sworn into office. I know of no other transition accomplished in such a very short space of time. I wish to thank everyone who helped; the opposition parties, the staff and the public service. It took a great deal of effort and co-operation and worked extremely smoothly. Speed was necessary because we recognized the importance of moving quickly to tackle the pressing

Without Walls or Barriers: The Speeches of Premier David Peterson, Library of Political Leadership Series, by Arthur Milnes and Ryan Zade, Editors. Montreal and Kingston: McGill-Queen's University Press,

problems confronting this province.

Before I discuss our plans for this session, I would like to be the first in the House to express respect for the Conservative Party's long reign. We have had many honest differences over fundamental issues through the years, but we recognize that the hundreds of Conservative legislators who sat on this side of the House sought to guide the province as best they could. I congratulate them on their ability to so often win the confidence of the people of Ontario.

The last election brought changes most of us, including my wife, did not expect. The people of the province supported our commitment to openness, to compassion and to competence. We who sit on this side of the House will spare no effort to justify their confidence. We will open new avenues to public participation and close old ones to arbitrary decisions. We will guard against any erosion in health care, equality of opportunity or help for the needy. We will show respect for every cent of every taxpayer's dollar.

We will act to preserve a clean environment. We will be bold in creating new jobs and vigilant in protecting those that now exist. We will fight for Ontario's interests and never let them be ignored. We will begin to reshape education to meet the needs of our society in a changing world. We invite all in this House to join us in the pursuit of these goals.

Our differences pale when compared to those that divide people elsewhere. We should never forget the blessing of living in a country where the phrase "political battle" is a colourful metaphor rather than a grim reality.

Six days ago, when I was honoured to be sworn in as the premier of this province, I spoke of the need for a government without walls or barriers. That is important inside this House as well as outside.

There is a proper place for partisanship. There is also a proper time for partisanship. It must not encompass every waking hour of every working day. We are committed to making minority government work and our aim is to make use of the talents of all legislators. In this House, everyone will count. We want to exchange ideas, not insults. We seek common ground with both opposition parties.

Many of our campaign proposals were included in the last government's throne speech. Obviously there are some basic points on which we can expect the support of all parties.

Nous occupons tous un nouveau poste. Nous devons tous faire preuve de patience. On ne peut tout faire en un seul jour, ni en une seule session. Il serait insensé d'essayer.

All of us in this House are new to our jobs. We all have to show patience. We cannot do everything in one day or one legislative session. It would be foolish to try. In the next few days, ministers of my government will announce a number of new policies. The treasurer will soon provide an economic statement. That is why I will not announce today every policy we intend to pursue or every goal we hope to reach. I offer not an exhaustive list, but a broad agenda.

We face many pressing needs. One that touches upon all of us is the need to make Ontario's government open, compassionate and competent, like its people. People can only achieve the changes they want and need if they are allowed to put their hands on the levers of power and shift gears when necessary. We joined an Accord to indicate the kind of policies we will pursue and the kind of support we can expect. We realized we owed it to the people to make it clear that our government will act from open plans. That is why we have placed a welcome mat at the front door of this House.

We have already gone beyond symbolic efforts in trying to involve people in the decisions that affect their lives. It is because of our belief in open government that we released long-withheld information on separate school funding less than 48 hours after we took office. We have reiterated our commitment to ensuring full debate on the manner of implementation. We want to hear what people have to say.

Notre approche ouverte s'appliquera à toutes les questions, y compris celles qui ont reçu peu d'attention dans le passé.

Our open approach will extend to all issues, including those that have received little attention in the past.

D'ici quelques jours, le ministre des affaires du nord annoncera la tenue des audiences publiques vers la fin du mois sur l'attribution des routes utilisées par la deuxième Dash 8 de NorOntair. De telles décisions ne se prendront plus sans que ceux qui doivent en subir les conséquences puissent se faire entendre.

Within a few days, the minister of northern affairs (Mr. Fontaine) will announce public hearings to take place later this month on the awarding of routes for use by norOntair's second Dash 8 aircraft. No longer will such decisions be made without giving a voice to those who have to live with the consequences.

We will move quickly to make this House the people's home. We will bring television into the legislature so what we do and say can be seen and heard in every living room in the province. We will soon introduce freedom-of-information legislation. Six years after a bill was first promised by the government, we will open that window to the fresh air of public access. The same bill will protect personal privacy, and guarantee every citizen the means to protect his or her reputation.

We will move quickly to bolster the role of members and committees of the legislature. We recognize their vital role as the direct link that allows the people to tell us their concerns. A legislative committee will be empowered to conduct a review of parliamentary procedures and appointments. It will be given two vital assignments. It will be asked to devise ways to make full use of the talents of elected members and determine what resources they need to effectively represent their constituents.

The committee will also be asked to develop means to attract and select the most dedicated and capable citizens to serve in government. It is our goal to seek out the finest minds and firmest hands. We are open to talent from every corner of this province. It is our duty to dispel skepticism about public and political institutions. Appointments made to repay favours have bred contempt among the public. Cynicism has been justified in the past. We will see there will be no grounds for it in the future.

Public service will regain the respect it deserves. We will replace the spoils system with the merit system. Public service must be viewed as its own reward.

We will remember that our commitment to open government is important only as a means to an end. The end we seek is government with the competence to lead and the compassion to deliver. In the past few days we have seen an example of how people can get through to government if the mechanisms are there. We congratulate the senior citizens of this country for their successful effort to right a wrong.

Nous tenons également à exprimer notre gratitude. C'est avec grand plaisir que nous avons instamment demandé au gouvernement fédéral de revenir sur ses plans de réduire la protection des intéressés contre l'augmentation des prix. Les personnes âgées du Canada ont fait bien plus pour nous que nous n'avons fait pour eux. Elles ont non seulement prouvé la valeur de la participation publique mais elles ont également rappelé à bon nombre d'entre nous d'un point qu'à notre avis nous ne devrions jamais oublier.

In a little over two decades, more than 1.4 million citizens of Ontario will be over the age of 65. Many of us will be among them, those who have not expired. Many of us must now work to plan how we are going to provide the senior citizens with services they have earned. That is why I appointed a minister without portfolio responsible for senior citizens' affairs. He has begun to work to develop an efficient, affordable and sensitive system of caring for the aged.

Those three goals come together naturally. By rationalizing services and improving seniors' access to local resources, we will make it possible for them to remain in their communities while keeping costs under control.

We will place a high priority on implementing homemaker and home-support programs. We recognize the importance of assessment and placement services and they will be reviewed. We will help senior citizens to remain as independent as they can for as long as they can.

If compassion means anything, it means support for guaranteed first-class health care for all. We will move to eliminate extra billing. Our minister of health will meet soon with representatives of the medical community to work out the fairest way of implementing this basic principle.

Compassion means recognizing people's rights and insisting they be met. Unfair discrimination against women, minorities, and the handicapped must go; full and equal opportunities must come.

We will introduce legislation to guarantee equal pay for work of equal value in the public sector. The attorney general will direct an interministerial task force to begin immediately to prepare a green paper on the means of implementing this principle in the private sector.

We do not underestimate the difficulties in bringing in an equal value system but we are determined to make a meaningful start and see the process through. This government will ignite the engine that will drive us to the long-sought destination of equal rights for all.

To advance to that goal, we will set up a $1-million fund to support court cases based on the women's rights guarantees in the Charter of Rights and Freedoms. Justice is always a sound investment.

We will also proceed with bills aimed at bringing our own statutes into line with the Constitution, and a Family Law Reform Act, and give teeth to court orders for support and custody. An important element in compassion is fairness. We will also introduce child care programs.

We are determined to build an atmosphere of improved labour-management relations. Workers have a fundamental right to organize for collective bargaining. Certification procedures provide means for the majority to decide the issue of trade union representation, but certification is a meaningless event when a first collective agreement proves unattainable.

To address this problem, the government proposes to introduce legislation to provide for the arbitration of first collective agreements. The objective will be to protect the right to organize while maintaining an incentive to negotiate a first agreement rather than rely on arbitration.

Notre proposition se traduira en meilleures relations entre le patronat et les travailleurs, une situation que nous recherchons tous. Pour cette question, la compassion et la compétence vont nettement de pair.

Our proposal will ultimately lead to improved labour-management relations, a goal we all seek. On this issue, compassion and competence most clearly meet.

This government will also introduce measures to reform the *Workers' Compensation Act* and the *Occupational Health and Safety Act* to ensure fair treatment for those injured in the workplace and further limit the risk to workers.

We must all work towards ensuring basic shelter for all. Today we wish to announce that rent review will be extended to all private rental dwellings, effective August 1. At that time, the legal limit on rent hikes will be reduced to 4 percent. Given the 90-day notice required for a rent increase, the new, lower limit will apply to all notices given on or after May 2.

Legislation on these measures will be introduced early in the fall, giving the new government time to prepare a fully comprehensive package. Meanwhile, I urge all landlords to act in good faith. There is little point in raising rents only to see them rolled back retroactively.

In extending controls, however, we will be fair to all. Any landlord who feels he can justify recent rent hikes on the basis of costs will be able to apply for rent review.

The minister of housing will give high priority to designing a rent registry so new tenants can find out the legal limit for prospective dwellings. Work on this will continue without delay to ensure the earliest possible date for implementation.

Our commitment to affordable housing is reflected by our decision to create a separate Ministry of Housing. A solution to this problem, which has reached huge proportions in our metropolitan areas, is going to require co-operation from all three levels of government. The minister of housing will be meeting with his counterparts at the housing ministers' conference in Calgary this week. He will urge there be a strong federal presence in the field.

We will seek the municipalities' ideas on how we can reverse the present trend and improve the atmosphere for residential construction. Compassion must always be accompanied by competence. Compassion without competence is like a talented orchestra without instruments: instead of harmony, it creates only silent frustration. Competence is not something you declare; it is something others must recognize.

The taxpayers trust us to put their money to the best possible use. We will not let them down. Any policy or program that is outside a framework of fiscal responsibility is nothing less than a boomerang that will turn around and smash social progress.

Reckless spending destroys our ability to meet our commitments in the future, erodes support for social programs in the present and sparks calls for a return to the simple notions of the past.

Nous devons aider ceux qui sont dans le besoin mais nous ne devons pas augmenter le coût que nos enfants auront à payer. C'est ici et maintenant que nous devons résoudre nos problèmes.

We must help those in need but we must not leave the cost to our children. We must deal with our own problems here and now.

There is no doubt that an early problem we have to deal with is our beleaguered credit rating. For months it has been a source of concern to all who are familiar with the issue. The treasurer will discuss this matter more fully in his statement in the next few days.

As one measure of this government's firm commitment to sound financial management, I am announcing today a government-wide review of all existing and planned advertising expenditures. Effective immediately, I am declaring a freeze on the execution of all planned advertising campaigns yet to be signed and committed. During this review, we will enter into no new advertising contracts. Of course, we will exempt summer tourism campaigns and other promotional programs which have been already contracted for. Legal notices required by various acts will also be permitted. But even those campaigns will be subjected to the same cost-conscious scrutiny as all advertising plans in our comprehensive review.

We also will review all new financial commitments made by the previous government between May 2 and its departure from office on June 26. We will take a very close look at the $181 million that was committed in special payments during the six-week period after May 2.

Members of this House will take an especially active role in saving money on behalf of the taxpayers they represent. We will bolster the powers of the public accounts committee and the provincial auditor to scrutinize all government spending and spending plans.

We will establish a legislative committee on energy with a special responsibility for bringing greater accountability to Ontario Hydro.

In keeping with an earlier commitment, the government will ask a legislative committee to review details of plans to commit $30 million to a domed stadium.

Looking further ahead to the long-term task of managing this government, we will initiate an assessment of all crown corporations and assets, and the economic and social environment in which they are functioning.

I am very pleased to announce today that the task will be taken on by John Kruger, who has agreed to serve as a special adviser to the premier with the rank and status of a deputy minister. Mr. Kruger, who is known to many members of this House and the public for his distinguished service in municipal government in Metropolitan Toronto, is superbly qualified for this major assignment. I am delighted that someone with his record as a proven problem solver has agreed to bring his impressive abilities to bear on behalf of the people of Ontario.

To this government, competence begins with a long, hard look at the pivotal issues as they emerge, not after they have created problems. Free trade is one such emerging issue. There is no doubt that any new bilateral trade agreement with the United States would have a significant impact on our economic future. Its influence would extend to our social, cultural and political institutions. Most important, it would have direct impact on the lives of our citizens.

To many, the phrase "free trade" has become a synonym for work without a future and a future without work. We need to know all its implications. For that reason we will be establishing a legislative committee on Ontario's economy to study the free trade issue and its potential impact on all of us. In order that I have the benefit of day-to-day counsel on this vital matter, I will appoint an adviser on free trade.

These are just our first steps to ensure that Ontario is not left out in the cold.

Our top priority is protecting the interests of the people of this province. Every policy we pursue, every piece of legislation we introduce, will be based on that principle. We will oppose any policy that does not pass our most important test: Is it fair to the people of Ontario?

That is a test that many recent federal policies have failed. When one in every five jobs in this province depends on a strong auto industry, we cannot sit by while Japanese import quotas appear to slip away. We call on the federal government to stand behind the quotas unless and until the Japanese auto firms boost their investment in Canada and Ontario receives economic concessions that will ensure jobs for our auto workers.

The same principle must apply to energy prices. Oil price hikes threaten the livelihoods of too many Ontario families to be ignored or wished away.

Let us keep in mind that Ontario has always supported measures to reduce economic disparities and boost the economies of our sister provinces. As far as this government is concerned, we always will.

However, in any new economic arrangements with foreign countries or other provinces, the federal government must bear one thing in mind. You have to keep stoking the engine that generates the nation's growth. That is good for all Canadians. We will constantly drive home that point.

We will also demonstrate that the provincial government has the ability to move the economy and create jobs. We will not sit by and accept the waste of half a million talents.

We will act on the basis of basic principles:

1. There is no single cure for unemployment. We need a wide variety of tools, including direct job creation.
2. Any assistance to business will be tied to actual job creation performance. Blind faith is no basis on which to give away taxpayers' money.
3. Unemployment knows not fairness. Young people, women, the handicapped, natives, and visible minorities require unique programs to deal with unique needs.

We must rationalize all our job creation programs and ensure they are understandable and accessible to the public. This is especially true of programs for young people. In recent years, many youth employment programs have failed largely because young people and other affected parties were not consulted beforehand. We will not make that mistake.

While we will meet the needs of all young people, including high school graduates and summer students, the focus of our efforts will be on those with the fewest skills. Two years ago, I proposed a program that would guarantee hard-to-employ youth meaningful employment in return for individual efforts at educational upgrading. The aim was to break the cycle of recurring unemployment, help these young people earn a fair chance in the workforce and reduce the social costs of unemployment.

I am pleased to announce that the minister of skills development is preparing to implement such a program before the summer is out.

A moment ago I listed three of the most important principles in employment programs. Of course, there is one more, and it is the most important: the principle of education as training for life.

For many years, I have been struck by the effectiveness of co-operative education programs in training our young people. Studies show that co-op students are far more likely to complete high school, go on to post-secondary education or successfully find employment than are other students. Moreover, co-operative programs are extremely cost-effective. Support for such programs will be a priority.

We will advance the vital long-term goal of restoring relevance to the education system. Young people entering the workforce must be given the tools to do the job. We must reassert standards and make education relevant to the modern world. At the same time, we must give educators enough room to do their job based on the needs they see every day.

Unfortunately, not all students in this province enjoy equal educational opportunity. Young people from some cultural backgrounds often find themselves streamed into non-academic programs before they have had time to make the necessary cultural adjustment. We will end that practice. We will leave no doubt about our commitment to equal educational opportunities for all.

We intend to honour the previous government's commitment to full funding for public separate schools. We will adhere, in so doing, to three guiding principles. First, there must be full, open hearings to allow for public consultation. Second, given the questions that have been raised, we intend to honour our commitment to seek a court reference to assure its constitutionality. Third, we intend to honour former Premier William Davis's commitment to proceed with funding this fall. The minister of education (Mr. Conway) will be making a statement in the next few days.

Par suite d'une décision du tribunal à propos de la question linguistique, le gouvernement présentera, comme il se doit, un projet de loi sur la gestion des écoles de langue française.

As a result of a court decision on the language reference question, this government will, as required, bring forward a French-language governance bill.

This government will ensure that environmental hazards do not eat away at the legacy we wish to leave our children. Part IX of the *Environmental Protection Act*, the long-awaited spills bill, will be proclaimed immediately. It will go into full force and effect this fall. We intend to meet next month with the interested parties to finalize regulations required for full implementation. Industry and insurers will have time to take all necessary steps.

No longer will there be any question of who is responsible for preventing spills or cleaning them up. No longer will innocent victims be left without a route to compensation.

This government will also address its concern regarding the source and impact of acid rain. One measure of a government's competence is its success in balancing growth across the province. I am pleased to announce today that the minister of industry and trade will instruct the Ontario development corporations to direct a greater percentage of their investments to northern and eastern Ontario.

I am also pleased to announce that the long-awaited report of the Royal Commission on the Northern Environment will finally be released this summer. We look forward to any guidance in evaluating plans for resource development in our northland.

In a further move to equalize conditions in northern Ontario, we will launch a study into differences in the price of gasoline in northern and southern Ontario. As well, the minister of health will begin the process of allowing those in remote northern communities to charge the Ontario health insurance plan for the full cost of medically necessary travel.

We will assist family farmers to maintain their role as the backbone of rural Ontario. The government cannot stand by while farmers are squeezed by rising debts and falling markets. We will soon unveil a farm credit plan to rescue the farmers under most serious assault.

We recognize also the importance of Ontario's other primary industries. The priority we give to mining was signalled by the appointment of a specific minister with responsibility in that area. He will be meeting with many members of the mining industry to look at new measures that could be most helpful in that sector.

The minister of natural resources will soon announce the terms and conditions of an independent audit of our forest resources. We shall take our rich forests for granted no longer.

The minister of consumer and commercial relations will act on another matter we raised during the campaign: the distribution of beer and wine in independent grocery stores. He will consult with business organizations, such as the Canadian Federation of Independent Business and the Retail Merchants Association of Canada, and representatives of the brewing, wine, and distilling industries, labour unions, consumer groups and other parties that have an interest in that issue. We on this side of the House are prepared to recognize that Ontario has come of age.

This government also wishes to state its belief in the importance of our arts and cultural groups, facilities, and organizations. We commit ourselves to ensuring an arm's-length relationship with such funded groups.

This government will not shrink from its commitment to change and progress in every aspect of Ontario life. The principles we fought for in the election—principles that won us more votes than any other party—

will continue to guide us.

We are determined to provide the people of Ontario with a government in which they can take pride and a lifestyle in which they can take joy. The people are ready for change; they are willing to participate, and able to contribute. We in this House must provide the competence, openness, compassion, and leadership.

LEARNING FOR LIFE: EDUCATION AND TRAINING IN THE '90S, DESIGNS FOR A CHANGING WORLD CONFERENCE
Toronto, Ontario, May 28, 1990

It's difficult to believe that there has ever been a time when the task of preparing young people for the world that awaits them has been more difficult or more complex.

As someone who is both premier and parent, I sometimes think that the task of being premier is the easier of the two jobs.

One reason why it's so difficult to help children prepare for the world is because the world itself is changing so rapidly.

President Havel of the Czechoslovakian republic—a man who in a matter of weeks went from prisoner to president—recently observed that things are moving so quickly that "we have no time to be astonished."

All of our old political and economic maps are now obsolete. There was a time when history was something that you found in books. Today, history is being rewritten on the front pages of our newspapers each and every day.

The rate of change in science and technology is no less astounding. I'm told that 85 percent of the technologies that will be in use in the year 2000 haven't even been invented yet.

Just to give you an idea of the kind of impact that new technologies are having, today an average researcher using an ordinary computer can check more correlations in an afternoon than Einstein could in his entire lifetime.

Then there's the down-side to change—the veritable minefield that awaits our children in the form of AIDS and crack—dangers that did not even exist in the relative innocence of our own childhoods.

I'm not going to try to discuss all of these changes and the impact they're having on our children's lives. Unlike my colleague in the legislature, Peter Kormos, I'm not sure that I'm capable of speaking for 17 hours—and I'm quite sure that you're not interested in listening that long.

But I would like to spend some time talking about the way in which our workplaces are changing, and what that's going to mean for the way in which we educate and train our children and our workers in the decade ahead.

There's little doubt that the workplace has dramatically changed. In the past, the majority of our workforce earned their livelihood by dexterity and stamina—we all remember Edison's dictum about success being 90 percent perspiration.

Today—with apologies to Edison—a little knowledge goes much further than a lot of perspiration. Consider the vast array of skills that the workforce of the '90s will require to succeed. They're going to have to be:

- literate enough to read and comprehend complex instructions and computer generated data;
- analytical enough to grasp the patterns, problems, and solutions embedded in that data;
- technical enough to program, operate, control, and repair high technology equipment;
- imaginative enough to exploit the full potential of innovative production processes and office-information systems;
- co-operative enough to work in teams, confident enough to speak up in groups, and sensitive enough to do so in a way that ignites, not dampens, the motivation of their colleagues.

With all of these skills needed to perform the most elementary jobs, it isn't surprising that employers of the future will be looking for workers with increasingly higher levels of education.

By the year 2000, the majority of jobs in this country—64 percent—will demand some post-secondary education. That's a 20 percent jump in the figure for 1986.

Another changing characteristic of the workplace is its unpredictability and volatility.

In Ontario one out of every four workers has a job that's directly dependent on exports. That's good if those exports are high-value added products like telecommunications equipment and computer technology.

But if they consist of raw materials and semi-finished goods—as most of our exports do—then some of those workers may be called upon to make some painful career adjustments.

Then there's the fact that 90 percent of all Ontario workers work in firms employing fewer than twenty employees—small business, in other words.

Small business, to be sure, is the greatest generator of job growth in this country. But it's also true that the average life-expectancy of a small business outfit in Canada is just five years.

What happens to the employees if one of these firms closes its doors? They have to shift jobs, adjust their careers, realign their expectations. In many cases they will have to develop new skills or update old ones.

As a province, we have two choices as to how we adjust to these changes in the workplace and the marketplace.

We can try to muddle through—propping up uncompetitive industries, hoping that our workers can pick up a few new skills on the job, giving them a bit of new training when their jobs have disappeared due to the ebb and flow of economic adjustment.

But consider the consequences of muddling through—it means becoming less and less competitive in the international marketplace, it means seeing jobs disappear and our tax base become smaller and smaller, and it means cutting back on expenditures in areas such as protecting our environment, health care, welfare reform, and programs to combat the spread of drug abuse.

It means not only falling further behind countries such as Japan and Germany, but being surpassed by countries such as Korea, Spain, and Brazil.

The other approach is to try to anticipate the changes that will take place and prepare for them.

That's the approach we've chosen in Ontario. That's why we're modernizing our traditional industries to make them more competitive, that's why we're supporting the growth of Canadian-based multinationals that deal in advanced technology goods, that's why we're generating creative sparks by spending $1 billion dollars on technological innovation.

At the same time, we realize that our industrial strategy will only be as strong as our workforce allows it to be. We are now in an era where the wealth of nations will be determined not by what they find beneath their feet, but by what they find between their ears.

Developing a competitive workforce will require us to take a somewhat different philosophic approach to the way we educate and train in the decade ahead.

First and foremost, it means we have to embrace both the concept and the reality of lifelong learning.

When most of us in this room went to school, education and training were seen as one-shot deals—something we did before we reached the age of 25, usually in formal institutions.

Today that notion is as obsolete as the Berlin Wall. To survive in the workplace of the '90s, our children are going to have to keep learning and relearning new skills into their 30s, 40s, and even 50s—perhaps even longer.

In order to prepare our children for this lifetime of learning, we're going to have to make some significant changes throughout our education and training systems—some of which we've started already.

To begin with, we're going to have to provide children with an opportunity to participate at a younger age in an environment that will build on their natural curiosity and their capacity for early learning.

We've already started doing that by requiring all school boards to offer half-day junior and senior kindergarten. But I can foresee a day when children as young as three will participate for a full day in a simulative learning environment.

As they move into the formative years in Grades 1 and 6, we're going to have to pay more and more attention to helping them develop literacy, analytical, and communications skills.

The development of analytical and problem-solving skills is particularly important. When I talk to employers, they tell me that one of the greatest problems they face is that workers can't seem to figure out how to solve new problems or adjust to new situations.

That isn't good enough. In the workplace of the '90s, it isn't good enough that workers remember the answers to old problems. They also have to be able to figure out the answers to new ones.

We're also going to have to place a greater emphasis on trying to instill a love and an aptitude for science and technology.

Our children arrive at school with a wonderful interest in science and technology. Oh, they don't call it that. But they want to know why the sky is blue and what keeps the clouds up, how the VCR and Walkman work.

Our job is not just to give them the answers—it's to help them learn how to discover for themselves. Science classes must spark questions, rather than spoon-feed answers; they must stimulate curiosity instead of stifling it.

And that emphasis on science and technology must become stronger throughout our secondary and post-secondary institutions.

At the moment we have a very disturbing trend line that shows that the portion of high school students who have taken at least one course in technological studies has fallen by 25 percent over the last decade, even as the scientific and technological requirements of industry have increased dramatically.

Personally I find it quite frightening to note that we're looking at a shortfall of 30,000 engineers over the next ten years.

I can tell you that in an age where the rate of science-based innovation will determine which nations are leaders and which are followers, we have good reason to fear the Japanese when we're graduating ten times as many lawyers as they are—and one-third as many scientists and engineers.

There are other areas where we could stand to learn a few lessons from the Japanese about how to prepare our children for the future.

For example, did you know that every student who graduates from a Japanese high school has to have six years of English? Every single graduate.

But how good a job do we do in this country in preparing our students for the reality that much of their working lives will be spent interacting or competing with their Asian counterparts? Sometimes I think we're too fixated on our status as an Atlantic country and forget that Canada is a Pacific country too.

Another area that requires our attention is the need to create stronger links between our schools and our industries.

At the moment, our whole education system seems to be based around preparing students for going on to a post-secondary institution. But the reality is that fewer than one-out-of-three actually do. The rest go straight into the workplace—or into the unemployment lines.

We can't afford to wait until students graduate or drop out of high school before they make a connection to the workplace.

That's why I'm pleased to see that a lot of secondary schools are connecting with business, industry, and labour through programs like school-workplace apprenticeship and co-op education programs.

To me, co-op education represents one of the great waves of the future. It's a trend line that must continue.

The final point I want to make is that we have to provide far more opportunities for those already in the workforce to retrain and upgrade their skills.

We live in a time where the average age of our workforce is getting older, and the stream of new workers is growing smaller.

We have to ensure that we have the highest possible skill levels in our existing workforce.

At the moment, Canada has a terrible record in industrial training. Our American friends spend between $30–$50 billion dollars on industrial training, while we in Canada spend only about $1.5 billion—most of which goes into training new workers rather than into upgrading the skills of older workers.

We have to find ways of getting our private sector to increase its commitment to training.

In part, this means getting our industries and our unions more involved in determining our training needs and mapping out our strategies for meeting those needs. They're the real experts; they're the ones who are in the best position to point the way.

My friends, these are just some of the directions in which I see our approach to education and training headed in the decade ahead.

If the past year has taught us anything, it's that we can't always predict the future. But if we can't always predict it, we can prepare for it.

With your help and support, we have already begun to prepare for it by charting a course of reform for our entire education and training systems. Let us continue to move down that road.

CANADIAN MENTAL HEALTH ASSOCIATION, C. M. HINCKS AWARD DINNER
Toronto, Ontario, May 3, 1988

Ladies and gentlemen, I am deeply honoured to receive such a distinguished award this evening. I will accept it not in recognition of anything I have done personally, but as an acknowledgement of the important change in the delivery of mental health services that we've all worked to bring about.

The history of mental health care in this province is a long—and at times disturbing—story going back more than 140 years.

As National Mental Health Week begins, I think it is useful to realize just how dramatically our notions of, and attitudes to, mental illness have changed.

Less than twenty-five years ago, more than half of patients in psychiatric hospitals had been there over seven years—and most of them would live out their days in one institutional setting or another. Today, two-thirds of psychiatric patients are admitted to psychiatric hospitals for less than two weeks, and nearly all stay less than a month.

Your association was among the first to recognize that the traditional methods of institutional care were not appropriate for all psychiatric patients, and that alternatives to hospitalization were required.

As more psychiatric patients began to receive treatment in the community, your association was also there—to help educate the public, to dispel the many myths about mental illness, and to build the foundations for more caring and supportive communities.

Mental Health Week is a good opportunity, then, to focus public attention on the nature, care, and treatment of psychiatric disabilities. This is a good opportunity to drive home the point that we all have a stake in the continued development of a comprehensive and flexible network of community and institutional care in this province.

For a moment, let's consider the dimensions of the challenge we face in caring for psychiatrically disabled: One in eight Canadians can expect to be hospitalized for a mental illness at least once during their lifetimes. Suicide is the second most frequent cause of death among Canadians aged 15 to 39. Mental illness is the second leading category in general hospital use among those aged 20 to 44. It's estimated that 1.5 million people in Ontario have some form of mental illness, and that 38,000 are severely disabled by schizophrenia, affective disorders, and other mental disabilities. And when we look to the future, we are told we can expect a doubling of mental disorders among the elderly, a 40 percent increase in chronic functional disorders, and little change in the numbers of acute cases.

Lying behind each and every one of these numbers—these statistics—are real human beings with a variety of psychiatric difficulties; human beings who look to the healthcare system and to our communities for the support and care they require.

This was the reason for shifting the emphasis on mental health treatment from institutions to community settings. Because with the right treatment programs, the right supports, we know that, in most cases, mental health can be restored.

Over the years, a flexible and responsive network of community mental health programs has been developed in this province. Supportive housing, geriatric services, self-help, and psychosocial rehabilitation programs, voluntary community support, drug and alcohol dependency programs are just some of the different methods that have been developed to help people from every walk of life and every strata of society.

Providing this care is a partnership that includes government, health professionals, social workers, volunteers, interest groups, and friends and families.

Tonight, I want to talk to you about our government's role in this partnership.

Governments are measured and evaluated by the goals they set for themselves. Ultimately, in the public mind, governments are judged by how well they have achieved those goals.

I want to say to you tonight that we have set the care and treatment of the psychiatrically disabled as one of our highest goals… and I want us to become known for achieving a new direction for mental health in this province.

During last year's election campaign, I committed our government to just such a course. I announced that funding for community mental health programs would be doubled to $130 million annually over the next three years—and that with this funding we would more than double the number of people served by these programs.

This commitment presents us with a major opportunity to bring change and new direction to mental health care and treatment here in Ontario. But we must be absolutely sure that the programs developed will genuinely improve quality of life and increase the potential for restoration to health. We must therefore have standards and evaluation procedures.

To answer these questions and prepare for this expansion, the minister of health last fall appointed a working group to develop a comprehensive community mental health model for the province. The group, under the direction of former Rideau Valley District Health Council Chairman Robert Graham, is taking an extensive look at what we have in place now, and what we will need to realize a fully integrated, balanced, flexible and accessible network of mental health services in this province. Strategically, we want this network to ensure that all residents of Ontario have access to mental health services in or near their own communities. We want to give priority to providing support to those individuals and families experiencing dramatic or prolonged psychiatric disabilities. We want to provide a range of formal and informal supports that will reduce the need for institutionalization and at the same time be sensitive to geographic and demographic needs. And finally, we want to improve quality of life for the psychiatrically disabled by supporting them in their own communities with housing and life skills.

We also want to ensure that this expanded network remains a true partnership. We recognize that community mental health services must be more closely integrated with other health and social agencies in the community, including general and psychiatric hospitals.

A key element in the successful implementation of this network will be our volunteer district health councils, which will plan for the provision of mental health services across their regions. We will offer our full support to DHCs in this exciting—and complex—undertaking.

For my part, I am certain that we will develop a community mental health model for Ontario which will allow us to effectively and efficiently expand upon our existing network of 471 programs. An expanded network of community care is also at the heart of another government mental health initiative now underway—the redevelopment of Whitby Psychiatric Hospital.

This ambitious redevelopment plan will provide an integrated, area-wide mental health system for the nearly two million people in the hospital's catchment area. It is a strategy that has never before been attempted in Ontario—or in any other province for that matter—on such a massive scale.

As part of this project, $7 million in new money is being made available over the next five years for the establishment of new community mental health programs in the area. While the details are being worked out in consultation with district health councils, general hospitals, community agencies, and interest groups, the thrust of this redevelopment is clear: More psychiatric patients will be able to receive all the services they need, and all the levels of care they require, in or near their own communities.

Within the health ministry itself, Mrs. Caplan and her senior officials are looking at ways in which the internal organization of mental health services might be strengthened to mark this renewed emphasis on program delivery.

I expect that you will be hearing more about this in the weeks ahead.

The changes we are planning for mental health care are part of my own personal commitment to seek innovation and new directions across the length and breadth of our healthcare system. With the creation of the Premier's Council on Health Strategy, I have brought together representatives from a cross-section of Ontario to map out some of the broad approaches we might pursue to improve the quality of health and the quality of life in this province. The mission of the Premier's Council on Health Strategy is to provide leadership and guidance to the whole government in achieving the goal of health for every citizen of Ontario. What is envisaged is a very broad concept of health. Health is not only the absence of disease or illness but is a positive resource that allows people to cope, adapt and/or influence the pressures of daily living. Health is not only an objective to be sought but an asset to be used to help us achieve our objectives.

I'd like to thank you once again for the very generous recognition you have accorded me tonight. I know I can count on your ideas, co-operation, and support as we enter a new era in health—and mental health care in Ontario.

Ontario Liberal Party Annual Meeting
Hamilton, Ontario, April 1, 1989

I stand before you today with an immense amount of gratitude in my heart and in my soul thanking all of you for being here and for keeping the spirit of this party alive. I've said to you before that one of great dangers of a party in power is that the parliamentary wing can subsume the party at large, and that the party will atrophy if it isn't alive, growing, dynamic and open, and yes, challenging itself on all issues. The party is far more important, as I said before, than any caucus or any leader at any point in time. What is important is the things and the values we represent, the positions we bring to build a better world, and a better country, and a better province. That's what important, that is what brings us all here, and I want to thank you because I value your help.

I have been the first minister of this province now for almost four years. When I look back to 1982, when I assumed the responsibility as the leader of your party, I don't think there were many of us that thought that we would be in this position some seven years later—not only with the capacity to look back at our successes and our failures but to look forward as well with great optimism into the future—holding the same values we held in 1982, now seized of a great responsibility of governing for close to 10 million people.

Very few people around the world understand the importance of our province and the importance of our province in our country. Some of you may not know it, but if Ontario was a separate country—and I am not advocating separatism—we would be the eleventh largest economic unit in the world. That gives you some sense of our size, our power, our scope, and our responsibilities. We are lucky because we have enjoyed in the last few years, the highest rate of growth in the industrialized world. We have seen enormous growth here. All of the good things and the pressures as well—pressures on our urban environments, pressures on housing, pressures on social services, pressures on individuals, pressures and tensions in our city. It is our responsibility to use these benefits that we have consistent with our philosophy to lead Ontario into a bright and prosperous future, and to make sure that we hold onto those values that are important to us and to other Ontarians.

That of course leads us into a Throne Speech that we are going to be having in just a matter of a few weeks. I have participated in a number of throne speeches as the leader of your party, and this year's Throne Speech will be a little different than others. It will be short, but focused. It will focus on our priorities. It will not be the traditional, shall I say, laundry list or grab bag that these things have become with a little something for everybody. Rather, it will deal with our main priorities of the economy, priorities of building a safe, clean, and healthy province, and safe, clean, and healthy communities. It will focus on education and focus on our kids as well. This Throne Speech will be followed up by a number of very specific announcements on programs and initiatives by the ministers pertaining to the Throne Speech, and other things in the days and weeks following.

I think we recognize that even though there is a down side to the enormous prosperity that we have enjoyed, and the growth that we have enjoyed, that we will not be able to advance our social agenda unless we have an economy that is performing well. Many of you know that we have been working through the Premier's Council, a consensus-building mechanism with leaders from the private sector, leaders from academia, leaders from our government, leaders from labour, to publish a document called "Competing in the Global Economy." This has formed the basis for our strategy for building a high intellectual value-added economy, now and in the future. None of these things can be accomplished in one day, but I believe we have set forth therein a path that is going to hopefully build and sustain our economy, build on the strengths, and assist us through these inevitable transitions that the world is going through at the present time.

A couple of weeks ago when I was in Boston, I had the opportunity to visit with Dr. Robert Solo. Many of you will know he was a Nobel laureate in economics last year; he teaches at MIT. He is an authority in industrial policy and on the impact of technology. He told me that [the document] is one of the finest pieces of work he has ever seen and he monitors the world. And so I can tell you we are going to implement aspects of that because we, as Liberals, believe that we need a strong, dynamic, changing economy. We are wedded to the future; we are not wedded to the past.

We are going to talk about our healthcare system as well. As you know we are enjoying an intense and broad debate about our health-care system. We in Canada have the second most expensive system in the world, second only to the United States which does not have public health insurance. We have wrestled with this problem as has Elinor Caplan, the minister of health, and we understand the threats on our traditional system. We understand the aging population, challenge of demographics; we understand the new technologies, the very high expectations. We also understand the limitations of the design in the system where the government has just become the insurer rather than the planner of the system.

We will be working more to change this system to move more to health promotion and prevention rather than just treatment after the fact. We will be moving toward a community-based system, rather than just an institutional system. I need not remind you that we, as Canadians, have more people per capita in institutions that any other country in the world. And we believe that it is more humane, more caring and more effective to treat people in their communities rather than just in institutions. So we are in the process of, shall I say, massive change—incremental but profound, and it is going to take, like a lot of other changes in society, time to do these things. And it is going to take the help and co-operation of the providers. But I can tell you that the Premier's Council on Health Strategy, which is a bunch of thoughtful people from the professions, consumers, and others, are coming to the conclusion that we have to make these changes. And as we make these changes, we are determined, as Liberals, to respect one basic principle—the principle that we have fought for in the past and will fight for in the future—that is that every single person in this province will have access to quality medicine regardless of their income.

I want to talk a little bit today about a matter that is distressing to me, and I think to all Liberals, and that is the matter of the two societies we are creating. There is an old saying that we do not inherit this land; we borrow it from our children. The question is, what are we passing on to our children? Are we giving them everything they need to deal with the challenges of the future? I see in some ways a province of contrasts—I see wealth unparalleled in the history of this province and in the history of this country, wealth unparalleled in the history of this world. When you look at our gross national product, when you look at our disposable income or some other indicators, or when you walk down Bloor Street, or walk down Hess Village in Hamilton, down Dundas Street in London, and look at all the shops, look at all this marvelous array of consumer goods, you say: "Gee, life looks pretty good."

And then you understand that there is another side to that. Even though we have record growth in GNP, we have record welfare payments as well, record numbers of people using food banks. And you ask yourself how could this be? That when we bask in the warm glow of the material comfort that most of us enjoy, we know so many others who are blown by the chill winds of deprivation. And that, my friends, is in spite of an enormous increase in our contribution to the budget for social services. As I said last night, and I repeat, we have increased that budget by 84 percent since 1984/1985—and in budgeting terms that is a remarkable increase. Yet, it still isn't enough. I think Bob Nixon would tell you if he was here, and he is down chatting with some of his friends across the way, that, I think, is the biggest single increase in our budget—in the range with health care.

So if it isn't just about money, maybe it is about taking a better approach. Maybe we have to use our values, our brains, and think creatively about how we are going to break the cycle of welfare and poverty. We have had a lot of serious looks at this matter including George Thompson's report, as many of you know. The philosophy is a good one, and the philosophy of that report, called Transitions, is one that we as a government share. Our job is to take people who are getting welfare cheques and turn those cheques into paycheques—and we are going to follow that with great determination. We have got to take people who are in the margins and put them into the mainstream. We have got to take people who live in a world of dependence and put them into a world of self-reliance. And that is the basic theme that we want to pursue in following a number of aspects of that report.

The first way we have to start is by removing disincentives. There are so many structural disincentives for people who are on family benefits or some kind of social assistance. They need a little help to feed their families and then they go out and make a few dollars and it is taken away.

It is like the old myth of Sisyphus rolling the rock up the hill. When Sisyphus gets to the top of the hill, just as he gets to the top, the rock slips and it goes back down to the bottom and he starts pushing and pushing it up again and it comes down again in perpetuity. And we have got to help Sisyphus get over the top of the hill and stay on top of the hill.

One of the aspects we have to help with is in the shelter area. We all know the enormous pressure on housing in a number of major communities; it is a function of our growth, the flipside of growth. When we have a 100,000 people a year moving into our community because it is so attractive—and, after all, we are not going to put up visas and say you can't move from other parts of Canada into Toronto or into Ontario—then it puts pressure on the system. And so we are going to help in the shelter area.

And we are going to help in the area of kids as well—an area I know touches many of us personally. Most of us have seen poor kids and you can see a certain pallor on their faces. You know kids are supposed to have a little twinkle in their eye and kind of get a little kick of out of life. Have you seen somebody that just isn't there? Kids weren't asked to be born you know. They are here; it seems to me that each one deserves an opportunity. I remember Shelley and I had our kids at Storybook Gardens one time, and there were a bunch of little kids walking around. Storybook Gardens is a little kids' park in London, and we were looking at some little kids with a group of social workers—and this little boy was walking in kind of a funny way. And I said to Shelley, what do you think is the matter with that little kid? And she said his shoes are too tight. That is a remarkable little observation that in 1989 a little child would have to walk funny because his shoes are too tight.

It seems to me we have the wealth, the creativity, and we have the will to make sure that doesn't happen; to make sure that kids have enough to eat so they can learn at school. This, my friends, is not a simple problem. It is not going to be solved in one day and there are many aspects to it—in housing and in education. It is not just a question of putting more money into welfare payments. It is going to require a commitment by governments and by many other institutions in our society. It is going to require the help of the federal government, which participates in our Canada assistance programs. And I say to you that it disturbs me when I hear the things I am hearing from Ottawa about potential cutbacks in this area. I say it is more important to help kids, to feed kids than it is to build nuclear submarines; that is where I come from.

So my friends, I think that we have a mission ahead of us. As I said I don't think it is going to be easy and I don't think it is going to happen overnight. But I think we can dedicate ourselves to assisting and breaking that cycle which has historically reinforced itself time after time after time. Let me just tell you that I spent Thursday night and Friday morning with the health council listening to some of the experts around the world, looking at the determinants of health—why are some people healthy and why are some people not healthy. What they have found is that there is a very direct correlation between poverty and health. The thing that has really helped advance the general health of the population is our growth in education and our growth in affluence and the social aspects of medicine, not the so called technical aspects of medicine after the fact. So we have got to see these things as cause and effect. We have got to see them in a holistic way, not in a way of little wee boxes unrelated to each other.

And I think we have to renew our determination to bring more people into the mainstream and help them to make their contributions to our society. There are people out there that want work at reasonable wages—who are prepared to work if we give them a little hand with education and child care and a few other things. And that is what we have to do my friends as Liberals; that's what we have to do as members of our society. We want to start in a measured and thoughtful way to make sure that we as Liberals respect one of the basic values that we hold and that is that each person, young and old, will be given equality of opportunity to participate to the full limits of their ability.

Hungry kids don't have that opportunity. You ask the teachers. You ask the teachers if they can teach a kid whose body is racked with hunger pains and they will tell you they can't. So we have to start with basics and we have to move it on from there.

And so my friends, I wanted to share with you the vision of your parliamentary wing and the kinds of goals in general that we'll be pursuing over the next little while. I think that the things I've talked about today are part of our values as Liberals, and part of our responsibilities as human beings, because one of the things we do know is that none of us individually can prosper unless others prosper as well. We cannot allow a society with great gaps to develop where there are stark dichotomies. Those of us that are privileged to have a little more than someone else have a responsibility to bring those others up as well. That is part of our mission and that is part of our goal and I want to thank you and the Liberal party for your support in these values and these goals as we elicit others in society to share our task with us.

Je veux dire en conclusion, que c'est une mission importante, non seulement pour nous maintenant mais pour l'avenir aussi. Nous respectons le droit et la capacité de chaque personne dans notre pays. Et c'est particulièrement important qu'ils aient les mêmes inquiétudes pour les jeunes, qui, en ce moment, n'ont pas les mêmes opportunités que les autres. C'est notre responsabilité de leur donner des opportunités que nous avons.

And that is why my friends we have to take on this mission with dedication and with clarity of purpose, and we have to make sure as Liberals that the mission continues.

CONSERVATION COUNCIL OF ONTARIO'S 35TH ANNIVERSARY DINNER
Toronto, Ontario, October 22, 1986

For 35 years, since before anyone ever heard of acid rain or dioxins and furans, the Conservation Council of Ontario has provided a common meeting ground for people who are concerned about conserving and restoring the natural resources with which our province is blessed.

Largely because of your efforts, the people of Ontario are better acquainted with our province's natural assets, and more determined to preserve and enrich them.

It was because of that record, and the respect it commands, that the Conservation Council was commissioned by the Ontario government to study the issues and factors involved in formulating a conservation strategy for our province.

The report, which we received earlier this year, reflects your longstanding commitment to Ontario's environment.

I can assure you that the government appreciates the expertise that the council brought to this task, and the effort you put into it. The report is under active study and consideration by not one, but three, ministries.

This is a good example of the approach we must take to ensure that we pass on to future generations Ontario's wealth of fresh lakes, clean air, rich forests, and fertile soil. An approach based on co-operation between government, dedicated organizations, and concerned individuals.

The task of preserving Ontario's natural heritage must be carried out by government and people working together, or it won't be carried out at all. We recognize that the tremendous wealth of this province has not been given to us; it has been placed in our trust.

The most important question our generation can ask of ourselves is, are we putting as much into our world as we are taking out?

If we do not leave our children a legacy of clean air, and fresh lakes, bountiful forests, and fertile soil, little else that we leave them will be of any value.

I've been to Grassy Narrows. I've seen the damage environmental neglect can cause—not just to rivers and streams, and land and air, but to whole communities.

In the past year and a half, environmental and resource management issues have reached the top of Ontario's agenda. It's safe to say that they will remain there for at least the rest of our lifetime.

Government has outlined the areas we regard as priorities for the next decade. We see protection of Ontario's environment and effective management of its resources as a vital aspect of each of them.

As was outlined in the Throne Speech, Ontario's most important priorities over the next few years will be restructuring of our industry, educational system, and social services in light of changing economic and demographic trends.

But even as Ontario's economic base shifts to catch up with a changing world economy, our natural resources will always be one of our most important assets.

No new technology can diminish our need for natural resources that are usable, accessible, and plentiful.

No improvements in our educational system will eliminate the need for our young people to be given an understanding of our natural heritage.

At the same time, the aging of our population and the growing importance of tourism can only increase our need for a secure network of recreational outlets.

A healthy economy and a healthy environment are not contradictory—they're complementary.

There is no question that when it comes to a healthy environment we still have much to do.

But we can be proud that in the past 16 months this province has become a recognized leader in environmental protection. One of the reasons for that can be summed up in two words: Jim Bradley.

Jim Bradley is the toughest environment minister in Ontario's history. Some leading environmentalists have called him the only environment minister in Ontario's history.

I just want to take a few moments to point out some of the ways in which government has moved to protect the Ontario environment since Jim Bradley became minister.

One of the first acts was to proclaim the spills bills—withstanding one of the heaviest lobbies in history.

A few months later, our environment ministry launched Countdown Acid Rain, the boldest initiative against acid rain ever undertaken by a government in North America.

In response to the chemical blob that was spilled into the St. Clair River last year, he introduced a program called MISA—the Municipal Industrial Strategy for Abatement—which will result in one of the largest efforts ever undertaken to improve water quality in Ontario.

Just yesterday, Jim announced our plans to prepare a similar abatement program for reducing air emissions. Just like our program for water, it will deal with the newer, more complex chemical emissions like dioxins and furans.

Last July, he introduced legislation to amend the *Environmental Protection Act* and bring enforcement provisions up to date, by raising fines, and in some cases giving the courts the authority to impose jail sentences and even strip polluters of ill-gotten gains.

In introducing every one of these measures, we gave all Ontarians a full opportunity to provide their views. Many knowledgeable and concerned individuals and organizations have put forward arguments that have persuaded us that the penalties we have proposed should be strengthened even further.

We recognize that the overwhelming majority of Ontario corporations conscientiously and consistently obey Ontario's laws. Our legislation is designed to ensure that those who try to skirt them do not receive an unfair advantage.

Of course, many of the environmental threats we face stem from outside our borders.

A year ago today I was in Washington putting forward Ontario's prime transboundary environmental concerns, such as acid rain and pollution of the Great Lakes.

Since that time we have made considerable progress in increasing co-operation with our neighbours. We reached agreements with the state of Michigan to strive for the virtual elimination of persistent toxic substances from our shared waterways, and to co-operate in the battle against acid rain.

We also recognize that ensuring protection of our environment and proper management of our resources requires an across-the-board effort, encompassing all ministries.

Soon after we took office, the Ministry of Natural Resources under Vince Kerrio launched a review of forest management procedures in the province, established new requirements for public involvement in forest management, and initiated extensive public consultation on a policy to protect Ontario's wetlands.

Recognizing the need to preserve farmland in a province where agriculture accounts for one in every six jobs, the Ministry of Agriculture under Jack Riddell has created a cost-sharing program offering farmers financial incentives for soil conservation and environmental protection, and proposed a strengthened foodland preservation policy.

I'm proud of what our ministers have accomplished in all of these areas, but we realize that there is still much to do.

I would like to discuss some of the steps we will take over the next few months.

First, we are now developing a policy to clarify the allowable uses of new provincial parkland. That policy will recognize and respect the fact that parks are meant to meet the needs of people.

Second, we will take steps to ease the property tax burden that threatens the preservation of land that is vital to Ontario's natural heritage. We will extend the principle that has seen the provincial government rebate 60 percent of the property tax on agricultural land and managed forests to provide the same kind of assistance to many heritage lands, such as Class 1 and 2 wetlands.

That is our short-term solution. For the long term, we are initiating an intensive review to determine the best way to ease the property tax burden on heritage land for the long term. We plan to complete the review and have changes in place by the beginning of 1989.

These are two examples of the approach we will take to resource management in this province.

At the same time, we will intensify our efforts to pursue a clean environment.

The Ontario government is proud of what the province has already achieved in the area of toxic waste clean-up, including a $10 million contingency fund established in the past few months.

But we also recognize the need for a national standard and a consistent approach.

That is why Ontario has proposed that the federal government and the provinces join together in a national contingency fund, similar to the US Superfund.

Just three weeks ago, the ministers of the environment of the ten provinces agreed to an Ontario proposal to develop a plan for such a fund.

I should point out that the Superfund has worked so well south of the border that it was recently extended there with increased funding.

In fact, there seems to be very little debate in Washington about its value, only the level of funding that can be afforded.

The same kind of approach is needed in Canada. Environmental concerns are not divided by provincial boundaries; we must be united in dealing with them.

For one thing, we need to ensure that no province suffers unfair disadvantages in industrial competitiveness due to efforts to guarantee a clean and safe environment.

Secondly, to maintain the principle that the polluter must pay, the generators of hazardous materials *across Canada* must provide the necessary funding.

Third, the participation of the federal government is critical in order to draw on its broader and more effective powers to raise specific taxes.

More than ever, we have the ability to shape our environment. Whether it becomes healthier and safer, or sicker and more hazardous, is ours to determine by our actions and our choices.

Round Table on the Environment and the Economy

Toronto, Ontario, March 28, 1989

I'm delighted to join you today to help launch Ontario's Round Table on the Environment and the Economy.

It would be easy for me to stand before you and make dire predictions concerning the fate of the world's environment. Every day the headlines are filled with ominous warnings: environmental degradation is spreading like a cancer throughout our planet; in the tropics, only one tree is planted for every ten cut; the greenhouse effect is dramatically altering the world's climate; and acid rain is spreading across national boundaries destroying our lakes, soil and forests.

If you believed everything you heard, watched, or read, you wouldn't think the future was very promising. But despite all the dire warnings, there's plenty of evidence that we're indeed beginning to clean up our act. Let's look at some examples.

In many of the world's industrialized cities, the air is getting cleaner and suffocating smogs are no longer choking us to death; many nations have taken the lead out of gasoline and paint; there are fish swimming again in formerly polluted rivers and lakes; we've stopped using phosphate detergents; and we're gradually cutting down our use of toxic substances.

And on a grander scale, big industrial and resource projects are starting to incorporate a new sensitivity to environmental impacts, and the development of new environmentally sound technologies have greatly decreased the risks to our environment posed by economic growth.

Here in Ontario, we've taken enormous steps to establish policies and programs which protect both our environment and our valuable natural resources.

Our Countdown Acid Rain program is an example of what can be accomplished when we set our minds to it. When we announced the implementation of this program, industry representatives said it couldn't be done.

Yet here we are today. We've convinced the major producers of acid rain to reduce their emissions. Under this program, sulphur dioxide emissions from these sources will be reduced in Ontario by 66 percent by 1994. Recent reports indicate that we're right on target in meeting our objectives.

And we've had other successes as well. Our Municipal Industrial Strategy for Abatement will ensure cleaner and safer waterways by eliminating discharges of persistent toxic substances. Our drinking water is cleaner and healthier.

As well, we're taking action to phase out the use of chlorofluorocarbons to protect the ozone layer, and we've launched an all-out war on waste by introducing a comprehensive waste reduction and recycling program involving millions of Ontarians. Through the four Rs—reuse, recycling, reduction and recovery—we aim to divert half of Ontario's waste from garbage dumps and incinerators by the year 2000.

Not only have we established some of the toughest pollution standards in North America—we've backed up those standards with strong penalties for polluters.

I'm proud of the province's commitment to the environment. And I'm extremely grateful for the co-operation and support we've received from private industry and environmental groups. By working together, we're taking giant leaps forward in turning our throw-away society into an environmentally sustainable society.

Today, we're taking another leap forward, beginning a new chapter in Ontario's history. We will continue with our efforts to rehabilitate and restore our environment. But today we're firmly establishing a second track of action to link environmental protection with economic growth. We are moving to a truly proactive and preventive planning approach.

Two years ago, the World Commission on Environment and Development, chaired by Norway's Gro Harlem Brundtland, released a landmark document entitled, "Our Common Future." The report provides long-term strategies for ensuring that economic development and environmental protection go hand in hand.

Many experts have referred to it as the "Michelin Guide to global survival."

Several Canadians—Maurice Strong and Jim McNeil—played a prominent role in the Commission's findings. As a follow-up to the Commission's visit to Canada, the Canadian National Task Force on Environment and Economy was created to foster and promote environmentally sound economic development in Canada.

Ontario Environment Minister Jim Bradley and other representatives such as Dow Chemical's David Buzzelli played a key role on the Task Force.

The Task Force recommended that each province establish a round table to help guide us towards better long-term management of our resources and protection of our environment.

Today, I'm pleased to help launch Ontario's round table. We've called together the best and the brightest from small and large industry, agricultural and environmental organizations, our native communities, labour, academia, and government to advise the province on ways to develop an environmentally sustainable society.

People like David Buzzelli and Bill James will give us a strong understanding of industry's role in meeting our common goals. Internationalist Maurice Strong—the creator of the concept of sustainable development and one of the world's leading advocates for environmental protection—will bring a wealth of experience to the table. And environmentalists Colin Isaacs and Toby Vigod, and labour leader Bob White will bring their diverse backgrounds to this forum.

You have a formidable job ahead of you. To people on the street, the term sustainable development is at best some vague abstract notion. In fact, when I first heard the term I thought it was the answer to a clue in a cryptic crossword puzzle.

As ambassadors and pathfinders to communities and businesses, I need you to articulate the changes that must be made to ensure the long-term health of both our environment and economy. You are the focus of this debate. You must draw up a framework and define the parameters of how we must change and how quickly we must make those changes.

I can't emphasize enough how important it is for us to alter our present course of direction. We need more than isolated changes. We need a complete and overall change in attitude, philosophy, and approach if we are to successfully implement this environmental educational process. And those changes must come at every level—from the householder discarding bottles and cans or the kid throwing away candy wrappers, to the boardrooms of big business and the cabinet rooms of the province, the nation, and the world.

Because when we talk about the environment, we're not just talking about clean air, lakes, and rivers. It's much more than that. Environmental protection goes to the very root of the way we live—it concerns our lifestyles, our personal health and our continued economic prosperity.

Our efforts aren't just for us today—they're for our children tomorrow and our children's children. I want to leave them a world they can be proud to inherit. I want to show them that we *can* protect our air and water, that we *can* husband our forests and fisheries, and that we *can* reverse 100 years of exploitation and neglect of our environment.

I see this round table as helping set the agenda for co-operative efforts for decades to come. It will build new partnerships and will help shape the decisions of the future by promoting greater understanding of the essential linkages between environment and economy.

In your deliberations and discussions, you could debate forever what sustainable development means. Instead, I encourage you to develop some common ground and identify a realistic and workable set of principles that will allow us to put into practice the goals of an ecologically sustainable society.

Your mandate includes the development of a conservation strategy, public education, and special demonstration projects. As well, I particularly encourage you to share your expertise with other provincial round tables and with our own Premier's Council on High Technology and Premier's Council on Health Strategy. Through this co-operative and action-oriented framework, I am confident we will succeed in achieving our objectives.

Because I believe we have the will and the commitment to bring about change at every level of our society. Government can't do it alone. Yes, we need to change our own approach and put our own house in order, but we need every industry, community, family, and individual to do their part as well.

Let's take the spirit of co-operation and leadership that characterizes this round table to seize the moment and make Ontario a safer, cleaner and healthier place to live.

And in so doing, I want to wish each and every one of you, the best of luck with this exciting endeavour.

ACHIEVEMENTS IN EMPLOYMENT EQUITY AWARDS DINNER
Toronto, Ontario, October 8, 1985

The Awards for Achievement in Employment Equity are not just the government's way of saluting those who have worked to advance the cause of equality. They are also our way of recognizing that equality cannot be achieved by government alone.

When it comes to driving society toward that goal, the private sector—the people of this province—must grab hold of the wheel. Government can only ensure that the vehicle is in good condition.

Tonight, I would like to talk about some of the things that need to be done to move Ontario along the road to true equality, some of the areas in which we hope you will participate, and some of the ways in which we can be of help.

First, I would like to talk a bit about the principles on which our commitment to equal rights is based.

We believe in an open society—one of open choices, and one in which the individual has the ability and resources to make those choices.

Educational, economic, and social mobility are all elements of an open society.

The essence of freedom is that each of us shares in shaping our own destiny. But not all start out on an equal footing. Those who have been left out, we must seek to bring in. Those who have been left behind, we must help to catch up.

Our commitment to equal opportunity is a commitment to providing each person in this province with an equal chance at the starting line, and an equal chance to go as far and as fast as their abilities will take them.

Some may feel threatened as we seek to include those who have been excluded. It is government's job to make clear how all benefit when all are encouraged to make full use of their potential.

In order to strengthen our ability to compete, we need to increase our productivity and ensure maximum use of our talents. Measures to encourage equal opportunity can enhance these objectives.

Equal opportunity for women can tap the full potential of 52 percent of the population.

It can increase job motivation, decrease turnover, and allow firms to fill more positions from within.

The goal of equal opportunity has been widely accepted for years. What has changed in recent times has been our understanding of how to achieve it.

In the '50s, '60s and '70s, governments addressed the issue of overt discrimination. Laws were passed to prohibit discrimination in hiring, and to require equal pay for equal work.

But when barriers have been in place for decades, it is not enough to simply remove them. Sometimes they take on a life of their own.

In the mid-'70s, it became apparent that positive steps were needed, and affirmative action was born.

Affirmative action, or employment equity, can boast many accomplishments.

Less than two decades ago, in 1967, the average annual earnings of women in the Ontario labour force came to just under 44 percent of the earnings of men. By 1982, it had reached 54 percent. In 1967, 40 percent of women in this province participated in the workforce. By 1982, the rate had risen to 56 percent.

Affirmative action has helped. But there are still wide gaps in wages and opportunities.

It is our task to eliminate those gaps and equalize those opportunities. That is why we are fully committed to employment equity.

We could best do that by adhering to two principles. One, *where possible*, equality should be advanced through co-operation and consultation with business, labour, women, and government. Two, equality can only be achieved through a wide range of measures, dealing with equitable pay, training programs, and child-care funding as well as opportunities for jobs and job advancement.

Sometimes one has to start with symbolic steps. Consider the need for child-care facilities. Recent statistics indicate that 85 percent of single-parent families in Canada are headed by women, and 60 percent live below the poverty line. In her recent royal commission report, Judge Rosalie Abella described child care as "the ramp that provides equal access to the workforce for mothers."

Clearly, government must take the lead in putting that ramp in place. That is why one of my government's first actions was to arrange for a child-care centre at Queen's Park.

We realize that government will have to do much more—to provide child-care facilities to those who cannot afford them, and to encourage the private sector to make such facilities a part of the workplace. But as an initial step we are pleased to set a positive example while providing an immediate benefit to our own employees.

Another area where government action is clearly needed is in ensuring that women receive equal pay for work that is equal in value to that performed predominantly by men.

Despite some positive action programs that have been in place for years, and equal pay laws that have been on the books for decades, the average wage for women in Ontario's full-time workforce is still only 63 percent of the average for men. Women continue to work predominantly in areas which have been undervalued compared to others.

That is why our government stands committed to the principle of equal pay for work of equal value. That is why we are committed to introducing the principle in the public service—covering 80,000 workers—and issuing a green paper to discuss ways of implementing it across the board.

That discussion paper will be tabled in the legislature this fall. Public consultation meetings will be held in several centres across the province.

We are anxious to hear all points of view on this issue. We do not underestimate the difficulties of implementing an equal value system, and we are committed to maintaining Ontario's competitive position. But we will not forsake an important principle just because it may entail difficulties. In the words of Winston Churchill, "difficulties mastered are opportunities won."

At the same time, we must develop new ways to increase acceptance of employment equity.

Last year, at the request of the private sector, the Ontario women's directorate proposed several principles to form the basis of an agenda for employment equity programs. It was distributed to 300 private-sector employers, ten employer associations, and several women's organizations and labour unions.

Tonight, I am proud to announce a final version of that policy statement, a seven-point agenda endorsed by the vast majority of those firms, organized labour, and other organizations.

It will put employers—who sign—on record as supporting employment equity, and the equal treatment principles of the Ontario Human Rights Code. Specifically, it commits employers to:

1. Review and evaluate regularly employee hiring and promotion procedures to ensure that standards, tests, and other selection criteria do not inadvertently limit opportunities for women.
2. Identify and change human resources policies and practices that may prevent or limit the provision of equality in employment for women in hiring, promotion, training, and working conditions.
3. Actively seek qualified women and encourage them to compete for all available positions and training opportunities.
4. Collect information on women's participation in the workplace, and ensure that progress is made in recruiting and promoting qualified women into job categories where they are underrepresented.
5. Consider parental and other family responsibilities when establishing working conditions and benefits.
6. Have senior management monitor progress and conduct regular reviews—to ensure that employment equity practices are being implemented.
7. And communicate the company's employment equity policy to all staff and to the public in order to provide leadership and an example of positive results.

In order to promote the policy statement, and encourage adoption of its principles, our government will, over the next few weeks, take two further steps:

First, we will invite key employers and labour leaders to participate in an employment equity round table—an ongoing effort to develop methods to encourage programs in the private sector.

Under the direction of the minister responsible for women's issues, the round table will meet regularly to develop ways to encourage adoption of employment equity programs, and assess their effectiveness.

Second, we will support employment equity demonstration projects, based in the private sector, to produce valid examples and information that can be shared throughout the province. Such projects will provide an opportunity to develop, refine, and adapt initiatives to the constraints faced in the business environment.

My colleague, the attorney general and the minister responsible for women's issues, will have more to say about these initiatives shortly after the legislature resumes sitting next week.

In attempting to reach the goal of equality, we all have a job to do. I congratulate all of you who are being honoured tonight on your contribution.

THIRD READING OF THE *FRENCH LANGUAGES SERVICES ACT*
Queen's Park, November 18, 1986

Comme certains députés l'ont dit, il s'agit d'une occasion historique à cette Législature. Je veux remercier tous mes collègues de tous les partis, et aussi mes collègues dans les galeries, qui nous ont aidé à préparer ce projet de loi, mais surtout mes collègues à la Législature.

Il existe maintenant une atmosphère différente. Il y a un nouvel esprit de charité maintenant, et je crois que tous les partis ont des attitudes différentes. Nous avons constaté quelque chose de bon aujourd'hui.

C'était mon collègue Albert Roy, comme nous le savons, qui a toujours parlé, dans cette Législature, des droits des francophones, et ce sont ses idées à lui qui, depuis cinq ou six ans, je crois, figurent dans la formation de ce projet de loi.

Nous avons connu des débats avant ce débat-ci, dans un parlement différent. J'ai participé à un tel débat à cette époque-là et c'était l'un des meilleurs débats que j'ai jamais connus à cette Législature. Mais comme nous le savons tous, la situation était alors différente. Il est intéressant de rappeler que tous les partis et tous les députés à la Législature ont appuyé le projet de loi en question, mais c'était l'avis du premier ministre de l'époque que ce n'était pas opportun de le faire dans les circonstances.

Je veux dire, encore une fois, merci à tous mes collègues pour le travail qu'ils ont fait sur ce projet de loi et pour le progrès que nous avons fait ensemble.

As my friend the leader of the New Democratic Party said, it is a great day for francophones, it is a great day for all Ontarians, and it is a great day for Canada.

Je veux lire le télégramme de M. d'Iberville Fortier, Commissaire aux langues officielles, qui dit :

«Retenu à Kapuskasing, je regrette de ne pas pouvoir être présent à l'Assemblée législative à l'occasion de l'adoption de la loi 8 qui marque un tournant historique dans la reconnaissance des droits des Franco-Ontariens.»

I want to translate this because I think it is extremely important, as my friend the leader of the New Democratic Party says, to say the same things in English as in French.

Il s'agit d'une occasion historique, où l'on ne peut pas dire une chose en français et une autre chose en anglais.

Mr. Fortier said to me in his telegram, "I regret that a visit to Kapuskasing prevents my being present to witness the passing of Bill 8, which is surely a turning point in the recognition of French rights in Ontario."

He goes on to say:

«Je félicite vivement son pilote, le ministre Bernard Grandmaître, les partis et tous les parlementaires ontariens. L'Ontario apporte ainsi une magnifique contribution au projet canadien de réconciliation nationale.»

He says: "I would like to convey my heartiest congratulations to its pilot, Mr. Bernard Grandmaître, the minister of francophone affairs, and all the parties and parliamentarians of Ontario. The province has made a major contribution to the Canadian goal of national reconciliation."

C'est comme je l'ai dit : il y a une atmosphère différente à la Législature. Je crois qu'il y a une atmosphère différente au pays aujourd'hui. Comme nous le savons, les relations entre l'Ontario et le Québec sont différentes maintenant, et ce n'est pas seulement entre le Québec et l'Ontario, mais entre toutes les autres provinces et le Québec.

Demain, je vais discuter, avec mes collègues et avec les autres premiers ministres, de la possibilité d'apporter des changements à la Constitution canadienne parce que nous voulons inviter le Québec à faire partie de la Constitution. Je suis optimiste ; j'estime que l'on pourra obtenir de bons résultats.

Mais les Québécois observent de très près ce que l'on fait ici, ce qui se passe à cette Législature, les voix des députés à la Législature. Maintenant, nous avons des débats en français. Ce n'est pas unique, ce n'est pas spécial, comme mon ami l'a dit. Cela fait partie de la période des questions orales de tous les jours et c'est une bonne chose.

Je me souviens de la première occasion où les chefs des trois partis ont discuté d'une question en français à cette Législature. C'était le député de York Sud qui posait une question à l'ancien premier ministre, le député de Muskoka (M. F. S. Miller), qui répondait en français ; et moi, j'y participais en tant que chef de l'opposition.

Ça, c'était une occasion historique aussi. Maintenant, je ne suis pas surpris que la majorité du débat aujourd'hui se fasse en français. Et je ne sais pas, il y a peut-être 20 députés à la Législature qui parlent français et se sentent à l'aise en l'autre langue et l'autre culture. J'espère qu'un jour, tous les gens de l'Ontario vivront cette réalité : moi, mes enfants et les enfants de tous les députés ici et tous les enfants de l'Ontario.

It is a great day. I am told by parliamentary historians, by people who study these matters, that this is the largest leap in the past 120 years for the francophones of Ontario. I am delighted to participate in that. I appreciate very much the support and help of my colleagues. We have much left to do, but now we are putting into practical effect the things we want to guarantee, real rights, not just rights in writing, not just words, but giving a real opportunity to our Franco-Ontarians to live and to work in their language.

Je veux remercier tous mes collègues de ce jour historique, de leur aide en ce qui concerne ce projet de loi. Il est important maintenant que nous utilisions toute la volonté et toute l'énergie nécessaires pour que la mise en oeuvre de cette loi réussisse. Il reste beaucoup de choses à faire. Nous devrons avoir la coopération de toutes les agences du gouvernement et de tous les ministres et tous les ministères.

Il reste beaucoup à faire, mais après aujourd'hui, ce sera la loi de la province. C'est la première étape et c'est d'une très grande importance. À mes collègues du Parti progressiste-conservateur et du Nouveau Parti démocratique, je dis merci beaucoup de ce jour historique.

To a Meeting of Ontario Public Service Executives
Toronto, Ontario, March 5, 1986

Anyone who truly desires to make government achieve all it can for the people it serves would be well advised to consider the words of Lord Dufferin, who in 1878, said:

> The civil service of the country, though not the animating spirit, is the living mechanism through which the body politic moves and breathes and has its being. Upon it depends the rapid and economical conduct of every branch of your affairs; and there is nothing about which a nation should be more particular as to secure in such a service independence, zeal, patriotism and integrity.

These words are as accurate and as relevant today as they were when first spoken 108 years ago.

The civil service of Ontario is still the living mechanism through which the people of Ontario achieve the goals they set for themselves as a province.

In the coming days we will distribute to all Ontario Public Service employees a letter outlining my view of the importance of your role, and how we plan to strengthen it.

Today I would like to discuss with you how we plan to improve the quality of government's service to the public by reaching for new levels of excellence in management, and recognizing that the employees of this government are a critical resource.

The chairman of management board will then announce some of the specific means we will implement to reach that goal.

In the past eight months, I have become more convinced than ever of what I said on June 26, when I was sworn in as premier: We in Ontario can be proud of the most dedicated civil service one could ask for.

Ontario is fortunate in having a proud tradition of dedication in its civil service, a tradition that has come home to me in your support over these past months. I want to thank you for an orderly transition and to assure you that we appreciate your positive attitude and professionalism. The smoothness of the transition was truly admirable—especially when you consider how unaccustomed Ontario is to changes of government.

Your commitment to your job is matched by your commitment to the community. We see evidence of that in outstanding generosity through such important group efforts as the United Way and Federated Health campaigns.

You are the best reminder that government is *people*, that *people* are essential to setting Ontario's direction and delivering Ontario's services. Both inside and outside the public service, our emphasis must be on people.

If the people of Ontario are happy with their government, a great deal of the credit for that must go to the Ontario Public Service. You—and those you supervise—are the only people who can give daily life to the directions we set in public policy.

We need your help, for example, to turn our goal of open government into reality.

If open government means anything, it means public servants who are open to questions and suggestions for innovation even while they are open in the day-to-day pursuit of the public agenda. It means being accessible, available for consultation, both to your colleagues and staff, and to the members of the public you serve. It means straightforwardness in explaining to anyone who asks all the reasons that led to government decisions. Open government is service by people who close the gap between appearance and reality.

We need to create a more forthcoming climate that makes the public see that *people* help them rather than a "bureaucracy" or a "system." We need to create a climate that allows smoother teamwork among those of us within government—and more welcoming service to those we all work for.

Our commitment to a clear agenda with no hidden guidelines is essential if we are to diminish public cynicism and allay anxiety on the part of groups we serve. It is just as essential if we are to make it possible for you—and all 80,000 members of the Ontario Public Service—to participate fully and effectively in meeting our goals.

That is why we sought to clearly set out—through the strategic planning process—what I see as the three prime long-term goals of this government: The need for Ontario to chart a course that will allow it to achieve lasting prosperity in the advanced industrial society, the need for Ontario to develop an education system based on excellence and training for life, and the need to come to terms with the shifting demands that will be placed on our health-care system and other government services in light of the major demographic changes we will see in the population of the province.

That process is a good example of how we intend to keep you apprised of our long-term goals, and fully involved in reaching them.

Just as we will allow no walls or barriers to separate this government from the people we serve, we will allow no walls or barriers to divide those of us who serve the people.

We will allow no walls or barriers to stand between us and your ideas on how to streamline government rules, processes and programs to allow us to better assist the people of the province.

Let there be no mistake about it: your ideas are welcome. The ideas of those you supervise are welcome. Indeed, they are eagerly sought.

Let there be no doubt that in this government no rule is irreversible, no process is sacrosanct, no program is unchangeable if there is a better way. We invite your help in finding that better way.

We will also allow no walls or barriers to prevent policies from being carried out in a way that will solve the problems they were meant to solve.

The importance of accountability must be stressed throughout the public service.

We must all be prepared to enter into a pact—an interlocking chain of objectives that are attainable, based on plans that are realistic.

We will allow no walls or barriers to block us from making our expectations clear to all in the public service.

I meet regularly with ministers and deputy ministers to ensure that our goals are clear and our efforts compatible. I expect deputy ministers to carry the word forward, and spell out our expectations to senior managers, and I expect senior managers to do the same for their staff. The onus is on you to see that our goals are clearly articulated to the people who must help us reach them.

In short, if we are to eliminate the walls and barriers *in front* of government and *within* government, you must be the people who tear down the bricks.

And if we are going to achieve the goals we set, you must be the people who make the most of our resources.

I do not have to tell you that demand for government services is growing while our access to resources is shrinking. You are the people who hear of the demand most often; you are the people who monitor the resources most closely.

Consider education, for example, which is Ontario's most important vehicle on the road to an advanced industrial society. We need a variety of new, innovative tools to help prepare people for the rapidly changing economy they will face over the next 30 years. But we must balance any increase in our capacity to pay for those tools against the risk of slowing the economy in its tracks.

There is only one way to create breathing room between the rock of rising needs and the hard place of diminishing resources. That is by making a supreme effort to harness the most important resource at the disposal of any government: people and their ideas.

That is why all of us who work in government must push ourselves to the utmost limit of our abilities. And that is why we in this room must provide the leadership that will tap the competence of all who report to us. By competence I do not mean just the unreproachable performance of specific duties day in and day out. I mean, rather, an understanding of how your work fits into a broad plan, and an alertness to the need for improving the overall efficiency of your government.

That attitude of those who work for the people must never be: "that's none of my business." Rather it must be: "doing a better job for the people of Ontario is *my* most important business."

That is why we are committed to introducing a systematic approach to developing a senior management pool, men and women with the ability to move across departments, and take on positions of leadership in any part of the government.

We need people with specific skills, but sufficiently developed as generalists that they can provide leadership in line ministries or central agencies, in the social, justice, or economic development fields.

We are going to have to develop key personnel, and train them to handle vital posts across the board. I'm going to be heavily involved, and so will my Cabinet. And so will you.

Quite simply, deputy ministers and senior managers are going to be held responsible for developing their ministries' human resources in the same way they are responsible for managing its capital, programs, and expenditures.

In Ontario's civil service resides the largest pool of talent and energy in the province. We have more PhDs than any university, more skilled executives than any corporation, more creativity than is at the disposal of any other employer. We must recognize the vast wealth of our human potential, and draw upon it fully.

In setting out on the review of human resources management, we set out to reach the potential of every public servant in Ontario. To reach that potential we must follow a path built on the bricks of clear direction, tight coordination, consistent two-way communication, and concrete recognition for those who meet new standards of excellence.

First, everyone must know what is expected of them. They must be familiar with the immediate goals of their ministry or branch, and how it relates to meeting the needs of the people of Ontario.

Second, everyone must understand how the immediate work of their department or branch helps to advance the long-term objectives of the government—and meet the future needs of the people of Ontario.

Third, everyone must be kept constantly abreast of whether their efforts help meet those goals and objectives—or whether they fall short.

Fourth, work that advances those goals and objectives must be rewarded. Work that does not must be redirected. And work that consistently falls short must be reassessed. You are the people who must ensure that the entire public service knows what is expected of them, understands how it fits into the government's overall plan, and receives regular feedback on their work.

That is why individual performance reviews and annual management reviews will be more important than ever. I am counting on you to provide that essential link that must connect all elements of government and ensure they work in harmony.

To help you fulfill that role, you will receive the resources you need to provide a positive work environment—one that allows you to train staff, and encourage excellence.

With shrinking resources, every position in government takes on greater importance. I am counting on you—our deputy ministers and senior managers—to ensure that we have the right people in the right places, with the necessary training and the necessary resources, to do the job as effectively as possible.

I hardly need to remind you that there is no easier scapegoat for the powerless and the frustrated than an impersonal, rigidly structured government. Remember Huck Finn's father? As Huck told it, "Pap would get hold of enough whiskey for two drunks and one delirium tremens, and, whenever his liquor begun to work, he most always went for the government."

It is partly an absence of compassion and sensitivity to the individual that inspired pap's unforgettable rages against the government of his time. My example is pointedly American and far removed from Ontario today, but it is useful as a cautionary lesson.

Openness and competence in government require a new effort of our minds and our will, but compassion in government can only come from the heart. If we can be sensitive as individuals, then our programs will be sensitive too.

We need to strengthen our orientation to people—to meeting their needs in a way that recognizes their unique nature and circumstances. In many ways, how we deliver is as important as what we deliver.

Those who work for this government demonstrate their commitment to that principle in a number of ways: prompt response to requests for assistance; friendly, courteous and helpful service; and service in a range of languages that reflects the changing multicultural character of this province.

Service to the public must be the common denominator in all of our work—from policy development to program delivery. The quality of compassion must be evident throughout government.

Compassionate government begins in this room. The need for compassion is just as great in our relations with those who work for us as it is in our relations with those for whom we work.

You will be making decisions that will allow us to improve service and re-adjust priorities. That must be done with efficiency, but it must also be done with humanity.

As we shift resources, and develop new approaches and mechanisms to better serve the people of Ontario, we cannot forget those who have given their best for many years.

As a government we are committed to retraining programs that will allow the people of Ontario to adapt to a changing society with new demands. We can offer our own employees no less.

I need your help to ensure that the Government of Ontario meets its central objectives: openness—both to the public and to our employees; competence—both in applying our resources and managing them; and compassion—both to those we work for, and those who work for us.

I have great confidence in the structures the chairman of management board will now outline. I believe they can set the course for the needed improvements—in setting goals, achieving them, obtaining input, providing feedback, measuring performance, and rewarding it.

ANNOUNCING THE HONOURABLE JOHN BLACK AIRD'S STUDY INTO CONFLICT OF INTEREST
Queen's Park, July 2, 1986

Government faces no issue more complex than the question of how it can ensure its actions and decisions are based solely and clearly on the basis of the public interest with no reasonable suggestion of a conflict in that interest.

This is not a new question, nor one that is unique to Ontario. Indeed, it has been raised frequently in every democratic jurisdiction. I am sure all parties in every jurisdiction would agree on the need to guarantee that nothing detracts from the basic public trust that is central to democracy. At the same time, our regulations and guidelines must be drawn so as to encourage the widest degree of participation.

I wish to make it clear at the outset that I have the utmost confidence in the ministers of my government. I appreciate their efforts to adhere to the guidelines that have been in place since 1972, but at the same time I must acknowledge that the rules and the system we thought worked well in the past may not be good enough today. It has become more and more difficult to determine what is a genuine conflict of interest as opposed to what might only be perceived as a conflict of interest and the consequences that flow from each one.

It is important to recall that former Premier Davis never regarded his 1972 guidelines as exhaustive or as encompassing all possible situations. They must change with the times and adapt to new circumstances. We must find a more impartial way to examine suggestions of conflict of interest and separate the perceived conflicts from the genuine ones. The tools we currently have at our disposal to do that are imperfect at best.

In the 14 years since guidelines were first introduced, society has undergone many changes, and government must catch up. We must ensure that the principles acted upon in 1972 are reflected in guidelines and regulations most appropriate to the 1980s and the 1990s.

The functions of government and the private sector are becoming increasingly interrelated. It would be difficult to think of a profession or business that does not require regular contact with government and is not affected by legislation and government actions.

Certainly it would be impossible to think of a single piece of legislation that affects none of us in this House. Every piece of farm legislation, for example, could affect every member who owns a farm. Legislation regarding teachers' pensions, to cite another example, affects members on all sides of this House.

Only a political, economic, and social hermit could claim to be entirely removed from the business of this legislature, because to be removed from the business of this legislature is to be removed from society.

The guiding principle that has been accepted by all is that no one should be hindered from participating in the development of a policy from which he benefits, so long as that benefit is not specific or unique to him. Are the people of this province not entitled to know, however, when their elected representatives may stand to benefit financially from legislation? That, it seems to me, is the other side of that principle.

Moreover, we are now well into the era of the two-career family. The families of politicians are no exception. To what degree are we prepared to limit the business and professional endeavours of the spouses, children and other relatives of those who serve the public? Obviously, the business and professional activities of the spouses of politicians add to the complexity of sorting out what may or may not constitute a genuine conflict of interest.

Fourteen years after guidelines were first adopted, we need to examine them to determine how they can be improved and how they can be most effectively implemented.

1. We need clearer guidelines to deal with issues of the 1980s and 1990s.
2. We need a better mechanism to provide advice regarding ministerial disclosure, a mechanism respected by all members of the House and universally across the province.
3. We need a better decision-making forum to determine what is in fact a genuine conflict of interest.

In bringing our standards up to date in this area, there are many broad questions we must address.

Do current regulations fully and fairly cover all situations that could suggest a conflict of interest in the decision-making process?

How far should we go in monitoring the business and financial arrangements of spouses and children and other relatives?

Even accepting the principle that no conflict exists in the case of members of this House voting on matters that could benefit a group to which they belong, should we nevertheless require all members to declare a connection each time such legislation is considered?

Should there be requirements of disclosure for party leaders?

Should all members of the legislature be required to file declarations of holdings, given the expanded functions we are trying to ensure for them?

Should there be a restriction on some forms of outside work for all members of the legislature? Should there be a moratorium before former ministers may accept an appointment to the board of a corporation with which they dealt in office, as federal guidelines require?

Should there be a moratorium before former ministers are permitted to engage in private dealings with the government or represent private clients in dealings with the government? How long should such a moratorium last?

This is by no means an exhaustive list of the questions that must be considered. There are many grey areas in this issue. No doubt, there are many questions of judgment, but there are also questions of whose judgment.

Obviously, all members of this House must always be free to raise any issue that concerns them, but would it meet Ontario's standard of fairness to prevent a minister who has received legal advice that he or she has complied with the conflict-of-interest guidelines to stand accused of a violation because of a conflicting opinion?

Should consideration be given to the establishment of a body that could advise on the appropriateness of arrangements before they are entered into and make recommendations to the premier after suggestions of perceived conflicts of interest have been raised?

These are just some of the questions that come to mind. They are not hard-and-fast proposals. I would be grateful for the help of all the members of the House in participating and tackling this issue.

We obviously cannot be expected to answer all the questions related to this issue today, but I wish to inform the House of actions I am taking immediately to begin to deal with these concerns.

I am pleased to inform the House that the Honourable John Black Aird has agreed to take on the job of sorting out this issue's long-term implications, ensuring existing guidelines regarding conflict of interest are met in the short term and reporting to me as soon as possible.

Mr. Aird has graciously advised me that he will perform this task at no cost. I requested him to retain whatever assistance he requires, including the use of members of his law firm.

Mr. Aird's mission will be threefold.

Mr. Aird will take on the task of examining the statements of disclosure that have been filed and ensuring and attesting that the guidelines have been fully and correctly applied to all assets held by ministers and parliamentary assistants. This will serve as a valuable addition to the system that has been in place for more than a decade. All his findings in this regard will be filed with the clerk of the legislature, it is hoped, by the end of August.

Mr. Aird has agreed to provide an independent assessment of the validity of any suggestion of conflict of interest that may arise between now and the completion of his long-term task. I ask all members, including those of the opposition parties, to provide Mr. Aird with any information regarding potential conflicts of interest. Mr. Aird's assessment will be provided to me for public release.

He will consider the entire question of defining and evaluating what is, in fact, a conflict of interest and devising the most appropriate regulations in this area. Mr. Aird will review and make recommendations regarding the value of a permanent independent commission to review suggestions of conflicts of interest and will also study the question of whether such a commission should be involved in ensuring, on a continuing basis, that the disclosure made by ministers and other affected parties is up to date.

He will make recommendations about the form of a commission and the process involved. Mr. Aird will review work that has been done in this area at the federal level and in other provinces. He will meet with the opposition parties and others who have done work in this area. At the very early stages of his work, he will discuss with the opposition parties questions relevant to its scope and the establishment of an appropriate time frame for his report.

At this time, I wish to thank Mr. Aird for his willingness to take on the assignment. I express the appreciation of the government and, I believe, the entire House for his time and effort. His readiness to assist us in this way is typical of the generous commitment he has displayed to the welfare of this province.

Mr. Aird's recommendations will be passed onto the Standing Committee on the Legislative Assembly to allow for the most thorough and open consideration by all members of the legislature. I seek the participation of all parties in dealing with this issue as openly, expeditiously and fairly as possible. We all have a great deal at stake. If we are to develop a system that will deal with these questions, all of us must participate.

60TH ANNIVERSARY FOR ONTARIO SEPARATE SCHOOL TRUSTEES' ASSOCIATION
Toronto, Ontario, April 20, 1990

It's a great pleasure to join you in celebrating your diamond jubilee.

Your anniversary celebration is taking place in the midst of an exciting week. I understand that over the past four days, more than 23,000 catholic educators from all over North America gathered in Toronto for the convention of the National Catholic Education Association.

Going through their program, I saw hundreds of seminar topics, and plenty of experts on every subject. It sort of reminded me of one of our Cabinet meetings—except that our agendas are even longer.

I found a number of seminar topics that some of the people here would find *very* interesting:

For example, I thought Sean Conway might benefit from the seminar entitled "Ontario Separate School Education—How it Works."

Then there was one that was just perfect for Cardinal Carter—"Major Gift Solicitation," except in the cardinal's case he should be teaching the seminar instead of taking it. In fact, I think he wrote the curriculum for the advanced course.

That was one side of the convention. There was another side that was a great deal more sobering.

Seminars on topics such as family violence, street proofing our children, and AIDS education for elementary students, bring home the fact that preparing our children for the world outside their school doors is a much more complex process than it used to be.

We can't hide our children from the world, but we can equip them to deal with the challenges that await them. We can do that by making children the centre of a strong support network that encompasses the family, the school and the community working in concert.

That, it seems to me, is one of the things the separate school system in this province does extremely well.

You treat students as a link that ties together parents, educators and the community. Indeed, the religious community has established a tradition in the separate school system that leaves no question about the fact that the child is the centre of the school, and the school is the centre of the community.

The OSSTA has played an important role in making that process work. Over the years, you have responded well to the challenge of providing the best our society can offer to the community you serve.

At times that has been a difficult task. Certainly, 60 years ago when the OSSTA was founded, the challenge to catholic education was great, and the road ahead was long. But you persevered.

For more than fifty years you persevered. My colleagues in the Liberal Party and I thought forty-two years was tough. But you broke our record.

One area where you have persevered very successfully is in achieving the completion of the separate school system in Ontario through the extension of funding through Grade 13.

It was an effort that involved changing a lot of attitudes—both government attitudes and public attitudes. It was a struggle that dates back to the 1929 Supreme Court ruling on Tiny Township—a ruling which led to the birth of the association whose success we are celebrating today.

Along the way there were some steps forward and some steps back. For example, in the 1950s things were so bad that when Premier Frost stood in this very hotel and announced that separate school funding would not be cut back from Grade 8 to Grade 6—not that it would be expanded, just that it would not be cut back—he was greeted with tumultuous applause.

In fact, reports of that day state "there was bedlam in the ballroom. The premier was engulfed in applause."

You can imagine the response he might have gotten for announcing an extension of funding.

But though the struggle was long, we all agree that it was worth it. And our pride in the final result was confirmed when Sister Catherine MacNamee, president of the NCEA, observed a couple of days ago that American catholic educators "think they've died and gone to heaven when they hear about Ontario's financing system."

The achievement of completion of separate school funding is commemorated in one of the four paintings that are just outside this room. I want to take this opportunity to thank the OSSTA executive for presenting me with prints to hang in my office.

There have been a number of other important areas where you've also persevered and succeeded.

For example in 1985, less than 4 percent of capital expenditures by the Government of Ontario were earmarked for education. By 1989, the allotment for schools rose to more than 9 percent of all government capital expenses. And we're letting you know earlier what the board by board allocations will be so that you can have more time to plan how to spend it.

Last fall, the minister of education, Sean Conway, introduced, and the legislature passed, legislation that is meant to help address an inequity in education funding. By introducing pooling of the assessment of public corporations we're ensuring a fairer distribution of revenues.

But the greatest change has taken place within the separate school system itself. You are creating centres for lifelong learning—an objective we're pursuing throughout our education system.

Lifelong learning means a number of things, including giving kids an early start.

All separate school boards already offer senior kindergarten, and fifty-seven out of fifty-nine boards offer junior kindergarten programs.

We strongly believe in this principle. We believe that providing a child with literacy and language development as well as social skills in the early years gives them a springboard to opportunity. That's why we're committed to full day senior kindergarten and half day junior kindergarten.

At the same time we've begun to address the need for child-care programs within the school environment for children who are too young for junior kindergarten. We have been actively consulting with separate school representatives on this policy, and we're carefully considering your views.

It's because of our belief in the importance of the early years that we have moved to reduce class sizes in Grades 1 and 2, so that teachers can devote the time that is necessary to help each individual child get off to a good start.

I was visiting a school a couple of months ago and the principal told me that the reduction of class sizes in the early grades was the biggest and best step forward for education in this province in decades.

We're giving our children a good start—a start they can build on throughout their school years and beyond. We're making sure they get a chance to learn how to learn—not just to memorize the answers but to know how to find the answers for themselves.

We're giving them the chance to learn how to use logic, how to solve new problems, how to prepare for a lifetime of learning.

Lifelong learning also means giving adults a second chance.

As part of the completion of the system, separate schools are becoming active centres of continuing education, with a rapidly expanding program of adult learning programs sponsored by boards all over the province.

The completion of the separate school system is broadening the learning process in another important way. Young people in your schools are getting an opportunity to bridge the world of learning and the world of work, through a rapid expansion of co-operative education.

Across this province, many separate school board co-op education programs have undergone dramatic growth. Three or four years ago, the Dufferin-Peel Separate School Board had only a few dozen participants. Today, it has more than 600 participants and over 1,000 training stations. The Metropolitan Toronto Separate School Board has more than 1,400 students participating in co-op programs.

I'm sure that these gains have not been made without pain.

But let's consider the rewards. Co-op is not only helping our children to find jobs, it's helping them build careers.

Students are treating co-op placements as an opportunity to sample future careers. They're spending time in hospitals to see if they would like being nurses or doctors, and if they have a knack for it. They're working in the tourism and hospitality industry to find out if their futures lie in resort management.

They're going to the Royal Ontario Museum to discover if a childhood passion can become a lifelong pursuit. There's scarcely an occupational area that has not been developed as a co-op placement somewhere in Ontario.

There are even cases of students accepting placements in spite of the fact that they won't get an OAC credit for the effort of completing a work term. They simply want to experience what it's like to work, and explore a career interest.

Co-op programs help kids gain confidence in themselves. They help kids find their future.

Co-op education is accomplishing something else as well. It's involving our whole community in the education process.

In Bruce-Grey, for example, a co-op program at the Bruce Nuclear Power Development Station has seen Ontario Hydro and the Canadian Union of Public Employees, in conjunction with *both* publicly funded boards, offer opportunities for senior students to use the community as a career lab.

It's a model of co-operative education—classes are conducted on site, with the support of both management and labour. But it's also a model of a co-operative approach to education, with both boards working together through joint staffing and monitoring arrangements. It's just one example of the many partnerships that have been forged over the last few years.

As I look ahead I see an even larger emphasis on co-operative education emerging as one of the great waves of the future.

Co-op and other programs help young people to prepare for the world of work. This is an area we have been putting more emphasis on—and it's one that will become an even more important priority.

Over the past couple of years, the area of skills development has been the prime focus of the Premier's Council—a group made up of representatives of business, labour, government, and educators that is helping to prepare Ontario to meet the future.

The Council has been conducting the most extensive studies in the history of the province into what our job needs will be over the next few decades, and what we must do to prepare our children to meet them. In the next couple of months we will be releasing the Council's report on how to ensure that our children are ready to compete, and soon after that we will be following up with specific policies and programs.

Ladies and gentlemen, we have a great deal to do to prepare our children for the twenty-first century, and only a little time in which to do that. We all have to be partners in this—and that must include *both* publicly-supported school systems, working together.

The completion of the separate school system has not been achieved without sweat and sacrifice. But your efforts have been rewarded; it has been worth it.

And now that the separate school system is complete, you can work together better than ever with your sister school boards, to create new opportunities for the students in both school systems, to create new opportunities for people throughout your communities.

On the sixtieth anniversary of the founding of your association, you can look ahead with confidence; you can look with pride. Congratulations.

DAVID PETERSON
THE POLITICIAN

LONDON CENTRE NOMINATION MEETING
London, Ontario, October 9, 1984

Ladies and gentlemen, welcome to the 1985 Ontario General Election.

Welcome to *Campaign Ontario*.

Tonight we begin the exciting democratic process of changing the way we govern ourselves in this province. Change is certainly required. The Conservatives have been in power in Ontario since 1943. Fully 41 years, longer than most of us have lived. Maurice Richard was a rookie when the Tories took over at Queen's Park.

The departure of Bill Davis does not change history. The Tories may change their leader, but they will not change their style of government. It is entrenched; it is rooted in the past. It is a government which must be replaced because it cannot be restored.

We all spent a lot of time this summer listening to Brian Mulroney, with Bill Davis at his side, telling us that it's time for a change because power corrodes. Well, if Brian Mulroney is right, then the Tory government in Ontario has rusted right through to the core. In fact, the Tories have been in power for so long—forty-one years—that they have taken the Ontario voters for granted.

There was a time when the Tories had a partnership with the people. Not now. Theirs is a partnership rooted in the past. Special interests. Big business. Partnership fashioned by opinion polls and greased by privilege.

We want to include young people. We want to include the unemployed, minority groups, senior citizens, women, farmers, tenants, northerners, citizens of Eastern Ontario...

The Tories will tell you they are partners with the people, much like Ontario Hydro would like you to think its customers are partners. But

Without Walls or Barriers: The Speeches of Premier David Peterson, Library of Political Leadership Series, by Arthur Milnes and Ryan Zade, Editors. Montreal and Kingston: McGill-Queen's University Press,
© 2017 The School of Policy Studies, Queen's University at Kingston. All rights reserved.

does anyone really believe that you, the consumer, have a say to how Ontario Hydro is run?

And what about the partnership promised by the NDP? Theirs is a partnership tied to the big union bosses and socialist ideology. They would nationalize our resource companies and banks.

These are not our priorities. It is clear socialist solutions will never work in Ontario.

The election we will fight, the campaign we are now waging, is about change—the change to a government that works for everyone.

The people of Ontario have the clear choice. They have the power to build a better Ontario.

During the election we will be talking about how to return excellence and relevance to our educational system, proposals to provide jobs and needed training, and quality health care for all.

We offer change from forty-one years of one-party rule. The Tories would like us to think that they have managed our public affairs wisely and well, yet I still hear the echoing cries of those many forgotten men and women who lost life savings in the collapse of trust companies for no other reasons than the failure of the government at Queen's Park to protect their interests. Ask them if the Tory partnership is working.

I am angered by a 41-year-old government which frets more about self-congratulatory advertising than it does about putting our young people to work.

I am angered by a 41-year-old government that finds $40,000 to spend on a plastic bookmark proclaiming its own virtues, yet withholds financial aid from the disabled.

I am angered by a 41-year-old government that has squandered billions on unused land banks and unnecessary Ontario Hydro plants.

I am angered by a 41-year-old government that would think of buying a $10 million executive jet for the premier while farmers are losing their farms.

I am angered by a 41-year-old government that squanders $650 million on an oil company. How can this be justified when, if Terry Fox had lived in this province, he would be denied help to buy an artificial limb?

The next election will enable those who have been excluded from the Tory partnership to be heard. The choice is clear. More of the same, or a change to caring, responsible government. We intend to restore Ontario as a province of opportunity, not a province of polls, patronage, and privilege. These are our priorities.

I am personally convinced that the people of Ontario are ready to change the government at Queen's Park. We Ontario Liberals have been a good opposition. Now, we Ontario Liberals are ready to be a good government.

We will offer an open and accountable government, in which people are served with justice and equity.

It's time to elect a government that works for people, not just for the bosses of big business or big unions.

The people have the power to build a better Ontario.

FIRST CAMPAIGN SPEECH AS LEADER

Toronto, Ontario, March 25, 1985

I'm ready for my first election campaign as leader of the Ontario Liberal Party.

This is a great opportunity for us to present our Liberal policies and programs to the highest jury in the land.

We've got a great slate of candidates... in every part of this province... and they are all anxious to get out of the starting gate.

Mr. Miller and I have an altogether different picture of the kind of Ontario that we want to build. During this campaign, I look forward to debating with him anywhere and anytime the future course of Ontario.

And I am also confident that he will want an opportunity to defend his record because what he has done to this province will be a very important part of this election campaign.

Between now and election day, May 2, the voters will be taking a closer look at Frank Miller's Ontario with its insensitive record of hospital closings and unfair taxation.

They will also be looking closely at the kind of Ontario offered by the union-dominated NDP.

And I believe they will reject both of those narrow-focus visions.

I believe they will vote for a much broader vision. A vision that embraces their kind of Ontario.

They will vote Liberal because ours is the only party committed to guaranteeing equality of opportunity for *all* of the people of Ontario.

The Ontario Liberal Party is the only party that is not in the back pocket of any special interest group—not of the bank presidents or of the union bosses.

That's why my party can offer the bold, uncompromised, leadership needed to build a better life for all Ontarians.

We can offer you an opportunity to vote yourself a better future.

We can offer you a better kind of Ontario.

You need a government that is open and accountable. A government that treats you with respect and represents your interests.

A government that doesn't owe anything to anyone other than to you, the voters, who put it into office.

That's the kind of government that I want to lead. And that's the kind of Ontario that my government would build.

That's why my party has been outlining policies and programs in every major area of Ontario life—in jobs and in health, in education and fair taxation, on women's issues and on racial tolerance, in the environment and in agriculture, in housing, on hydro and in small business and in equality of opportunity.

There will be no more giveaways without guaranteed jobs in our programs. We have too much respect for the taxpayers.

We will ensure that tax money creates jobs that increase productivity and opportunity.

There will no longer be one standard of health care for the rich and another for the poor. We'll ban extra-billing, bring in denticare and abolish the OHIP premiums. We'll ensure quality treatment for all and put a much greater emphasis on preventing illness.

I want a real Ministry of Health—not a ministry of treatment.

My children and your children will have an education system that will equip them with the skills and attitudes needed to compete in this tough new technology-based world. And we'll ensure a better linkage between the world of education and the world of work and jobs.

Women will have equality of opportunity and participation. They will know that they will receive equal pay for work of equal value in a Liberal Ontario. Government will lead the way on that. Affordable child care will be available to all.

Our ethno cultural minorities, our handicapped, and our women... all citizens will be guaranteed equality of opportunity—in every line of endeavour. They will participate fully in the institutions that govern their lives. We will have no second-class citizens.

And these aren't policies or programs that we have cooked up for the purposes of this election.

We're not like the Tories who wait until three days before calling an election—four years after they were last elected—to announce something like Frank Miller's Enterprise Ontario program.

We don't believe in doing nothing for four years and then having the taxpayers foot the bill for a media extravaganza to announce what you're going to do in the *next* four years.

We don't believe in such manipulative deceit as the Enterprise Ontario program—a hodgepodge of something old, something new, something borrowed, something blue. All fancied up with a $1.3 billion tartan ribbon.

That's why the policies and programs that we will be expanding on during this election campaign are all there on our record—in speeches across this province and in the legislature.

Throughout this election campaign, the voters are going to discover the darker side of Frank Miller's Ontario.

Despite the folksy Miller's Ontario song they played at the Tory leadership convention, Mr. Miller whistles an altogether different tune when it comes to getting tough with our hospitals, our poor, and our senior citizens.

This election campaign will give the voters an opportunity to look more closely at the record of a Tory premier who believes he can weigh lives against dollars.

They're going to discover a man who went around this province closing down or cutting the funding for community hospitals because he had other priorities.

And they'll wonder why, to this day, Frank Miller says: "I still think I was right."

Just this Friday, in Stratford, he was at it again. Saying "no" to hospital funding. Don't be misled. That's the real Frank Miller.

I want them to remember that Frank Miller stuck the sales tax on hamburgers and ice cream cones, feminine hygiene products, and other items so he could yank more money out of the pockets of ordinary Ontarians.

I want them to remember that Frank Miller supports extra-billing.

That's Miller's Ontario. That's the reality of the Ontario that Frank Miller has always believed in. Always will believe in. Most Ontarians will soon realize that Miller's Ontario is not their kind of Ontario.

Youth, women, young families, people from minority groups, those who have been left out in Northern and Eastern Ontario will soon realize that there isn't a place for them to stand and a place for them to grow in Frank Miller's Ontario.

They will reject a premier who supported calls to abolish the minimum wage, end Medicare, and lift rent controls, because removing them would be returning to "the way the world was as I thought it should be." A world without social justice.

Frank Miller isn't going to build your kind of Ontario.

And you know that the union-dominated NDP isn't going to build it either.

By the time the NDP government finished nationalizing Inco and Falconbridge, and the other primary resource companies, and creating a state-owned car company, there would be no room left for entrepreneurs anywhere in Ontario.

They'd bring in a 32-hour work week with no cut in pay, but—and this is a big but—there'd be nowhere to work. The job producers would have been forced out of business because they couldn't afford to pay the same pay for less work.

The NDP is not going to build your kind of Ontario.

But we will.

Only last week, the Liberal Party said it was about time we allowed the sale of beer and wine in grocery stores in *your* Ontario because it makes sense and were mature enough as a society to handle it.

It's convenient. It's good for small business. It creates jobs. It's good for the consumer. And it's time to cut government regulations which interfere in every aspect of our personal lives.

That is just another good example of why the Liberal Party rejects Miller's Ontario. And the NDP's Ontario.

There is no beer and wine in the grocery stores of Miller's Ontario because that would upset the cozy relationship between the government and the brewers who monopolize the beer industry in this province

There would be no beer and wine in grocery stores in the NDP's Ontario because that would upset the big union leaders who control the NDP.

Throughout this election campaign, I will be asking the voters of Ontario to think hard about the kind of place they want to live in. To think hard about the place they want for their children and for their children's children.

And I'm asking you, the people of Ontario, to vote yourselves a better future.

To vote for your kind of Ontario.

Thank you very much.

ELECTION NIGHT
London, Ontario, May 2, 1985

This is truly a magic moment! And it just proves what we have been saying. Tonight, there is a sunrise in Ontario. C'est un nouveau jour pour tous les Ontariens.

So I want to say to you, my very dear friends in this room tonight, and indeed to everyone who worked in this campaign, for every party across this province, for everyone who exercised their democratic rights today, of participating in the greatest expression of democracy, I thank you. I thank you.

We all won something tonight. We won an opportunity to work together, to solve our problems in common. And I must say I am very proud to have led the party that received the most votes in this election.

[I learned] on this campaign we have far more which unites us in this province than divides us. And our job is to build on those strengths, not to tear apart.

The message to all of us is very clear: that the people of Ontario see value in what each of us has to say. Now our job, our job is not to fix blame for the past, but to move courageously and boldly into the future. That is the challenge for everyone.

The next legislature—let me tell you this—the next legislature will only work if we who are elected work in the spirit that has been generated in this great province, a spirit that truly represents the people of this province, and that is a spirit of goodwill, a spirit of generosity, a spirit of co-operation. And I believe we can do that.

But there is in the result tonight a very strong message and that is that the people of this province want forward-looking and compassionate government. On vous dit que nous devons batir un meilleur Ontario, tous ensemble.

Our job is to harness that spirit, to use it to deal with our problems and in order to do so we must do so immediately in calling the legislature back. We must deal immediately with the problems of jobs, unemployment, education that is meaningful and relevant to our young people, reforms in health care to make it fair for everyone. We must deal with women's issues to bring women to full, equal participation in our Ontario. And, we must attack our environmental programs with courage, not looking backwards. That's the Liberal agenda; those are the Liberal reforms.

This legislature will be blessed with tremendous talent. And I want to welcome to our vigorous new team people like Joan Smith, Doug Reycraft... Ron Van Horne and I will be proud, proud to serve with this new group. And I want to say to all of our new team, all of whom I know, we are going to have a vigorous, vigorous, vigorous legislative contingent in our party.

And to all the new men and women who have been elected for all the parties, I say welcome and I look forward to facing the challenges of this province with you. And to those, let me say, let me say something else, many good men and women were defeated tonight. I know many of them, I understand how it feels, and my heart goes out to them, and I say to them, continue to serve this province. It's worth fighting for, and there are many ways to serve.

And I say to those who lost tonight, no one loses when they participate in the democratic process. And to some of my good friends, Cabinet ministers, Keith Norton, Gordon Walker, and other neighbours, I am some understanding of how they feel tonight and I give them my personal best wishes.

But you know, one person I have to thank most of all—who is standing beside me tonight—my wife Shelley, who has been with me every single step of the way since 1975. I can tell you we have done this together and I couldn't be more happy. There were times in this party where there were only two real believers; they're standing right here tonight. But I'll tell you, there are many more now and I am grateful for that. And my son Benjamin, who is representing the other two, I am most... the other two went for a little nap. But to my Mom and Dad who are here tonight... and I am... my brother Jim and my sister-in-law Heather, Aunt Vi, and my brother Tim, and to Shelley's mom and Shelley's sisters, I can tell you I am blessed to have such an extended family that is so supportive. And I do appreciate it.

And I say tonight to Premier Miller and to Mr. Rae, my congratulations on their re-election and I look forward to working with them both.

Well to you, for making this the second greatest day of my life—the first was my marriage to Shelley and I'll tell you, this is close—I thank you all for all you have done for our great party. Thank you for your support.

Je veux dire à tout le monde et à tous les jeunes de cette province: merci, merci beaucoup. For I am going to need your help and your strength in the months and years ahead, and I know I can count on you all. For I have always believed that if one advances confidently in the direction of one's dreams, he will meet with success unexpected in common hours. We did that tonight together. My friends, I thank you for tonight and I thank you for the future. Merci du tout la monde!

Reply to the Speech from the Throne
Queen's Park, June 7, 1985

I am very proud to open the discussion on behalf of my party. As you know, Mr. Speaker, we have all faced some very interesting times in the last little while, and I am one of those who [is] persuaded they will continue to be interesting. I believe our party is ready to assume the challenges that lie ahead, whatever they may be. I believe, in spite of some of the differences, we have developed many things in common among the members of this House that are going to serve us all well in the future.

That being said, the people of this province did speak for change with a very clear voice not too long ago. I have been here for ten years, and I believed change was necessary for all that time. The people spoke in the last election and confirmed that view.

For anyone who had any doubts, watching the Conservatives in action for the past three weeks has confirmed very clearly that change is the order of the day. The performance of that party in the past three weeks has turned many of its supporters against it. It is a record of which none of the Conservative members individually should be very proud.

I have never seen such philosophical harlotry. I have never seen such lack of dignity in facing the inevitable. They know and I know about the appointments putting in their friends and abusing the situation that lies in front of them. They know and I know the daily reports of the purging of files. I do not think history is going to treat them very well. This is not their finest hour as a party. It is not something any of them should be very proud of.

I am very proud of the new group with whom I stand. The many new members in this House are evidence that the people of this province did want change. We are prepared to join with others in being agents of that change. When people cast their ballots on May 2, not only did they give the Liberal Party more votes than any other party for the first time in 48 years but also they brought this House and this parliament into the 1980s in one quick spring. They injected our party with a great new dose of talent to bolster the already proven talent we have.

One of the things I am proud of is the fact that our party, more than in the past at least, represents the mirror of the new face of Ontario. I can assure the House the difference is more than meets the eye. The difference is a new perspective, new points of view unencumbered by the past and perspectives that will give a new voice to many in our society who have not previously been heard in these chambers.

Let me be charitable and congratulate the government on the Speech from the Throne, at least for the assistance it gave to the lieutenant governor in the preparation thereof. There is little in it that we would not have said ourselves; in fact, there is little in it that we did not say ourselves.

But at the very least the speech proved one thing: that the government of the day can interpret election results as well as anyone else can. It reminded me of the words of a commander in the French Revolution who said: "There go the people. I must follow them, for I am their leader." That is the spectre of what we have seen in the past few weeks.

There is one fundamental problem with the Throne Speech: it should have been delivered years ago. Also, many of the promises it contains should have been acted upon years ago.

We understood, and I think we have understood for some time, the depth of the people's real desire for change in this province. The people had before them a very clear option. They could have maintained the government of the day, but instead they voted by a margin of more than two to one a mandate for that change, and that is the reality of May 2.

It is not surprising that a number of things on which we campaigned were shared by the other parties, the New Democratic Party in particular and latterly the Conservatives as well. We obviously do not agree on everything. What has been established is not a coalition. We are not trying to persuade New Democrats to become Liberals; they are not trying to persuade us to become New Democrats any more than we are trying to persuade the Conservatives to become Liberals or vice versa.

But there has developed during and after the campaign a clear consensus on a number of issues. I do not expect it will always be easy going; I have some understanding of the difficulties and vicissitudes of a minority House. But I am also persuaded that we can all make it work.

As I said, it is also clear in many ways that we were brought closer together during this campaign and after, and I very much hope this spirit of co-operation will continue in the important things, because it is a reality of life and a reality of politics that no one person has a monopoly on good ideas, no one party has a monopoly on good ideas. That is why it is going to be incumbent upon every single member of this House to make the best of how the people have spoken.

We do have one very basic thing in common, and that is that we all believe in our system of democracy, the system of free people making free choices. When one looks at the relatively few places in the world that have our system, we are, in spite of our differences, fortunate to be here and fortunate to be participating.

As I said in this House last year, each legislator has a special responsibility. Each legislator brings something unique, individual perspectives and talents, to the process. In this House, there are no nobodies.

The people of this province must also be guaranteed an opportunity to participate. I do not have to remind anyone here that we are the servants of the people; they are not our servants. May I remind members of the words of Sir Edward Blake, who led my party more than a century ago. He said, "The privileges of parliament are the privileges of the people and the rights of parliament are the rights of the people." I think it is going to be incumbent upon all of us to try to match the spirit of those words.

We can do that by encouraging everyone in this province to play a role in the process of government. We in the legislature must say to the people of this province: "This is your House. This is your parliament." Our job is to unlock the door. We must make everyone feel welcome here. It is time we gave government a human face, one with eyes that have a clear vision, ears that listen and, indeed, a smile as well. That is the way we would govern if we were given the opportunity, because we realize the essence of government is not command, but consent.

We must share all information freely and openly with those who belong to other parties and with those who belong to no party. We must give people the information they need to participate in the process of government. That includes not only freedom-of-information legislation but also the release of all information that can help people participate actively in the process.

For example, why should it be the exclusive prerogative of the government to see polls taken with public money? They should be available for all, for opposition parties and for everyone in this province to study, examine and draw one's own conclusions. Our guiding rule should be simple. Any information that helps the government to shape policies should be available to all so that they can assess those policies.

We have seen an example of that in the last two days in the discussions that have gone on in this House. I disagree fundamentally with the approach of the government on the matter. It should be shared now; we have been waiting almost a year with no public information. There is not one member in this House who is insensitive to the divisions that have been caused, essentially, I believe, not through lack of goodwill but through lack of information, consultation, and discussion. We have failed, and I say even more critically, the government has failed in its responsibility in that regard because part of our responsibility is to restore people's faith in the good intentions of government.

It is not my view that the government of the day has been possessed by bad intentions, but there is little reason to believe that for the most part those intentions have always been matched by deeds. We must reverse that mentality. For example, we must change the rules on untendered contracts. We have to end cronyism. We have to make sure that public appointments are not based on friendship or political affiliation, but are based on merit. Our responsibility will be to establish public service as the highest calling in our society and to persuade people of all points of view, be they Liberal, Conservative, or New Democrat, or be they the many who have no particular affiliation, to come forward to serve their province and their country.

I believe one of the strong messages that came from this election is that we have a mandate to end cronyism. When I see that cronyism continued in the past couple of weeks, as the Conservative Party tries desperately to hang on to power, I do not think it speaks well of its judgment in this matter.

Perhaps the worst thing about the cynical manner in which the government has repaid its political debts in the past is the impact on the way in which people view the public service. It has made those who are willing to serve the public the subject of scorn rather than the object of respect. Cynicism breeds cynicism. That is the greatest debt this government bears at the moment. We must agree together to restore respect for those who serve the public. Our civil servants must not become part of the political battleground; neither should they be among the casualties when there is a change. Our civil service must not be expected to carry out our political tasks or to take any action to curry favour with this government any more than it should be permitted to obstruct the policies of this government.

We should be very careful not to take a narrow view of our job and our responsibilities. Our job obviously includes legislation, management of policy and the public purse, and charting a course for economic growth. However, it includes something more, something intangible. It is the job of government to raise the public will, to summon the public spirit and to motivate people to go the extra mile to aid their fellow citizens. From what we have seen recently, I believe every one of us has reason to believe that when summoned, when inspired, when called upon, people will respond.

Government and politicians have been displaying a tendency to shrink from challenges, sometimes when people have been displaying a tendency to seek out those challenges. In our own country, we have recently seen two marvellous examples of people willing to rise to those challenges. We have seen a young man from British Columbia, afflicted by the most dreaded disease of our time, battle that foe on behalf of himself and millions of others. In Steve Fonyo we have proof that a journey of even 5,000 miles begins with a single step.

In our own province, in response to the tragedy of last weekend, we have also seen people rising to fight a common foe. Amid the terrible devastation that hit the central part of our province last week, one positive thing stood out very clearly. There were far more volunteers wanting to help than there were victims. When challenged, people respond, and proof of that was provided in Barrie, Orangeville, Tottenham, Holland Marsh, and Grand Valley.

We must summon that spirit to help mould the kind of Ontario we want to leave to our children. One of the prime goals of this government should be to develop ways to unlock that spirit, to marshal that strength and find solutions to many of the problems that confront us. We must develop new ways to develop that potential for good.

The government's responsibility is to lead. Looking back for a moment, there is no question that in more than four decades there have been many accomplishments. We have achieved much that we in our party and I am sure those in other parties would want to preserve. We owe great debts, collectively, to Leslie Frost, George Drew, Bill Davis, John Robarts—someone whose seat I now hold, redistributed as it is. I have always been very honoured to have that distinction. The history of Ontario is lined with testimonials to their dedication and their contributions.

But we must start facing today's problems. We must not saddle our children with yesterday's problems. It is easy to see why that approach was considered reasonable forty years, or thirty years, or even twenty years ago. When times are good, it is tempting to think times will always be that way.

One can understand how governments can be deceived into believing the good life was easy, always there and impossible to lose. What is difficult to understand is why we were still deceived after the blinders were ripped off us with such force in the early 1970s. What is sometimes difficult to understand is the self-deception. Over the past four decades, governments of this province, when faced with long-range problems, have often shuffled them aside. If that would not do, the premier would simply shuffle the Cabinet, but many of the problems did not disappear in those shuffles.

We have to think of the problems of an aging population. We have to think about the fundamental changes that are affecting industry. We have to ask ourselves where our young people are going to work ten years and 20 years from now. Do they have the skills? We have to set on course now the plans and the motions to make that happen. We must not let the deficiencies of the past become ingrained in the name of false progress.

We have to think about the environmental problems we are still creating today, in 1985—a major subject of discussion in this House because of our failure to lead and our tendency to apologize, to be always behind.

Many of these problems were predicted or could have been predicted. We have had many discussions in this House and it is probably not productive to go back and say, "We told you so, because we talked about this ten years ago or five years ago." The reality is that many of these things were not acted upon.

The Tory Throne Speech is a perfect example of that. It is a 37-page apology, an admission of where things were wrong and perhaps a misreading of the political mood of this province. I have no idea. It is living witness to the fact that we have a number of problems we have not faced in the past and now we have to take up that challenge.

We have seen policies that could stand the test of politics, but they have not stood the test of time. We have failed to prevent many of the things we could have prevented and we have failed to deal with our potential problems. It is as though this government has been late for every deadline. It is like trying to catch a train without a schedule.

The important thing now, however, is not to fix blame, but to chart the course for the future. One thing we have learned is that government must not only be concerned about the next election. Politicians tend to see the future in terms of the next election, but we must see it collectively in terms of the next decade and the next generation.

In the past four decades we have passed through an era of rapid growth, an era of consolidation and an era of retrenchment. Now we have to go back and build the new opportunity. Before we enter this era, we must decide where we want it to take us and how we are going to get there. It is not good enough to get off to only a fresh start; we must get off to a good start.

We have to do that with our eyes open. We must enter this era thinking about where it will lead us and planning the course we will all follow, unlike the way we embarked on the previous eras in our post-war history. The prospect of change often brings with it apprehension, but I am sure it will become very clear in the near future that there is no reason for that concern if we confront that future and discuss collectively the kind of change we want to see.

We have to stop telling people to expect less. It is this kind of talk that blunts ambition and saps the spirit, because it is a desire for a better life that motivates people in a free society. We have no reason to curb our expectations. We just have to use more ingenuity in the future to achieve them. Over the next few years we can expect major changes in industry, job creation, education, training, and health care, especially for a growing and aging population.

I want to speak very briefly about what I consider to be three of the fundamental challenges any administration faces in this province today. There are the day-to-day concerns, the things that have to be dealt with, and good management is obviously the order of the day. There are some basic things as well, however. We must not let the events that intercede in our political lives take us off the path of our basic commitments to change society.

I am very mindful of the influence of events on political life. I once saw an interview with Harold Wilson. He was asked by David Frost what the chief influence in his life was. It was a very in-depth interview. Mr. Frost was looking for an answer that would give a philosopher, teacher, or mother some credo Mr. Wilson lived by. He asked, "What is the major influence in your life?" Mr. Wilson turned to him and in one word answered, "Events." We all know how events conspire to shape political life but let them not take us off our basic course.

Our party is dedicated to fundamental reform in work, in school, and in health. It is a cliché to say that the nature of our industrial economy is changing very rapidly around us. We have had a minister of industry and trade, and I am not being critical of any particular one, who has done essentially two things. He has travelled abroad selling our products on trade missions, all quite wonderful and worthwhile, and he has run around bailing out and trying to prop up failing industries.

Both of those activities belie the fundamental changes that are going on in our society today, the move to high technology, the move to freer trade around the world, and international competition. These are dramatic changes that I do not believe have been fully comprehended or worked into public policies in this province.

Many of our traditional industries are under siege today, and many may not be there, at least in the same form, five, ten or twenty years from now. We have to ask ourselves where our kids are going to work. Where are they going to find the kind of opportunity to allow them to make their choices to build their kinds of lives and have their own economic opportunities?

When I look at the slow erosion and at the changes that have gone on, I become very concerned at the fundamental inability of our system to deal with those matters. I do not think they can be solved with a conference once every four years, bringing together 150 players from various sectors and with nothing happening but the publishing of a very glossy and attractive report. That is neither the kind of dialogue nor the kind of leadership we are going to have to have. It is going to take a lot of time, sleeves rolled up, a lot of work; people from all sectors working together, identifying common objectives, and working towards them.

I do not suggest for a minute that the solutions are simple or easy. I do not suggest for a minute that it is not one of the most complex questions we face as a society. But we have no choice other than to address it, and I hope to do so with the help of all my colleagues in this House and to start that process now. That is one of the great challenges we face, and we will not know the results of it for many years down the pike. But when its history is written, I hope it will be written that this legislature, this group, understood the depth of the problem and was prepared to address it in all its various forms—high tech, aging industries, smokestack industries—making sure that people are not displaced unduly by these changes, that we approach them in a compassionate and thoughtful way, not clinging to the past but moving ahead with courage and a sense of direction.

I believe as well that another of our great challenges is to make our school system—our education system—relevant today. We have had many discussions about this in the past. Interestingly enough, for probably one of the great areas of jurisdiction of this legislature, it is an area that has probably had less discussion. Unless a bill comes around, such as Bill 127 or a forced universities reference, there is very little real input from this legislature in those matters.

You know, Mr. Speaker, as I know, the great consternation in the education community on the part of both the practitioners and the consumers—parents, young people, and everyone else. When one throws in the number of things that have been thrown in, such as the separate schools question, something we believe in, that consternation rises even more.

We must now reassert our commitment to quality education at all levels, recognizing that it is the single most important resource we have: trained, educated, entrepreneurial, and creative young people. Without going into detail, Mr. Speaker, because you will know some of our discussions in this party, there are many things we have to do and do quickly.

Again, we will not see the results in six months; we will not see them in two years; we may not even see them in five years. But I hope when history is written, the direction of the ship of state will have been turned and we will be making our system more relevant and more meaningful.

Those are basic challenges we face, just as we face basic challenges with respect to our healthcare system, an aging population, and tremendous pressures on every facility that exists across this province. That, too, is going to take major and fundamental rethinking.

We have talked about non-institutionalized programs; new, thoughtful and, I think, sensitive and cost-effective ways of dealing with some of these problems in the future. We are prepared to chart new directions, we are prepared to deal with these fundamental problems, and we do believe we can turn the direction of the ship of state and make a meaningful contribution over the years.

Those are things that we in our party believe in because the Liberal Party has never feared change. The Liberal Party has historically been an agent for change, believing it is our responsibility to move forward with courage and not to seek the security blanket of some twenty years ago.

Just as we have major problems in our environmental area—and I will not go into detail—the deathbed conversion of the Tories on this matter is not credible, to say the very least. But we are going to move ahead with courage in that area as well.

One of our great responsibilities is to change the face of the way this province is governed, to make sure that the great majority receives equal treatment. I am talking about the 52 percent of women in this province. Those of us who believe in the ideal of equality cannot rest easy when 52 percent of our population still faces discrimination that is a residue of age-old prejudices and misconceptions.

It is not too soon to change that, and we intend to do so. We will not listen to excuses or accept bureaucratic delays or half-committed leadership to slow down what I believe is a legitimate aspiration of women across this province. So too with minorities, who have a legitimate right to participate in all our institutions. We intend to change that as well.

It has always been said that Ontario did not have any particular sense of identity, that Ontarians always saw themselves as Canadians first and that we did not have the sense of regionalism that perhaps some of the other provinces in this country have. I think we saw in this campaign a sense of Ontario more than we have seen in the past, a sense that we are not prepared to sit by and see Ontario's interests sacrificed to bilateral deals made with the federal government for other provinces when our interests are not protected and not considered.

We have seen the interests of many people in this province threatened by unilateral federal moves in the last little while. Our seniors are going to lose enormously as a result of the federal budget. Obviously, there was very little consultation, if any, with this government. If there was any consultation, it was not taken seriously.

We need to stand up for Ontario's interests. We need voices in Ottawa that will be taken seriously and we are prepared to provide that leadership. We cannot sit by, Mr. Speaker. You know the things we believe in; the things we are prepared to do. You know the government's record on these matters as well; at least you know the record today. There are no guarantees that it will not be different tomorrow.

Recognizing the inevitable is going to happen, it now becomes our responsibility to summon the most thoughtful people from all parties to work together and fulfill the dreams, hopes, and aspirations of the two thirds of the people in the province who voted for meaningful change.

This government has had its chance. When it went to the highest court in the land, it failed. It was judged to be guilty. People want change. I only hope the government can recognize that with some equanimity. I have some personal understanding of failure and I know it is not easy, but I hope they will not take it personally or do things that will embarrass them when history is written.

This government has lost the confidence of the people of the province. To paraphrase the words of Oliver Wendell Holmes, sometimes government must sail with the wind, sometimes it must sail against the wind, but it must always sail. It must not drift or lie at anchor. This government was drifting, it was lying at anchor, and it was not providing leadership on the things that mattered to the people of this province.

SWEARING-IN OF THE FIRST PETERSON CABINET
Queen's Park Lawn, June 26, 1985

Your honour, Mr. Chief Justice, mes chers amis:

I would like to like to express how I feel about following in the footsteps of nineteen dedicated leaders of this province. But first, I ask you to join me in a moment of silence and sorrow on this national day of mourning for the loss of so many of our fellow Canadians in Sunday's devastating tragedy in the air.[1]

Thank you.

Today I ask you to join with me in giving renewed meaning to the words of the Canadian artist Paul-Émile Borduas who said, «c'est avec joie que nous assumons l'entière responsabilité de demain»—"it is with

---

[1] Air India Flight 182 was destroyed by a bomb on June 23, 1985 over the Atlantic Ocean, claiming the lives of 329 people.

joy that we take the entire responsibility of tomorrow."

Et j'ai besoin que vous partagez avec moi la grande heure du moment présent. En effectuant le changement de gouvernement, nous célébrons une unité, une liberté rare en ce monde. And I am grateful for the opportunity to swear an oath to preserve that legacy.

And in taking on a new challenge, it is inspiring to do so in the presence of so many whose help I will need. And I include on the top of my list my wife, Shelley, my children who are here—Ben, Chloe, and Adam—my mother, my father, my brothers, and Shelley's family as well.

And I'm very grateful to all who joined in marking this moment, the leaders of the opposition parties, our colleagues in the legislature, and many members of the most dedicated civil service we could possibly ask for. But most of all, I am honoured to see so many people on whom our success will ultimately depend: the people of this province. In this government, you will have the most important role to play.

This is a humbling experience, but not an overpowering one, because our task will be made easier by the help of nine million people. We know that we will not reach all of our goals overnight, we will not accomplish all of our objectives exactly as we set out to do, and we will not solve the province's problems without difficulty. But with time and the help of people who are sworn to serve, there is no doubt, there is no task we cannot perform, no burden we cannot bear, and no obstacle we cannot overcome.

All of you who were kind enough to join me this afternoon are helping to symbolize the kind of government to which Ontario is entitled: a government without walls or barriers. This province must offer to us what it offered those who came before us: a vision of opportunity. Many came to this province seeking the opportunity to participate. Many sought the opportunity to prosper. Some sought the opportunity just to survive. But all sought opportunity.

So let us take this as our mission: where opportunity is fragile, to make it strong; where it is fleeting, to make it permanent; and where it is unknown, to make it familiar. It must be available to women as well as to men; newcomers as well as those whose roots go back centuries; young people and seniors, as well as those of us who are somewhere in between.

Today is the first day for many things. But above all, it is our first opportunity to express by symbol what we hope to accomplish in substance. And I hope those who made time to join us this afternoon will also take time to tour the legislature and to visit my office. Moreover, I hope you will take every opportunity to participate in our work. Because one thing on which we all agree—no matter our political stripe— the building that stands behind me stands for the people of Ontario. And in building a better life for our children, all of us must do our part to build the foundations now.

Thank you. Thank you for standing with me today on the new threshold of a new era for your Ontario. Merci.

Ontario Liberal Party Heritage Dinner
Toronto, Ontario, May 14, 1986

I can't help but notice that there are a couple of you here who couldn't make it last year.

What do you know. The cheque *really was* in the mail. Back when we were in opposition, I think we heard "the cheque is in the mail" almost as often as we heard "the fullness of time." When we were organizing a heritage dinner a couple of years ago, we were told several times the cheque was in the mail. And that was smack in the middle of a postal strike.

This year, so many more people finally got around to ordering tickets, I think I might finally give a different speech. It's gotten so that some of the regulars were starting to read it along with me. But that's okay, there weren't *that many* regulars.

Let me fill in those of you who couldn't make it for the past 42 years or so. All of the previous heritage dinners were the same as this one, except there was one less course, several hundred fewer people, and almost no red ties.

But we always knew that at some point, our day would come... "in the fullness of time." Praise the Lord... and the Accord.

Now, I want you to know, we can make as much noise as we want tonight, you can boo as much as you like, you can even applaud if you feel like it, don't let me hold you back. I happen to know the fellow who built the place.

Just think, at this rate, in a couple of years we could be holding this dinner in the domed stadium. And if we're lucky, we'll raise as much money as Dave Steib makes every time he gives up a run.

And in that context, I want to thank Don Smith, who over the past couple of years has proven that all his experience in the construction industry doesn't hurt when you're trying to build a political party. Although I might also point out that when pay equity is passed, chief whips will have a strong case for getting paid as much as construction company presidents.

In the words of a great philosopher, Yogi Berra, I want to thank everybody who made this night necessary. It took a great deal of work, and I appreciate it. And I want to thank all of you who showed up tonight. I realize that many of you aren't Liberals, and some of you never will be—although I want you to know we're selling memberships at the door. I appreciate the support you are showing for the party system.

It's nice to see so many people are willing to support the political process. It's good to know so many people are prepared to encourage us. It's interesting to learn so many people didn't expect the St. Louis Blues to push the Calgary Flames to seven games.

We're not going to let this excellent turnout go to our heads. It reminds me of a fellow who once told Sir Winston Churchill that he must be very proud so many people turned out to hear him speak. Churchill paused for a moment and responded: "It is quite flattering, but whenever I feel my head getting too big about it, I remind myself that if instead of making a speech, I was being hanged, the audience would be three times as large."

At least if I hang tonight, it will only be on my own words.

But I do want to thank you for coming tonight, to this $250-a-plate dinner. Just think, to look down and realize that stain on your tie cost you $18.45 not including the tax credit.

I know that there are a number of attractions that could have kept you away, especially with the sales tax exemption now covering meals up to two dollars. Then there is CFTO's newest show, celebrity wrestling with Ted Steubing and Pat Marsden. And I understand they're having a bingo night at the Albany Club. First prize is a Senate seat. Second prize is two Senate seats.

I especially appreciate the fact that Art Eggleton cut short his trip to China to be here. Art, you were gone so long we sent the prime minister out to find you.

But there are a couple of specific points I want to make tonight. I find that what most banquets need is an express podium—for speakers with six thoughts or less.

In his kind introduction, Dean talked a bit about last year's Heritage Dinner. A fair bit has happened in the past year, and I thought I might say a few words about that, and a few about what we can expect of the years to come.

At the time of last year's dinner, if you had asked people our chances of forming a government, most would have cited the words of the legendary producer Samuel Goldwyn: "in two words—im possible."

But sometimes the impossible just takes a little bit longer, or a little more work. So now, for the first time, as Dean points out, a Heritage Dinner is an opportunity to celebrate a Liberal government.

And it's different, speaking at one of these dinners, coming from the other side of the House.

In government, we call a crisis a problem, a problem a challenge, a challenge an opportunity, and an opportunity an achievement.

I am proud to say that since we have formed the government we have had several achievements, quite a few opportunities, a couple of challenges, the odd problem, and not a single crisis—unless you count the time I had to sing on the steps of the legislature.

But I'll tell you, I'll take on the opportunities, the challenges, the problems, even the crises—so long as I am working with the team we have in our Cabinet, and the team we have in our caucus. That's a team that reminds me of this year's Montreal Canadiens, or last season's Toronto Blue Jays. A team with character.

We've got the smallest Cabinet this province has seen in decades—but I'll take it over any Cabinet Ontario has ever known.

They've taken on a big task—half of them without any legislative background at all. And they've done a remarkable job.

We started by recognizing that all wisdom is not automatically conferred by having the title MPP added to your name.

We learned from the example of the Harvard professor, who prayed for humility, saying: "Dear God, please protect me from the sin of intellectual arrogance, which, for your information, means…"

Our first job was to open up the process of government, to let the sun shine in on Queen's Park. So we moved immediately on a bill to guarantee freedom of information and privacy.

And we're continuing to open up Queen's Park, to make that House the people's home.

Starting this session, the legislature is being televised every afternoon.

We want to call the show, "Love of Life." But the NDP likes "Search for Tomorrow," and the Tories are kind of stuck on "Search for Yesterday." Actually, a couple of the Tories are producing their own spinoff— Dennis Timbrell and Alan Pope in "The Young and the Restless."

But partisanship aside, I hope you'll get the chance to tune in, and watch democracy at work.

We are reforming other aspects of our political system. For people like you, who are regularly asked to come to these dinners, the good news is we will introduce election financing reform. The bad news is we may raise the limits on contributions.

Other challenges, other opportunities. When we formed the government, we did what any prudent group of men and women would do. When you take over a business, you examine your assets, you decide what is worth holding onto, what is not, and what must be reorganized.

That's the nice thing about choosing a new government—every 42 years or so. It gives you the opportunity to rummage through the attic, clean up what can still be used, and discard what cannot be.

That included oil companies, transit companies, and land corporations. That was a big part of our first budget.

More challenges, more opportunities: When we formed the government, we had a number of commitments to fulfill—commitments we made in the last election, commitments many of you heard me make at previous Heritage dinners. Commitments to justice for some who have been denied it, such as pay equity, and employment equity; and to justice for all who require it, such as protection of the principle of equal access to a first-class healthcare system.

And we had to move on one of our most important commitments—our commitment to future generations, to leave them a legacy of clean air and fresh lakes. So we moved to cut down acid rain.

Patrick Moynihan tells how several of his fellow officials in President Kennedy's government used to wonder what they would do in the second year of his term, when all of the nation's problems would be solved.

Well, we have always realized that it would take a lot longer than one year. But I am encouraged by the start we've made.

Now, we are beginning to address the challenges and the opportunities of the decade.

In the past three weeks our government has presented its first Throne Speech and second budget. They represent a new accord—an accord with Ontario's future.

Some budgets are like a 28-inch snowfall. They're deep, they seem to cover everything—and six months later you'd never know they happened.

Not for nothing was our treasurer's budget presented in May. People's recollection of this budget will be long and green because this budget was based on several principles that will stand us in good stead for years to come.

It is based on the principle that we must pay for what we get—in this generation. We cannot tax our children and grandchildren, just because they cannot vote.

The *only* costs those future generations should help bear, are those for improved infrastructure and capital facilities that they will benefit from—those that strengthen the province's ability to ensure prosperity and provide needed services in years ahead.

It is based on the principle that Ontario's social conscience will always have a voice, and our better instincts will always prevail.

That is why, for example, yesterday's budget included a special $850-million allocation for hospitals. For one thing, that might be the only way I could make sure I could find a doctor who would admit me if I needed it. Now all I have to do is find a lawyer who never wanted to be a QC.

The people of Ontario long ago accepted the canon that wealth must be shared.

That is why we have committed ourselves to maintaining and improving social programs.

The budget is based on the principle that in order to share wealth, we must ensure our ability to create it.

At the moment, the Ontario economy is extremely buoyant. Over the past year, 175,000 new jobs have been created in this province. The first three months of this year saw the creation of more than 70,000 new jobs. Ontario's unemployment rate is down to 6.8 percent, the lowest in Canada.

Now, I'm not here to take credit for that. The prime minister has already done that. But I would like to remind you that housing starts are up by more than 75,000. Consumer confidence, if reflected in growth of retail sales, by 11.6 percent. Business investment will be up by 10.9 percent this year. Manufacturing shipments in 1985 were up by 8.8 percent over the previous year.

In other words, now is an excellent time to plan for the future. It is always best to build from strength.

We must build new industries, and revitalize established ones.

That is why our budget, and our Throne Speech, focused particular attention on three things we must do to ensure for our province a bright economic future.

One, we must move boldly to ensure our position as a world-class leader in innovation, technology, and the new knowledge industries. One step in this direction will be the creation of a council to direct a $1 billion special technology fund to steer Ontario into the forefront of economic leadership and technological innovation.

We recognize that technology does not just include high technology, and computers. It includes all ways to do things better, faster, and more efficiently. Our goal is to increase Ontario's know-how.

Two, we recognize that the most important investment this province can make is in its people. That includes not just their know-how, but their know-why, and where, and when.

In order to invest in its people, Ontario must invest in its universities and colleges. And our investment must be well-targeted. Schools of higher learning must avoid unnecessary duplication, and find the niches in which they can develop excellence.

Three, we must create a new spirit of entrepreneurship. And we must start in our schools, by encouraging young people to develop entrepreneurial qualities such as self-motivation and the ability to originate better ideas, and better ways of doing things. We are encouraging entrepreneurship and risk-taking through a number of measures, including several that were included in the budget and the Throne Speech.

In examining recent economic statistics, one fact jumps out: prosperity and employment belong to those who seek them out.

In the past year in Ontario, 99,000 new businesses were formed. Of these, about 34,000—little more than one in every three—were firms that hired employees. These firms created more than 180,000 job opportunities and generated $500 million in new investment.

It has been estimated that half of the companies in Canada in a few years will be firms that do not even exist today.

It would be difficult to estimate with assurance how many jobs new enterprises will create. Entrepreneurship is an invisible source of future prosperity.

But we realize that government cannot build an entrepreneurial society on its own.

Earlier I thanked you for coming tonight. As a Liberal leader, I appreciate your support. But as premier of Ontario, I need your help. Your province needs your help.

We need the help of people who care about their community and its future.

We need to determine Ontario's priorities in developing new technologies. We need to gear our education system to our future needs. And we need to promote a climate of enterprise.

Business, labour, schools, municipalities, the provincial government—none of us can do it alone. But we *can* do it together.

QUETICO CAUCUS RETREAT
Atikokan, Ontario, September 8, 1988

Let me begin by saying what a worthwhile exercise this retreat has been. We've had the pleasure of hearing from four outstanding individuals and I want to thank Michael Adams, Bob Evans, Roy Aitken, and André Saumier for providing us with their insight and knowledge.

This retreat has served a dual purpose. It has given us an opportunity to get away from the political urgencies at Queen's Park. But more importantly, it has allowed us to reflect on the trends and changes that will place tremendous challenges before government in the future.

An ancient philosopher once wrote "there is nothing permanent in the world except change." Looking at the twentieth century, or even the last ten years, that would be considered an understatement. Since the beginning of this century the world has undergone profound and dramatic changes. Our planet's population has grown from 1.6 billion to 5 billion. Before the year 2000 it will increase by another billion. The use of fossil fuels has grown nearly thirty-fold; industrial production has increased more than fifty times; between 1940 and 1980 water use has doubled. By the year 2000 it will double again.

Ontario has experienced its share of change. In 1900 this province was overwhelmingly agricultural. As late as 1941, the Census found that as many Ontarians were employed in agriculture as in manufacturing, 23 percent of the workforce. By 1981, agriculture had shrunk to 3.5 percent of Ontario's working population. In Ontario today there are more chartered accountants and auditors than farmers.

Demographically, the composition of our population has changed too. In 1871, the English, Irish, Scots, and Welsh comprised 82 percent of the population. Today, their domination has dwindled to a mere 43 percent. A century ago Catholics formed a small minority of 17 percent. Even in 1941 they formed only 22.5 percent of Ontarians. Today Catholics outnumber Anglican and United Church supporters combined.

Economically, Ontario has undergone a dramatic socio-economic transformation. A massive rural-to-urban population shift has accompanied intense industrialization. Cheap and plentiful energy, easy access to skilled immigrant workers and the overspill of a booming American industrial economy has transformed our province from an agrarian-based economy into an industrial power.

I've just highlighted some of the historical trends and demographic shifts that have influenced Ontario's development. But as we gather here in this beautiful setting, we must ask: what about the future? What is the Ontario government's role in dealing with the challenges ahead? What kind of province do we want for our children and our grandchildren?

The social scientists have told us we're now living in the post-industrial age—the new information society. We work in a global economy where computers, robotics, and telecommunications networks are international in scope and design and are unrestrained by national or provincial borders. Knowledge has become the major factor of production rather than labour or capital. The economy is shifting from one based on the production of goods to one focusing on the consumption of services.

By the year 2000, 75 percent of Ontario's labour force will be employed in the service sector. It now accounts for 73 percent of employment and 73 percent of gross domestic product. Not only is Ontario's population growing but people are living longer. More women are entering the workforce. The number of two-career families will continue to rise. In the 1950s and '60s we experienced the baby boom. The 1970s and early 1980s turned into the baby bust. Now the projections indicate we're headed into another mini-baby boom. As more and more women enter the workforce, they're discovering that having a career and a family are not irreconcilable.

To meet the needs of our changing population, we as a government, as a caucus, as a party must constantly reassess our priorities. We must constantly readjust our policies and programs.

That's why we're making changes to our healthcare system—so that our aging population can live their golden years in dignity. That's why we're reforming our education system—so that our children obtain better-than-adequate skills to help them compete in the information society. That's why we're reforming our social services—so that every Ontarian has the same opportunity to a home and a decent job. That's why we're reassessing our transportation needs—so that people in our cities can travel with ease from home to work. That's why we're developing new skills and retraining programs—so that our workers can adapt to new and emerging technologies.

The future will bring some difficult choices. I don't have to remind you of some tough decisions we'll soon have to address: nuclear power, our energy needs, waste disposal, education reform, health reform, global restructuring, child care, and cleaning up our environment.

My friends, it's a great privilege to govern. But governing is much more than winning votes. To govern is to take the initiative, set the agenda and assert our priorities. To govern, we must dominate the agenda. We must control the agenda. We must show we have a vision, a course of action, and a plan to not only deal with the crisis situations but the long-term challenges as well.

I'm proud of what our caucus has accomplished. This past year has been one of the busiest and most productive sessions in the history of the Ontario legislature. We've provided leadership on the tough issues. We've shown we have the philosophy, the determination, the will, the sensitivity, and the vision to get things done in this province.

Nobody can accuse this government of lacking the drive for reform. No one can say we lack commitment.

Let the record speak for itself—conflict of interest, auto insurance, free trade, Meech Lake, intervenor funding, Sunday shopping, Worker's Compensation, Northern Heritage Fund, French language school boards, protection of rental housing, protection of our water and natural resources, co-operative housing, educational reforms, environmental protection, Premier's Council on Health, the Premier's Council on Technology. And while we've been enacting legislation at a record pace, we've been busy behind the scenes developing long-term strategies in areas critical to the future development of our province.

In education, we've launched an aggressive agenda of reform that will improve basic learning skills and raise education standards. We've reduced class sizes in Grades 1 and 2 and allocated funding for more computers and educational software. We're helping ease the transition to adulthood by doubling our expenditures on co-operative education. We're encouraging potential drop-outs to remain in school.

But much more remains to be done. We must continue to make more improvements in elementary education by constantly reviewing the curriculum. We must provide new focus for guidance programs to reduce the drop-out rate. We must upgrade our education standards through province-wide achievement benchmarks and indicators.

Finally, we must extend education in the community by placing more day-care centres in schools. And we must strengthen the link between government, educators, parents, business, and industry.

To find new and innovations strategies to guide our healthcare system into the next century, we formed the Premier's Council on Health Care Strategy. We must work towards a system of health care that will be flexible in response to changing times.

That's why we're developing new directions in a number of strategic areas: community-based services, the role of public hospitals, the involvement of health professionals, prescription drug use, outcome management, and the role of health consumers. We must stay on the right track to keeping our healthcare system effective, fair and affordable.

If there's one critical question that every citizen of the world will be asking themselves in the 1990s and beyond, it concerns the environment and economic growth—can they be reconciled? Can we have strong economic growth and a clean environment? Can the two co-exist?

In Ontario, a healthy economy and a healthy environment are not contradictory—they're complementary. The protection of the environment has been a priority—and will continue to be a priority—for this government. Our aggressive program of environmental reform has made us the leading jurisdiction in environmental protection in North America.

In a few weeks, Jim Bradley will name members of the Ontario Round Table on Sustainable Development. It will be a permanent body made up of fifteen to twenty senior people from government, industry, and public interest groups. It will work in much the same way as the Premier's Council on Technology. The Council will emphasize that Ontario will only tolerate development which is sustainable. In other words— Ontario won't allow an enterprise to cut its costs by dumping wastes which threaten to mutate our genetic structure. This is a forward-looking development and will have a substantial impact on the formulation of public policy.

In housing we've shown leadership and compassion in providing creative solutions for affordable housing. We extended the *Rental Housing Protection Act*. We introduced the home ownership savings plan to give first-time home buyers an opportunity to own a home. In the budget, we announced a $2 billion housing initiative to help build 30,000 additional rental units over the next three to five years. We're also developing a medium and longer-term housing supply strategy using government lands and streamlined approval processes. Our integrated approach to solving the housing crisis will prove that we're a government of vision and action.

My friends, one year ago this Saturday, we were handed an enormous mandate by the people of Ontario. We were entrusted to chart a course for the future direction of our province. I believe we are taking significant steps in that direction.

As we enter the second year of our mandate, we must constantly remind ourselves of what we stand for. We must continue to be seen as a government that is honest and caring, not arrogant and haughty. We must strive to be seen as a government that stands for hope and justice, not indifference and apathy. We must strive to be seen as a government that is open and forthright, not closed and cynical.

We've all made incredible sacrifices to be here. It's the price we pay in public life. But we are having an impact. We are changing the course of history. We've made an incredible start. But there is so much to do.

In Defence of the 'L' Word

John F. Kennedy School of Government, Harvard University, Cambridge, Massachusetts, March 15, 1989

Ladies and gentlemen, I know that it is in the great intellectual traditions of Harvard that even the most controversial subjects, even the most hotly disputed activities, can be discussed openly and freely. And so I want to take advantage of that tradition and be very candid with you here today. I want to admit to something that I know a lot of people would be nervous about acknowledging almost anywhere else in the United States these days.

I am a liberal.

Not only that, but I am a liberal twice over: a small-l liberal, and a capital-L Liberal... in fact the leader of the Liberal Party of Ontario.

And not only that, but I'm *proud* to be a liberal.

To a Canadian like myself, it's a matter of some amazement that the l-word really has become a pejorative term in American politics. It has become an accusation that requires no further elaboration, and an accusation that is widely believed to permit no other response than frantic denial.

In my own country, any politician who tried to savage an opponent simply by accusing him of small-l liberal tendencies would be laughed right off the stage.

Indeed, it's still a fact of Canadian political life that capital-L Liberal parties lose elections when they allow themselves to be perceived as too conservative, and capital-c Conservative parties and small-s socialist parties can only win elections by convincingly presenting themselves as small-l liberal.

Canada is probably one of the most intuitively small-l liberal countries in the world, and that is one of the very important differences between your country and ours despite our apparent similarities.

It's only a slight exaggeration, in fact, to say that on social issues the whole spectrum of Canadian politics—from the socialist New Democratic Party on the left to Progressive Conservatives on the right would fit within the liberal wing of the Democratic Party in the United States.

These differences between our respective countries can be traced back to their earlier days.

The United States was born in revolution and tempered in the crucible of civil war. The history of Canada has been predominantly one of peaceful evolution. Your country had to fight for democracy—our country inherited it.

From the earliest days of our respective countries, Americans have prized individualism and a spirit of every man for himself, while Canadians have preferred a collective spirit of helping each other.

The mythic image of the American frontier is the lone gunfighter riding off into the sunset. Our counterpart image in Canada would be the barn-raising—the neighbours all pitching in to help new settlers build their barn in a day.

You can still see the reflection of that today: In Canada, no one could get elected by campaigning on the right to bear arms. Canadians believe that the individual's right to bear arms is superseded by the right of the rest of us not to get shot by someone bearing arms.

Government has always played a bigger role in the development of our country than of yours, because our circumstances required it. To develop Canada as a distinct, cohesive and prosperous nation extending from coast to coast, we had to defy geography, climate, and the continental pull of a giant nation on our southern border.

There was no way this could have been done except through a constant act of collective will, expressed in a far higher degree of government involvement than would be considered appropriate in the United States.

It was the Canadian government that created a national railway, a national broadcasting system, a national airline and other elements of national infrastructure without which Canada as we know it could literally not have existed.

Over the years, Canadian governments have also developed a national network of social support programs that are the envy of people in much of the world—including many, I believe, in this country. This network includes our universal medicare system, our unemployment insurance and our old age pensions.

And nothing causes Canadians to speak out more vocally than when we sense that there is a threat to such programs.

But liberalism has had a proud tradition in your country as well as in ours. Some of the finest achievements in modern American history, including Franklin Roosevelt's New Deal and the end of racial segregation in the South under the Kennedy and Johnson administrations, were the products of direct intervention by explicitly liberal governments.

The emergence of the world liberal as an outright epithet is a relatively new, and I hope temporary, development in American politics. I am, of course, thankful that the situation remains different in my own country.

But I know that American cultural and political attitudes do have a way of spilling over across our friendly and undefended border from time to time. The United States is always a backdrop to Canadian politics, and we are always in the process of redefining our identity in terms of what is happening in our southern neighbour.

And I also know that any political philosophy can only be as strong in the long run as the conviction and clarity of purpose of its practitioners. Any political philosophy that is worth believing is worth vigorously defending and advocating.

And so it saddens me when I see liberals, anywhere, believing that the times call for keeping a low profile and even taking on some of the political coloration of their adversaries. That only makes the task easier by default for those who want to argue that liberalism cannot be defended and advanced in today's world.

Whenever I see that happening, I am reminded of those poignant lines by the poet Yeats: "The best lack all conviction, while the worst are full of passionate intensity."

I say "the best" because I happen to believe that liberalism is by far the finest political philosophy the world has yet evolved.

I'm a practicing politician, not a theorist, so I don't want to stray too far into the realm of political scientists. But I believe that liberalism is the philosophy that best balances the needs of the individual and the collectivity, it is the philosophy that best tempers the pursuit of progress with the dictates of compassion, and it is the philosophy that provides the best framework for pursuing the true freedom and fulfillment of the individual that should be the purpose of all societies.

I don't believe that liberals, in my country or anywhere in the world, have anything to apologize for, or be defensive about.

There are, of course, many different definitions of liberalism, some friendlier than others.

Ambrose Bierce wrote that "a conservative (is) a statesman who is enamoured of existing evils, as distinguished from the liberal, who wishes to replace them with others."

But I much prefer the view of John F. Kennedy, one of the many distinguished alumni of Harvard, who said:

> Liberalism is not so much a party creed or a set of fixed platform promises as it is an attitude of mind and heart, a faith in man's ability through the experiences of his reason and judgment to increase for himself and his fellow men the amount of justice and freedom and brotherhood which human life deserves.

To me, freedom and justice are what liberalism is ultimately all about.

Both conservatism and liberalism are dedicated to the pursuit of individual freedom.

But conservatives tend to equate freedom simply with the absence of constraint by the state, and so to them the best government is the least government.

I believe, as do other liberals, that it's much more complicated than that. Every man-for-himself freedom is the freedom of the jungle—it's a freedom where the rich, the smart, the powerful, and the influential are free to thrive, while the weak and the vulnerable are free to get trampled underfoot.

I believe that it's the role of societies to provide an environment where *all* their members have the freedom and the opportunity to lead fulfilling lives.

That sort of freedom is more than merely the absence of overt oppression or constraints.

A single mother is not really free to fulfill herself and participate fully in society if grinding poverty forces her to spend every waking moment struggling to figure out how to feed, clothe, and shelter herself and her children. She is not free if she is forced to depend on the state, with no incentive to work and to invest in her family's future.

A sick person is not really free if lack of money cuts off access to first-rate health care to cure a debilitating illness or prevent a premature death.

A willing worker is not really free if either patterns of discrimination or inadequate economic policies prevent him or her from finding a job—both to earn a living and to have a sense of playing a meaningful role.

A child may never be really free to live up to potential if inadequate or uncaring education systems leave him or her without the knowledge and the skills needed to participate fully in an increasingly knowledge-intensive world.

People who live in economically disadvantaged regions of our country are not really free to fulfill themselves if leaving everything up to so-called "market forces" requires them to choose between moving away from the places they love or enduring permanent poverty and unemployment.

The elderly are not really free to enjoy their retirement years if inadequate incomes or inadequate care and support facilities leave them able to do little more than wait out their remaining time.

We are none of us free, if our individual efforts to promote good health are subverted by collective neglect of our environment—if we poison our air and our water, and turn our cities into giant garbage dumps.

Those are some of the dimensions of individual freedom that the conservative philosophy of hands-off and every-man-for-himself ignores.

I believe, as a liberal, that real individual freedom means not only freedom from oppression, but also freedom from fear of poverty, sickness and unemployment.

Freedom without social justice is only freedom for some, not freedom for all.

That's why I'm proud to be a liberal, because liberalism stands for the values of caring and sharing that go right to the heart of why people live together in society in the first place.

We liberals believe that as much as possible should be left to the private sector.

We don't share the socialist view that government should be the first resort for every problem, because that sort of approach leads to needless bureaucracy and inefficiency, and it can ultimately erode both initiative and freedom.

But where the private sector is unable or unwilling to do what is necessary in the public interest, then government has not only a right but a duty to intervene.

It has that right and duty, because a democratically elected government is not some threatening outside force, as conservatives would have us believe. It's us, the mechanism for putting into effect our collective will as citizens.

And so I don't believe in needlessly big government, but I believe in government ambitious enough to meet the legitimate needs of all the citizens it was created to serve.

I don't believe in a rigidly planned economy—but I believe that an economy without *any* coherent plan for its development and evolution is an economy heading for disaster in today's changing world.

I don't believe in a smothering welfare state—but I believe that a state that does not put the welfare of its most vulnerable members ahead of other considerations is a state that cannot justify its existence.

This liberal philosophy is one of compassion, but it is also one of enlightened self-interest, the choice between social justice and economic prosperity is a false dichotomy. I'm firmly convinced that one cannot exist without the other.

History has taught us that a free society cannot achieve or maintain a high degree of prosperity without a high degree of consensus and social peace and we know also that there cannot be sustained social peace and consensus without sustained social justice.

If we try to achieve industrial adaptation on the backs of the workers who are affected, without sensitivity to their needs and concerns, then our labour force will surely resist and frustrate the imperatives of that adaptation.

If we allow regional economic disparities to fester unaddressed until they set region against region, then in time we will see not only the erosion of our internal common markets but also the erosion of the sense of common purpose without which no society can thrive in the world.

If we allow racial tension to exist in our streets, it will inevitably exist in our offices and shop floors, destroying productivity and competitiveness as surely as the efforts of any outside rivals.

If we allow our downtowns to become the exclusive preserves of the heedlessly rich on one hand and the desperately poor on the other, then the desperate will eventually prey on the heedless and the rest of us will hardly dare set foot in their midst.

But if maximizing our prosperity requires a high degree of social justice, it is equally true that maximizing social justice requires us to pursue a high degree of prosperity.

If we want to maintain and expand social programs, we have to generate the money to pay for them and so the liberal view recognizes that the crucial role of government is not merely to redistribute existing wealth, but to play a proactive role in helping to generate new wealth for our society.

I'm pleased to note that in this regard, over the past half-dozen years Ontario has led the industrialized world in economic growth. During this period, our real output has expanded by 42 percent and we've created nearly 900,000 new jobs.

In an effort to build on this record of success, one of my top priorities was to create a new body, the Premier's Council, with a clear mandate to forge new partnerships and steer Ontario into the forefront of economic leadership and technological innovation. The twenty-eight members of this Council are a representative cross-section of dynamic and forward-looking leaders from business, organized labour and the academic and research communities, together with four Cabinet ministers. I attend and chair all the Council's meetings.

Last April, the Premier's Council completed the most in-depth analysis of Ontario's strengths and weaknesses ever undertaken in the history of our province. They developed a blueprint for establishing Ontario as a world leader in technology and innovation.

We've acted quickly on the Council's recommendations. For instance, we established seven Centres of Excellence to carry out ground-breaking research in areas ranging from artificial intelligence to lasers and light-waves. We're positioning Ontario at the leading edge of a number of leading-edge industries. The program has been so successful that not only is the federal government implementing this concept on a national scale, but we're receiving inquiries from around the world.

At the same time, we've been pursuing our liberal commitment to social justice by introducing and following through on what I believe is the most comprehensive, activist social agenda of any jurisdiction in North America.

We are acting in the spirit of Hubert Humphrey, who more than twenty years ago observed that, "the true moral test of government is how it treats those in the dawn of life—the children; those who are in the twilight of life—the aged; and those who are in the shadow of life—the sick, the needy, the handicapped."

We are revamping our early education system to ensure that our children will have the tools they need to realize their ambitions and dreams. We've dramatically lowered the pupil-teacher ratio and put new emphasis on literacy and mathematical skills, science, and technology.

We're revamping our healthcare system to place new emphasis on the prevention of disease rather than treatment after-the-fact.

We're also moving to take many of our health services out of our hospitals and put them into our communities where they can be more responsive to local and individual needs—to the needs of women and natives and diverse cultural groups.

We have passed pay equity legislation to ensure that from now on wages will be based on the value of the work being done, and not on the gender of the person doing the job.

We have passed ground-breaking new occupational health and safety legislation.

And we have established the toughest environmental pollution standards in North America, and we've backed them up with tough penalties for polluters. I take great pride in the fact that when it comes to environmental protection, Ontario is a world leader not a follower.

And so we've introduced the toughest acid rain reduction legislation in the world. We're on target to cutting our sulphur dioxide emissions in half by 1992. And we look forward to your country introducing similar legislation because acid rain is a problem that recognizes no international boundaries.

I'm not saying all this to boast about our accomplishments. I'm acutely conscious that a great deal more remains to be done, in my province and in my country as a whole.

Rather, I want to make the point that not only the theory but also the practice of liberalism remains very relevant to life in North America today—and that it can command wide public support. Our challenge as liberals is not merely to defend our accomplishments, but to keep moving forward. Liberalism is a restless faith, and at its core is a constant belief that we can do better.

That is very much the thinking of the government I am privileged to lead.

We look at an education system whose current practices we established in the 1960s, and we see the urgency of further adjustments to make sure that our children are fully prepared for the very different world of the twenty-first century.

We look at all the mounting evidence of devastating damage to the environment, and we see an absolute imperative to come forward with new initiatives to reduce our contaminants and recycle our waste products—to safeguard the future for ourselves and for our children.

We look at the number of people still suffering hardship and frustration despite one of the most generous social support systems in the world and we see a challenge to fund new ways of equalizing opportunity, encouraging initiative, and breaking the cycle of poverty.

We look at the growing stridency and effectiveness of special-interest groups in pursuing their own narrow advantage and we are reminded daily of our obligations to govern for all the people, not only the vocal and the powerful.

What I *don't* see, amid all this, is any evidence that we need to conceal or apologize for our liberalism, nor even to redefine it into some so-called neo-liberalism.

Our horizons are limited only by our vision. Our promise is limited only by our perseverance, and our capacity to make this a better world for ourselves and our children is limited only by our courage and our confidence in our ability to do so.

And so, I stand in front of you today as someone who is very proud to call himself a liberal, and as someone who is very proud to be associated with that great set of principles known as liberalism. And I stand ready and eager to associate myself with the words of John F. Kennedy—in whose name this school of government was established—and to state that, "I believe in human dignity as the source of national purpose, in human liberty as the source of national action, in the human heart as the source of national compassion, and in the human mind as the source of our invention and our ideas. It is, I believe, this faith in our fellow citizens as individuals and as people that lies at the heart of the liberal faith."

1990 ELECTION CALL
Queen's Park, July 30, 1990

Ladies and gentlemen, I've just spoken to His Honour the Lieutenant Governor and I've informed the leaders of the opposition parties that on September 6, an election will take place in Ontario.

Choosing the most appropriate time for an election is never an easy decision to make, and over the past few weeks I've given this matter a great deal of thought and consideration. I've reviewed the issues and challenges that lie ahead of us, and having weighed the alternatives, I have decided that the time for an election is now.

In the three years since Ontarians last went to the polls, we've experienced many dramatic economic and political changes in Canada and around the world. We can see the challenges of the future clearly today, and I have a clear and full agenda to meet those challenges.

Ontario industries are facing increasingly tough competition from the United States and around the world.

We are all confronted by the need to adapt to new technology. Indeed, experts tell us that 85 percent of the technology that our people will use in the year 2000 has not yet been invented.

Federal policies such as free trade, a high dollar and high interest rates, and the proposed GST, have each created considerable anxiety.

People are anxious about the future—about the security of their jobs and homes—about their ability to continue providing a high standard of living for themselves and their children—about the stability of our country.

I am confident of our ability to meet future challenges. But to do so, we must set our own agenda for the decade ahead.

I am setting out today to seek the confidence of the people to proceed with an agenda to build a stronger economy, to protect our environment, and to preserve safe, healthy, and caring communities.

Only with a strong economy can we create and protect jobs at home, compete and succeed abroad, and move forward with our program of social reforms.

In the days ahead, I will put forward detailed policy initiatives to assist Ontarians to improve our skill levels, and to create new opportunities for training and upgrading.

I will present a plan to provide new support for entrepreneurship and export development; to expand our scientific and technological capacity, to strengthen our agricultural communities, and to ensure employment opportunities for all segments of our society.

I shall introduce proposals to ensure that we can protect Ontario's economic and political interests regardless of any changes that may take place in the structure of federal-provincial relations in the years ahead.

To achieve this goal, I will soon announce initiatives to involve Ontarians in a broad consultation to protect Ontario's interests.

Together we will ensure that Ontario's economic future and standard of living will not be jeopardized as a result of bilateral discussions between the federal government and other provinces or regions.

We've worked hard to earn our standard of living in Ontario, and now we have to work hard to maintain it.

I will announce new initiatives to ensure cleaner air and water; to protect the safety of our food supply; to reduce and recycle wastes; and, to conserve our greenlands, river valleys, farms, and forests.

I will also announce new initiatives aimed at preserving our communities as safe, healthy, and caring places in which to live.

These measures will improve safety on our roads and waterways, reduce drug abuse, provide better nutrition for children from low income families, and provide better care for seniors and the disabled.

I want to discuss all of these proposals with people across Ontario in the weeks ahead and listen to their thoughts and ideas on how we can work together to build a more prosperous, safe, and caring society.

I invite the leaders of the opposition parties to discuss these proposals, as well as their own ideas, in a televised debate. I believe that there are very real and significant differences among our three political parties. A debate will assist people to decide who can best represent and protect their interests, and who can best chart a clear course for the future of Ontario.

In the next few years, we are facing a number of important challenges and pressures. Some of these pressures are international, others are national.

Ontario is well-positioned to meet those challenges.

In each of the past two years, Ontario has brought in a balanced budget. This provides us with the financial flexibility to adjust to the challenges ahead.

Ladies and gentlemen, we all take a great deal of pride in Ontario. Ontario is a good place to live, a good place to work, and a good place to raise a family.

Ontario didn't become that way by accident and it won't stay that way through inactivity. It will only stay that way through a clear and meaningful agenda for the '90s.

The time has come to chart our course for the decade ahead.

I am asking the people of Ontario for their support.

PAYING TRIBUTE

Unveiling of the Portrait of Premier Frank Miller
Queen's Park, December 1, 1986

Your Honour, Frank and Ann, members and friends of the Miller family, Mrs. Miles, I'm delighted that you could be here today for the unveiling of the official portrait of Ontario's 19th premier, Frank Stuart Miller.

In his fifteen year career at Queen's Park, Frank Miller has worn many hats—fortunately none of them quite as loud as his jackets.

Some you know him best as the MPP for Muskoka, some as a cabinet minister, some as premier. All of us know him as a friend.

All of us know Frank as a man of tremendous personal warmth and humour. As a man of honesty and integrity who does not run from challenges, but seeks them out. As a man of traditional values in the very best sense of that term. As a man who came from simple roots and never forgot those roots. As a man who isn't afraid to take a position. You may not always agree with Frank, but you never leave a discussion wondering where he stands.

And we know Frank as a man whose vision of his province extends well beyond its boundaries. When the subject turns to economic development, it is almost a cliché to say that Ontario and Canada must follow the arrow leading to the untapped markets of the Pacific Rim. Let us not forget that it was Frank Miller who was among the first to point us in that direction.

The portrait of Frank that we will soon unveil is a special one for many reasons. First, because it was painted by one of Canada's foremost artists, Anthony Miles. And sadly, because it was Mr. Miles' last work. Only days after he put the final brush strokes to canvas in early June, he

Without Walls or Barriers: The Speeches of Premier David Peterson, Library of Political Leadership Series, by Arthur Milnes and Ryan Zade, Editors. Montreal and Kingston: McGill-Queen's University Press,

passed away.

In choosing Anthony Miles to paint his official portrait, Frank chose a man whose quest for realism took him from coal mines and slaughter-houses and the slums of Glasgow to sea on an Icelandic fishing trawler. His work includes the original sets for the television series *Coronation Street* and many of the murals for the Man and his World exhibits of Expo '67. His famous subjects include Sir Winston Churchill, and of course, Frank Miller.

We are deeply saddened that Anthony Miles did not live to be with us here today, but we are honoured that his wife Ailsa is able to join us. Mrs. Miles, the memory of your husband lives on around the world in the form of his paintings. We're privileged that this House will be a home to one of them.

The portrait of Frank Miller will soon be hung on the second floor where it will sit alongside those of his predecessors, George Drew and Mitch Hepburn, John Robarts, and—in the fullness of time—Bill Davis.

If you want to know my definition of an intimidating experience it's walking to your office every morning and knowing that these gentle-men are looking over your shoulder.

But then I also remind myself that these are the great men who built this province. These are the artisans who crafted all that we hold dear. Today, we add to that gallery of honour the portrait of another man of courage, who had the vision to dream and who dared to build that dream for the betterment of all of us. Frank Stuart Miller, your portrait will sit well in that company.

UNVEILING OF THE PORTRAIT OF PREMIER BILL DAVIS
Queen's Park, October 19, 1989

Your Honour, Bill, Kathleen, friends and members of the Davis family, ladies and gentlemen, it's a great pleasure to welcome you to Queen's Park this morning.

Normally at events of this nature I like to begin by extending an ex-tra-warm welcome to those who are visiting Queen's Park for the first time.

But looking out at this sea of familiar faces, I'm not sure that there's anyone here who fits into this category.

We're here today to pay tribute to Bill Davis, Ontario's 18th premier, and to honour the tradition of hanging the portrait of former premiers in the corridors of Queen's Park.

It's a little known fact, but this tradition was actually started by some of our earliest premiers themselves, who, being men of wisdom and sound judgment, realized that hanging portraits was a far more benign tradition to encourage than hanging premiers.

Today we're following a modified version of that tradition.

The real tradition calls for each premier to preside over the unveiling of the portrait of his immediate predecessor. But in this case, Bill took so long in choosing an artist that the portrait of Frank Miller has been hanging in our halls for nearly three years.

I know that some have stated—rather uncharitably, and I might add, incorrectly—that the reason it took so long is that Bill couldn't make up his mind about the artist. Certainly anyone who knows him personally could never believe that.

Others have told us that we should have known we'd be in trouble the minute Bill said he'd forward the guest list "in the fullness of time."

But I can now confess that the real reason for the delay is that Bill insisted that the portrait be painted by numbers—and it took Hugh Segal three years to collect the numbers.

When the numbers finally came in they showed that 66 percent of Ontarians wanted Bill to wear a blue suit in the portrait, 85 percent wanted a white shirt, and 53 percent said that Bill should have a pipe in his mouth.

Unfortunately for Bill, since he left Queen's Park we outlawed smoking in this building—so the pipe had to appear as an unlit prop.

Now that the portrait is finally ready—and when you see it, I think you'll agree that the artist, Istvan Nyikos has done a really wonderful job—we're going to find a very special place for it.

In fact I've personally arranged for it to hang in between the portraits of Mitch Hepburn and Harry Nixon. That way, Bill will live through eternity surrounded by Liberals.

In addition to unveiling the portrait, this occasion provides us with an opportunity to reflect on the career of Bill Davis, a man whose loyalty embraced family, Queen, country… and the Toronto Argonauts.

Sometime during the course of his more than a quarter of a century of public service, "Brampton Bill" was credited with saying that "bland works."

But if you look at Bill's career, there was nothing very bland about it at all.

In fact I think I agree with the journalist, who in summing up Bill's career observed that "it's not so much that bland works, it's calling yourself bland that works."

During his tenure as minister of education and minister of university affairs, he presided over a period of expansion of our post-secondary system that was unprecedented in the history of our country.

And during the course of his 13 years as premier, he presided over a period of unprecedented expansion of our economy.

Bill was more than just a great public servant and premier. He was, and is, a great Canadian.

He is a man, who in the words of another leader of his time—and forgive me Bill for quoting a Liberal on this blue tie occasion—recognized that "masters in our own house we must be, but that house must be all of Canada."

Bill was a man, who in the great tradition of Ontario premiers, reached out to embrace all Canadians.

It was his understanding of Canada and Canadians—his willingness to place the national good above regional interests—that made Bill Davis a national statesman and an essential player in bringing home our Constitution in 1982.

Bill, in lasting tribute to your great contributions the beautiful portrait which we will soon unveil, will now hang in the corridors of Queen's Park.

From your perch on the second floor you'll be able to look over my shoulder every day as I walk into the building and enter the premier's office. I think there's a nice touch of poetic irony in that. After all, as the leader of the opposition, I spent many, many months looking over *your* shoulder as you walked into that office.

You will find that your picture will place you in good company.

The portraits of Ontario's premiers, extending from the office of the premier, along the second floor corridor to the legislative library, represent a portrait of vision—a vision of eighteen men, who along with the dedicated men and women whose names are engraved on the marble walls of this legislature, have served to build a strong province within a great country.

It's now time for your portrait to take its place along this distinguished corridor.

On this very special occasion, I want to share in the gratitude of the people of Ontario and thank you for your commitment, dedication and service to a province you truly love.

Fundraiser with Premier Frank McKenna

London, Ontario, April 12, 1989

I'm delighted to have the pleasure of extending a warm welcome to our special guest from New Brunswick—Frank McKenna.

If there was ever a book written that described the classic Canadian success story—it would probably be entitled "The Life and Times of Frank McKenna."

Every chapter would contain the same recurring themes over and over again—determination, hard work, and a driving passion to succeed. Because in every sense of the word—Frank McKenna is a winner.

Forty years ago, in a small New Brunswick hamlet called Apohaqui, Frank McKenna was born into a large and loving family. From day one, he faced little opposition.

From the time he learned how to walk on the family dairy farm, he was expected to help his two brothers and five sisters with the household chores.

Of course, Olive and Durwood McKenna didn't realize at the time they were raising a future premier of New Brunswick. If they did, they wouldn't have let him spend so much time in the barn practising his slapshot.

In fact, Frank made so much noise working on his shot—the cows stopped giving milk.

When he wasn't practising his slapshot, he excelled at his studies—and while achieving top marks, he served as president of his high school student council and played on half a dozen sports teams.

In fact, Frank was such a good hockey player, he was once offered a contract to play for the Montreal Canadiens. But he turned them down because he wanted to make a living stickhandling all year round.

He even got a call from Harold Ballard. But he had to turn down the Leafs—he couldn't get used to the idea of being pummelled by the opposition.

At St. Francis Xavier University, he won several awards in political science and graduated with honours.

He then moved to Upper Canada to do some post-graduate work at Queen's University. After a brief stint as special assistant to the wily fox of the Trudeau Cabinet—Allan MacEachen—he returned to the University of New Brunswick to study law.

Plunging into the practice of law with his customary zeal, Frank fought hundreds of criminal and civil cases in every corner of New Brunswick—establishing himself as a tough street-smart lawyer. It wasn't long before he got the itch to run for political office.

In 1982, he accepted the nomination to run in the provincial riding of Chatham. In the face of a Tory majority, he campaigned tirelessly and won the seat by 81 votes. Three years later, he was elected leader of the New Brunswick Liberal Party. And the rest is history.

It wasn't long before he got the chance to test himself before the people of New Brunswick. In a historic victory, he ended Richard Hatfield's 17-year Tory reign. His party swept every seat in the province. And at 39, Frank McKenna became Canada's youngest premier.

When you look at Frank McKenna today, he's probably smiling—and it's not hard to figure out why. He's living a politician's dream.

He has the luxury of leading a government that doesn't have to face an elected opposition. No hecklers, no interruptions, no interjections, no verbal abuse, no non-confidence motions, no supplementary questions.

Of course, being a member of New Brunswick's opposition has its good news and bad news. The good news is that the government has consented to respond to written questions. The bad news is that Canada Post has been hired to deliver them.

In fact, Canada Post has already screwed up. Last week, Frank received letters from ten New Brunswickers signed "lonely and forgotten." Then he got call from Dear Abby—she'd received letters from ten New Brunswick Tories—signed "lonely and forgotten."

He has the looks of Huckleberry Finn, the grace and charm of Jean Beliveau and the toughness of Yvon Durelle.

His sizeable majority hasn't made him complacent and the people of New Brunswick have responded to his brand of reform politics.

He's the leader of one of the most activist and progressive governments in North America. Of course, some would say he leads the second most progressive government in North America.

Whatever you say about Frank McKenna, I can tell you that he's a man of conviction, a man with a vision, a man with a quiet sense of purpose.

Ladies and gentlemen, please join me in giving a warm London welcome to Frank McKenna.

FEDERAL LIBERAL PARTY CONFEDERATION DINNER TRIBUTE TO JOHN TURNER

Toronto, Ontario, November 1, 1989

Ladies and gentlemen, it's a great pleasure to join you in paying honour and tribute to a great Liberal and a great Canadian, my friend John Turner.

As you know, this isn't the first evening of tribute to John, and I dare say it won't be the last.

In fact I'm rapidly becoming convinced that if everyone who is now thanking John Turner had voted for John Turner, then there wouldn't be any need for these kinds of evenings at all.

John, the film that we're about to see will demonstrate quite vividly how the story of your career is a tale of honour and achievement.

It's a career that has been punctuated by many accomplishments—one filled with exciting and historic moments.

In fact, knowing of the highlights as I do, I'm reminded of the old observation that "following Canadian politics is a lot like reading the comic strip *Pogo*. It's not the plot line, but the cast of characters that keeps you coming back for more."

John, I know that the going has not always been easy for you. But I also know that, like Vince Lombardi, you have always acted in accordance with the belief that "it's not whether you get knocked down that matters; it's whether you get back up again that counts."

You've gotten up time and time again, and as you've risen, you've carried the Liberal Party with you.

You've worked tenaciously to bring together a divided party, travelling long distances, spending many hours talking to Liberals across the country, attending countless dinners and policy sessions.

You've always known that the strength of the Liberal Party rests in its grassroots, and you've worked tirelessly to rebuild the party and bring people together to fight for the causes we hold dear.

In doing so, you've never shied away from a challenge, or from venturing into unwelcome territory. There were times when you travelled to parts of the country where the only protection a Liberal enjoyed was under the provisions of provincial game laws.

I know what that can be like. There was a time earlier in my career when I spoke in a place that up to then had been barren land for our party. When I was introduced as a Liberal the entire audience started booing—except for one man—and he was cheering the people who were booing.

But the result of your determined effort, is that there isn't a single seat in any part of this country that a Liberal doesn't have a chance of winning in the next federal election campaign.

John, there's an old saying that goes "the hardest steel is forged in the hottest fire." You have come through some of the hottest fires of any politician of our generation, and you did so with your integrity intact and your convictions stronger than ever.

You made the future of our country the cause of your life, and every citizen in this country owes you a tremendous debt of gratitude for inspiring us to take a close look at what it means to be Canadian, and to appreciate the uniqueness of our country.

I truly believe that when the record of this era is written it will state that when a strong and clear voice was needed to stand up and speak for Canada—John Turner was there.

John, every one of us in this business—or perhaps I should say this vocation—knows that politics can sometimes be a difficult soulmate. There are good times and bad times; there are times when you're up, and there are times when you're down.

We also know that you don't measure a person by the votes he receives on election day or his standing in the popularity polls. You measure a man by the strength of his character, by the courage of his convictions, and by the clarity of his vision. By that yardstick, you always have been, and always will be, a winner.

John, all Liberals, and indeed all Canadians owe you a tremendous debt of gratitude for your strength, for your character, and for all that you have done. We are privileged to have worked with you. We all wish you, Geills, and your family good health, happiness, and every success in the future.

Dinner for Michael Dukakis, Governor of Massachusetts
Toronto, Ontario, May 31, 1989

Governor Dukakis, Mrs. Dukakis, it's my great honour, as well as my great personal pleasure to extend a very warm welcome to you on behalf of the people of Ontario.

We're delighted to once again see you in our midst. I recall reading an article about your last visit here, which quoted the governor as saying "I came to meet businessmen, buy transportation vehicles, and watch the Red Sox get their butts kicked in."

We're most willing to accommodate you again in regard to the first two points. As for the butt-kicking, if we can persuade you to return in about a month to our new SkyDome, we'll be happy to oblige on that count as well.

We're very honoured to have such distinguished guests from the State of Massachusetts.

As I'm sure most people will know, Massachusetts has given the world some of its greatest liberal spokesmen—Oliver Wendell Holmes, John F. Kennedy, and Tip O'Neill.

Massachusetts has also given the world some of its greatest writers: Horatio Alger, Ralph Waldo Emerson... and Tip O'Neill. And of course Massachusetts has given the world some of its greatest stick-handlers: Bobby Orr, Phil Esposito... and Tip O'Neill.

And how can you not love a state that gave the world Walter Brennan?

The people of Ontario have long felt a great kith and kinship with our friends in Massachusetts.

And as part of that friendship we've always tried to help you out when you were in need.

When you needed someone to play goalie—we gave you Gerry Cheevers.

When you needed someone to play guard we gave you Danny Ainge. When you needed someone to play God we gave you John Kenneth Galbraith.

And each and every one of them was an all-star.

These are just some of the links that exist between our two jurisdictions.

Over the past several years we've built a very strong trading relationship. Two-way trade between Massachusetts and Ontario exceeds $3 billion per year and is growing at an annual rate of 20 percent.

And we're constantly looking for new ways to expand upon that relationship. For example, this past March when I visited Boston to give a speech at Harvard University, I had the opportunity to have breakfast with a large group of business people, and to highlight for them why Ontario is a good place with which to do business and in which to invest.

Now there was a time, when an Ontario politician at a Boston business breakfast might have been as welcome as Wade Boggs at a nunnery. But I can assure that on this visit, as has been the case in recent years, I found great interest in this province.

That interest is being followed up on an ongoing basis by the very talented people working in our Ontario government office in Boston.

In addition to these trade links, there are a number of other issues that draw the people of Ontario and Massachusetts together.

Each of us is very concerned about the protection of our environment, and particularly about the disastrous effects that acid rain is having on our lakes, rivers, and cityscapes.

I had the opportunity to discuss this issue with the Great Lakes governors when they held their annual meeting here in Toronto a couple of weeks ago, and I look forward to further discussions on this subject with Governor Dukakis and his fellow New England governors at their meeting next week.

And let me take this opportunity to very candidly note that when it comes to the battle against acid rain, Canada has no better ally in the United States than our good friend Governor Dukakis.

I am very grateful for the role that Governor Dukakis has played and is continuing to play in establishing a new level of dialogue between Canadian premiers and American governors.

I'm also very appreciative of the fact that we're able to learn from each other and from our experiences in dealing with common concerns.

For example, when I visited Boston I also took the opportunity to take a close look at a program that the Governor established called the Employment Training or E.T. Program. It's a program designed to help people get off welfare and into the workforce.

The program has been so successful that nearly three-quarters of its participants have been able to break the cycle of welfare and find employment. That's a truly remarkable achievement.

As you know, converting welfare cheques into pay cheques is very high on our agenda in Ontario and we're looking very closely at Massachusetts' success in this area.

In a similar vein, Governor Dukakis and Senator Kennedy have looked very closely at our universal Medicare programs as an inspiration for changes at both the state and national levels in the United States.

Ladies and gentlemen, before I introduce Governor Dukakis, I would like to say a few words about our guest of honour.

A few moments ago, you heard me mention the name of Horatio Alger. We have here, in the form of Governor Dukakis, the human embodiment of a Horatio Alger story.

Governor Dukakis is, to use his own words, "a son of immigrants." His father arrived in the United States at the age of 15 with $25 in his pocket and not a word of English in his vocabulary.

But he arrived here with a dream, a dream that through hard work and perseverance he could make a good life for himself and his children.

He worked his way up from the textile mills of New England to Harvard Medical School. And he passed on his passion for hard work and service to people to his son Michael.

Michael grew up into a brilliant student at Harvard law school. He later successfully ran for State legislature, and in 1974 was elected governor.

Under Governor Dukakis's leadership, his state has undergone a period of economic growth and renewal that many refer to as the "Massachusetts miracle."

Through it all Governor Dukakis has never lost touch with the person on the street. He still takes the subway to work, still carries a paper bag lunch and still plants his own tomatoes. In fact, I think that when he was booking his trip here we had to talk him out of staying at the YMCA.

I'd like to tell you a little story which I think is typical of the man.

A few years ago the governor was having dinner at the home of Barney Danson—who at the time was Canada's consul general in Boston. The governor disappeared for a while and Barney went to look for him.

Eventually Barney found him—he was in the kitchen speaking in Spanish with the maid, Maria, seeking her advice on how to run the State of Massachusetts.

Governor Dukakis, each of us here followed with a great sense of respect and admiration your campaign for the presidency of the United States.

When you described your vision of a humane and caring America—a society that provided opportunity to all who sought it, and support to all who needed it—we felt you to be a kindred spirit of ours

Each of us in political life knows that you do not measure success by the number of votes you receive.

You measure success by measuring the person—the quality of his convictions, the strength and dignity with which he pursues them and the impact he has on influencing the thinking of people for the better.

By these standards, sir, you are truly a winner—and always will be.

Ladies and gentlemen, would you please join me in giving a very warm welcome to our good friend and neighbour, the governor of the great state of Massachusetts, Michael Dukakis.

WELCOME TO HER MAJESTY QUEEN ELIZABETH, THE QUEEN MOTHER
Queen's Park, July 6, 1989

Your Majesty, it's my great honour, as well as my great personal pleasure to extend a very warm welcome to you on behalf of the people of Ontario.

The people of this province always look forward with great anticipation and excitement to visits by the Royal Family. On this special day, we welcome your visit with particular delight. This year marks the golden jubilee of your first visit to Canada. Fifty years ago, you accompanied King George on a coast-to-coast tour that was celebrated by millions of Canadians.

At every stop along the way, thousands gathered to express their loyalty and devotion to their King and Queen. Today, the memories of that visit still endure and there are many who fondly remember the grace and charm that dignified your every step.

Your Majesty, since that first visit in 1939, Canada has changed a great deal. Notre société a évoluée depuis ses origines. D'une nation composée de deux cultures fondatrices, elle s'est transformée en une société multiculturelle dont les membres viennent des quatre coins du monde. Aujourd'hui, des gens de plus de cent cultures différentes vivent et travaillent ici, chacun et chacune apportant une contribution unique qui enrichit notre province en ajoutant à sa diversité et à sa vigueur.

While our society has changed, one thing has not. Canadians have not forgotten, nor have we forsaken, the fundamental values and beliefs bestowed upon us by our British heritage: a belief in parliamentary democracy, a sense of compassion and decency that compels us to meet the needs of the less fortunate, a sense of honour, and fairness. Your visit allows us to reaffirm our dedication to those beliefs and provides us with an opportunity to strengthen the strong and enduring ties that exist between our peoples.

Over the course of the next few days, you will meet Ontarians from all walks of life. In a few moments, you will unveil a plaque commemorating the 50th anniversary of your namesake—the Queen Elizabeth Way—a highway that symbolizes the growth and prosperity of our province over the last fifty years. Tomorrow you will visit the beautiful City of London where you will unveil a statue of one of Canada's most distinguished medical researchers, Sir Frederick Banting. Later, you will open a new wing for veteran servicemen at Parkwood Hospital.

On Saturday, you will inspect the Canadian regiments at the Fort York Armoury and on Sunday you will watch the 130th running of the

Queen's Plate Stakes—Canada's oldest and most prestigious thorough-bred horse race. The Queen's Plate has a distinguished and celebrated history and your attendance will greatly add to the excitement and pageantry. May I add, Your Majesty, that when the field paraded to the post to begin the 1939 Queen's Plate, the King focussed his attention on a splendid chestnut colt—who went on to win by over ten lengths.

Should you have any tips to pass on this year, we'd be honoured to receive them. Your Majesty, we are delighted that you have chosen to visit us again and I know that everybody here today joins me in wishing you an enjoyable and memorable stay.

Once again, on behalf of the people of Ontario, I bid you a very warm welcome.

INTRODUCING NELSON MANDELA
Toronto, Ontario, June 18, 1990

Ladies and gentlemen, it's a great honour to welcome to Ontario and to Queen's Park a man whose name is synonymous with the struggle for justice and democracy in South Africa—Mr. Nelson Mandela.

Mr. Mandela, I should have said that it is a great honour to welcome you in person, because you have been with us in spirit for many years. Throughout your long years as a political prisoner, you have very much been in our hearts and in our thoughts.

I wish you could have been with us on that wonderful February evening of your release to see the tremendous feeling of jubilation that enveloped this city. I still remember the thousands of people who gathered outside the ANC office on Danforth Avenue—black people, white people, people of all races—celebrating together. It is our strong wish that this binding together of people of all races in common purpose will soon be found in a democratic, non-racial, and united South Africa.

Another great freedom fighter by the name of Martin Luther King once observed that "the ultimate measure of a man is not where he stands in moments of comfort or convenience, but where he stands at times of challenge and controversy." History will show that at times of challenge and controversy, Nelson Mandela stood tall. You stared at the face of tyranny and oppression, and forced it to back down. You have shown the world that you can imprison a man, but you can never stop the march toward freedom and justice.

Mr. Mandela, Canadians are with you in your fight for a democratic, non-racial, and united South Africa. As long as South Africa is a state where there is oppression of the mind, the heart, and the body, we must all work together for change. Your release from prison gives us all great hope that change will come sooner rather than later. We look forward to your guidance and advice on how Canadians can help speed along the great march to freedom.

Ladies and gentleman, would you please join me in giving a very warm welcome to the conscience of South Africa, Mr. Nelson Mandela.

Eulogy for Dalton McGuinty, Sr.
Ottawa, Ontario, March 20, 1990

My friends, we gather here today to celebrate the life and mourn the passing of a good family man, a good friend, and a good person, Dalton McGuinty.

It isn't easy to sum up a life in a few words, particularly when that life was as full and rich as Dalton's.

Perhaps each of us here remembers him best for his commitment to his family. Dalton was a man whose love for his wife Elizabeth and his ten children knew no bounds.

He spoke endlessly of his love and affection for them, and whether you were a casual acquaintance or a lifelong friend you felt an intimate attachment to his family. So I hope that Elizabeth and the children, in their time of sorrow and loss, will also feel the warm embrace that is reaching out to them from all of us here and people across Ontario who today consider themselves to be members of the McGuinty family.

As anyone who knew Dalton was aware, he was a man who greatly loved his children. But he was also a son of Ireland who loved all children. Children were the driving force in his life.

Dalton studied at Harvard, worked as a management consultant in Chicago and New York and earned a PhD here in Ottawa. With those kinds of credentials, he could have written his ticket to success in any number of business ventures that would have brought him great riches and material wealth.

But instead, he chose to dedicate his life to the very special task of developing the minds of young people. Whether it was as a father, a board of education trustee, a professor of literature at the University of

Ottawa, or a member of the provincial legislature, his goal in life was to make sure that every child possessed the skills needed to enjoy the blessings that life has to offer.

Dalton was a religious man with a deep commitment to his church. And he touched the face of God not only in his worship, but in the way he lived his life. Dalton truly loved people and he loved being with them. He loved to write about people, and to send out inspirational messages to those he knew.

This morning, I took a look—a second look—at a diary which he used to keep, and in which he would write about his days in the legislature. I was very much touched by one passage where he wrote that "at Queen's Park I never met anyone I didn't like. And I liked even those which others would dislike me for liking."

Something else which grew out of Dalton's religious beliefs was that tremendous Irish wit for which he will always be remembered. He truly saw humour as an extension of religion. He loved to quote the oriental mystic who observed that "God must have had a sense of humour or man wouldn't have had one."

Dalton once wrote that a sense of humour is what inspired him "to face the sunrise always with peace and hope, aware that life will forever have its feasts as well as its fasts, its crowns and its crosses, its midnights and its high noons, that it is always morning somewhere—that flames are often tempering cleansing flames—that lamps are bright and trimmed somewhere, however dark the night—that clouds will always break."

Because Dalton's humour sprang forth from his religious convictions, he never used it in a cruel way to cut a person down or to put them in their place. He never saw humour as a tool to demean, embarrass, or humiliate. He always saw it as means of bestowing upon people the gift of joy and laughter—a gift with which he was amply endowed, and which he generously chose to share. And so whenever Dalton was in a room, it wasn't just Irish eyes, it was all eyes that were smiling.

My friends, I know that we will want to shed many tears today, and many a tear will be shed. But when the tears have dried, let us, in the grand Irish tradition, hoist a glass in toast to Dalton—to a life well-lived, to a man well-loved, to a memory well-cherished by all who knew him.

Goodbye Dalton, dear father, dear husband, dear friend. In the words of the Irish blessing, "may your soul reach heaven an hour before the devil knows you're dead."

SOURCES

First Campaign Speech as leader

Archives of Ontario. F-2093-30-0-50. David Peterson Fonds.

Opening Statement by Ontario Liberal Leader David Peterson Campaign Ontario '85. March 25, 1985

London Centre Nomination Speech

Archives of Ontario. F-2093-30-0-50. David Peterson Fonds.

Excerpts from an address by Liberal Leader David Peterson to London Centre Nomination Meeting, October 9, 1984.

1990 election night speech

Gagnon, Georgette and Dan Rath. *Not Without Cause: David Peterson's Fall from Grace*. Toronto: HarperCollins, 1991. pp. 387–388.

Election Night, 1985

Courtesy Steve Paikin and TVO.

From Ontario Hansard

Reply to the Speech from the Throne, Queen's Park, June 7, 1985

Speech to the Ontario Legislature on the New Liberal Government's Legislative Program, July 2, 1985

Address to the Legislature of Ontario on the failure of the Meech Lake Accord, Queen's Park, June 26, 1990

Third Reading of the *French Languages Services Act*, Queen's Park, November 18, 1986.

From Newfoundland and Labrador Hansard

Address to the Newfoundland Legislature, General Assembly of Newfoundland, St. John's, June 20, 1990.

All other speeches are:

Archives of Ontario. RG 3-80. David Peterson Fonds. Premier David Peterson Speeches.